THE A OK

This book is sold subject to the Standard Conditions of Sale of Net Books and may not be re-sold in the UK below the net price

© 1975 by FOCAL PRESS LTD

ISBN 0 240 44709 3

All Rights Reserved. No part of this publication may be reproduced, stored in a retrieval system, or transmitted, in any form or by any means, electronic, mechanical, photocopying, recording or otherwise, without the prior permission of the Copyright owner.

First printed	December, 1939	Forty-first Edition	July, 1958
Second Edition	September, 1941	Forty-second Impression	September, 1958
Third Edition	June, 1942	Forty-third Edition	August, 1959
Fourth Edition	June, 1943	Forty-fourth Impression	September, 1959
Fifth Edition	April, 1944	Forty-fifth Impression	February, 1960
Sixth Edition	December, 1944	Forty-sixth Edition	August, 1960
Seventh Impression	June, 1945	Forty-seventh Edition	September, 1960
Eighth Impression	September, 1945	Forty-eighth Edition	June, 1961
Ninth (Indian) Edition	October, 1945	Forty-ninth Edition	August, 1961
Tenth Edition	July, 1946	Fiftieth Edition	December, 1961
Eleventh Impression	October, 1946	Fifty-first Edition	March, 1962
Twelfth Impression	November, 1946	Fifty-second Edition	January, 1963
Thirteenth Impression	January, 1947	Fifty-third Edition	June, 1963
Fourteenth Edition	May, 1947	Fifty-fourth Edition	March, 1964
Fifteenth Edition	June, 1947	Fifty-fifth Edition	September, 1964
Sixteenth Edition	June, 1948	Fifty-sixth Edition	October, 1965
Seventeenth Edition	July, 1948	Fifty-seventh Edition	March, 1966
Eighteenth Edition	January, 1949	Fifty-eighth Edition	February, 1967
U.S.A. Edition	February, 1949	Fifty-ninth Edition	August, 1967
Twentieth Impression	July, 1949	Sixtieth Edition	February, 1968
Twenty-first Impression	March, 1950	Sixty-first Edition	August, 1968
Twenty-second Impression	August, 1950	Sixty-second Edition	July, 1969
Twenty-third Edition	May, 1951	Sixty-third Edition	December, 1969
Twenty-fourth Impression	June, 1951	Sixty-fourth Edition	September, 1970
Twenty-fifth Edition	March, 1952	Sixty-fifth Edition	March, 1971
Twenty-sixth Impression	April, 1952	Sixty-sixth Edition	November, 1971
Twenty-seventh Impression	May, 1952	Sixty-seventh Edition	May, 1972
Twenty-eighth Edition	March, 1953	Sixty-eighth Edition	November, 1972
Twenty-ninth Impression	April, 1953	Sixty-ninth Edition	March, 1973
Thirtieth Impression	April, 1953	Seventieth Edition	June, 1973
Thirty-first Edition	May, 1954	Seventy-first Edition	January, 1974
Thirty-second Impression	June, 1954	Seventy-second Edition	May, 1974
Thirty-third Edition	April, 1955	Seventy–third Edition	December, 1974
Thirty-fourth Impression	June, 1955	Seventy-fourth Edition	March, 1975
Thirty-fifth Edition	February, 1956	Seventy-fifth Edition	July, 1975
Thirty-sixth Edition	February, 1956	Seventy-sixth Edition	November, 1975
Thirty-seventh Impression	July, 1956	Seventy-seventh Edition	February, 1976
Thirty-eighth Edition	January, 1957	Seventy-eighth Edition	May, 1976
Thirty-ninth Impression	February, 1957	Seventy-ninth Edition	August, 1976
Fortieth Impression	March, 1957		

in Spanish TODA LA FOTOGRAFICA EN UN SOLO LIBRO
Ediciones Omega, S.A., Barcelona

in Italian NUOVA GUIDA PRATICA DEL FOTODILETTANTE
Edizioni del Castello, Milano

in German DAS KLEINE FOTOLEHRBUCH
Verlag Wilhelm Knapp, Düsseldorf

in Finnish PIENI KAMERAKIRJA
Kustannusosakeyhtiö Otava, Helsinki

in Portuguese GUIA PRATCO DE FOTOGRAFIA EDITORIAL PRESENCA

Printed and bound in Great Britain by W & J Mackay Limited, Chatham
for the Focal Press, 31 Fitzroy Square, London, W.1

THE ALL-IN-ONE CAMERA-BOOK

The Easy Path to Good Photography

By W. D. EMANUEL

Seventy-ninth Edition

THE FOCAL PRESS
London and New York

CONTENTS

PARTNERS INTRODUCE THEMSELVES

A brief description of some very important objects

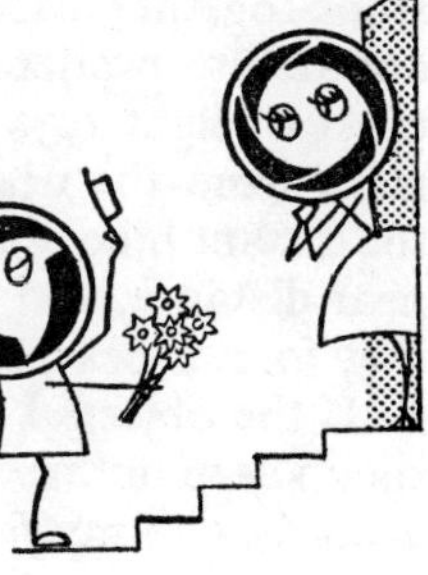

ESSENTIALS OF EVERY CAMERA

I am the Lens

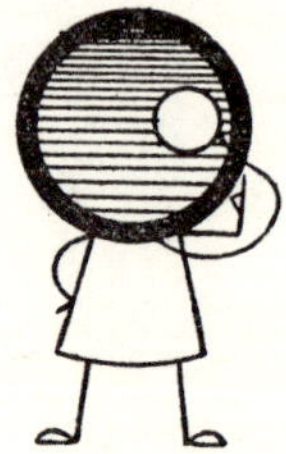

My family goes back to the year 1000 A.D.

My ancestor was a glass bottle filled with water. The historians say that even in those far-off days people had noticed that an image of the world was formed by the sun's rays streaming through the water in the bottle. True, this image is upside down: but everything is there all right: the brightly-lit window-frame, the blue sky, the trees and the houses on the other side of the street. And if somebody stands at the window and waves, his or her image and gesture will be faithfully recorded.

But the image thrown by the bottle is very imperfect; the details are somewhat blurred. So clever men set to work and made countless experiments and horribly complicated calculations until at last they invented me.

Being composed of a number of carefully ground lenses stuck together, each lens made of a different kind of glass, I am able to produce a faultless image. I take the disorderly mass of light rays as they come rushing through me, the glare from the near-by roof mixed higgledy-piggledy with the distant blue of the sky and the rays from the wood in the near distance, and I put them all in their proper place until they form a clear, bright image of the outside world.

If the objects I have to reproduce are a long way away, their sharp outline will appear 2 or 3 or 4 inches behind me, according to my *focal length*, as it is called. The nearer the objects come towards me, the farther their images retreat. True, this is only a question of millimetres and fractions of millimetres. But if you want me to produce a sharp picture you must be careful to catch the image at exactly the right spot. You must *focus* your camera. If you don't, you will get a blurred picture, and it's no use blaming me for it.

There are cameras which make it very easy to get the right focus. Those reflex cameras, as they are called, are fitted with a ground-glass screen on which you can see the picture and on which you can focus it sharply. There are also automatic focusing cameras which are fitted with a mechanism for measuring distances. These, too, ensure a sharp image of the object.

I am the Film

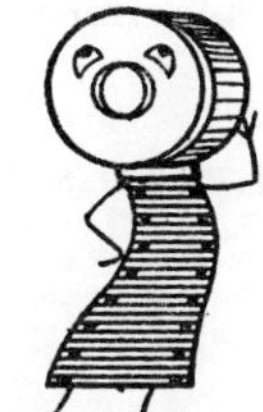

I have an extremely sensitive skin compared to which the delicate epidermis of a young girl is like the toughest pig-skin. A few fleeting beams of daylight are enough to make me sunburnt. That is why I am always packed in a light-tight box. My skin must only come into contact with the air in the dark interior of the camera. Photographers—cunning fellows—exploit my peculiarities in order to capture the fleeting image of the outside world cast upon my skin by the lens of their camera.

If this picture does not come out so well as the man with the camera hoped, I really cannot take the responsibility. I do my best and I know that the people in my birthplace, the big film factory, took a tremendous amount of trouble and used the best scientific brains and instruments to endow me with the very best qualities.

Above all I was given a certain degree of ***sensitivity***, expressed in ASA, or DIN figures, and printed on my packet. There are films with 50 ASA, others with 80 or 200 ASA, the higher the figure the greater my sensitivity to light.

There are two of us, actually. One of us makes only black-and-white pictures, but the other can reproduce things in their natural colours.

But for both of us, the greatest care must be taken to see that the image remains on our skin just long enough, neither too long nor too short. For our ***emulsion*** is highly sensitive to light. Otherwise one gets pictures which are either ***under-exposed*** or ***over-exposed.***

I am the Shutter

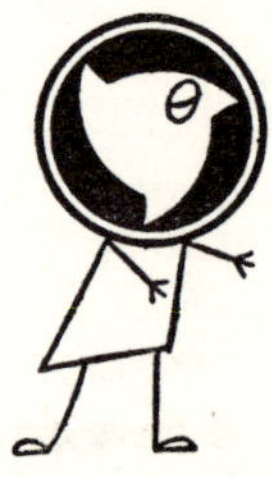

I am sometimes placed between the lens components. I decide whether the light is to pass into the camera and how long it is allowed to remain there. I act as door-keeper. To ensure rapid opening and closing of the door I am often provided with over a hundred beautifully-made metal parts.

I can move extremely fast, when necessary, for light rays are slippery customers. They dash through the gateway at 186,000 miles per second. If I were not snappy, one would have more light in the house than one could use, and the poor film's skin would be ruined.

Some of my colleagues, who, as a matter of fact, do not look much like me, and who live farther back in the interior of the camera, can bring off record speeds. These *focal-plane shutters*, as they are called, will give you an exposure of 1/1000 or 1/1250 second and even less, not once, but as often as you like.

Of course, both of us can easily do the longer times, such as 1/60 or 1/30 second, and when required, can remain open ten seconds, or ten minutes or even ten hours in exceptional circumstances.

If the object is brightly lit, I need let light in for a short time only, because it only requires the fraction of a second to work on the skin of the film. But a dull image, such as is thrown by unfavourable lighting or from dark objects, has to remain longer on the film.

I am the Diaphragm

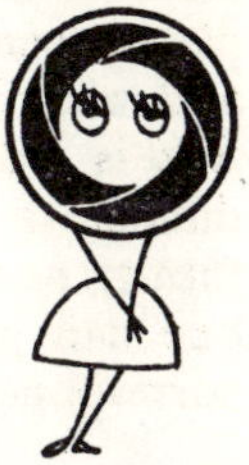

I am made of thin steel plates cunningly set in a metal ring. If a certain lever is moved, my plates close in and the opening in the middle gets smaller and smaller, until it almost disappears. If the lever is moved in the opposite direction my plates open out and the *aperture* gets bigger.

My place is in the empty space between the lens components, near the shutter if the lens has one. When I am opened wide, a lot of light can get in, and the image within the camera is bright. But if the steel plates close in, only a narrow bundle of rays can force its way through. The image remains dim and dull, because it is formed of so few rays of light.

So I control the number of incoming rays. The size of my aperture is expressed by certain numbers: 2.8, 4, 5.6, 8, and so on. The smaller the number the larger the aperture of the diaphragm (and the brighter the image within the camera). *Aperture* (or *stop*) 2 indicates a wide opening, whereas 16 means a small aperture and a correspondingly dark image.

The numbers indicating the size of the aperture are so arranged that by moving the lever from one mark to the next higher one the brightness is halved—by moving to the next lower one the brightness is doubled.

Strangely enough, the size of my aperture influences not only the picture's brightness but the sharpness of its details. If my aperture is kept small, all objects, whether near or far, are sharply reproduced. If the size of my aperture is increased, the area of sharp definition shrinks as the steel plates open wider and wider. With a very wide aperture such as 2, and with the camera focused at 3 to 6 feet, this *depth of field* is reduced to a couple of inches, so that it becomes difficult to get a person's nose and ears equally sharp—even though he may not be particularly thick-headed. Fortunately one can generally use the smaller apertures, covering a correspondingly greater depth.

We Work Together

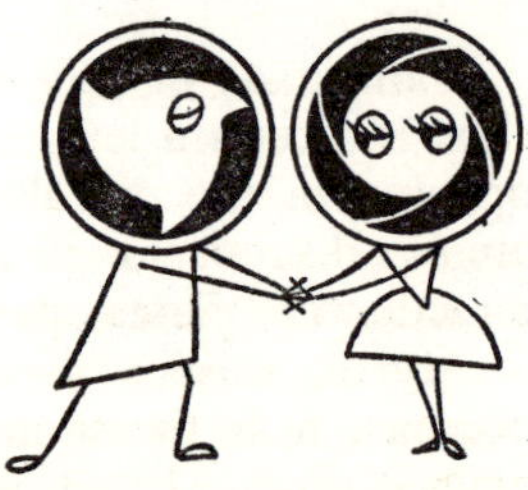

It is our job, Diaphragm and Shutter, to see to it that the film gets enough light and so we work hand in hand.

If you want a picture with great depth of field, you must make my (the Diaphragm's) opening fairly small. That means that the image inside the camera will be very dark. This is where friend Shutter comes to the rescue in allowing the image to remain longer on the surface of the film, so that, despite its weakness, it can leave an impression.

In other cases the shutter must only remain open for a short time, so that quickly-moving objects can be snapped sharply. This means that the image remains for a short time, 1/125 second or less, on the film. Now I, the Diaphragm, must compensate for this by keeping my aperture wide to make the most of the light available.

So it is rather like a see-saw; when one of us shoots up into the air, the other comes down with a bump. Speed of shutter and size of aperture, therefore, are complementary and in inverse ratio to each other. If the light is poor, however, we must both of us go all out; I, the Diaphragm, must provide the widest possible opening, and friend Shutter must remain open a long time, so that our combined efforts overcome the unfavourable lighting conditions.

The see-saw game between us, Diaphragm and Shutter speed, has in some modern shutters been automatically coupled and our relationship is expressed by an exposure value (some call it light value) which you can set on the exposure value scale of such a shutter. Once the exposure value is set you can change either of us—the shutter speed *or* the diaphragm opening—without changing the exposure. Through the exposure value coupling we are mechanically connected so that when you alter one of us, the other adjusts itself automatically to keep the effective exposure the same.

One thing must not be overlooked: before we share out the work, we must know how much light is necessary to get the picture on to the emulsion. Sometimes the sky is covered and at others the sun is shining and objects vary greatly in brightness. The light that comes rushing towards the lens is, therefore, of different strength every time.

Hence the existence of exposure meters.

I am the Flash Contact

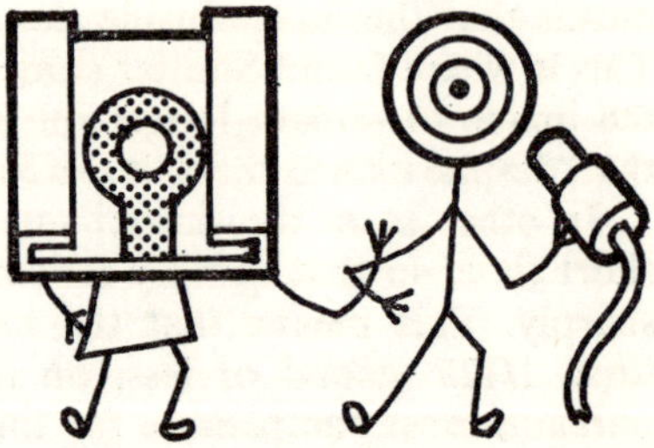

I am really an electrical switch wired to a socket on the camera body. I complete an electrical circuit when the shutter opens. So, if you connect a flashgun or flashcube to me, the flash goes off when you release the shutter.

I let you take pictures indoors or anywhere else where the light is not bright enough for instantaneous pictures. Because of me, even the simple camera without a fast lens has much more scope.

For the simple details of working with flash, turn to page 108.

I am an Exposure Meter

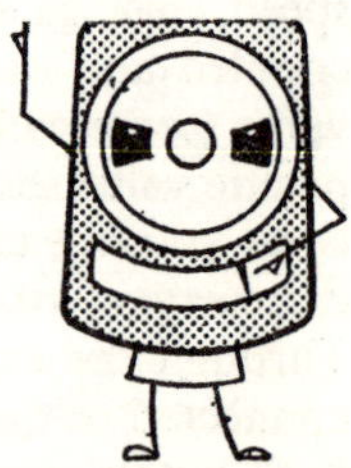

I am a sort of miniature electricity works. Strong light makes my needle swing through a big arc. If the light is weak, on the other hand, the needle only makes a faint movement. And on that depends my use for photography.

I measure the light which the various objects reflect, and indicate the correct exposure which will produce a clear image of these things on the film. If I am aimed at a dark object, my needle does not go much beyond the zero mark, and shows that a big aperture and/or a slow shutter speed is needed to take the picture. When I am pointed at a bright, well-lit object, however, my needle moves much more and indicates less exposure, i.e. a smaller aperture and/or a faster shutter speed.

Many cameras have one of my smaller brothers built into the camera body so that you do not need to carry me around separately. Some of these are connected to the aperture control and sometimes to the shutter, too. These give a certain amount of automatic working. See page 23.

And These Are Cameras

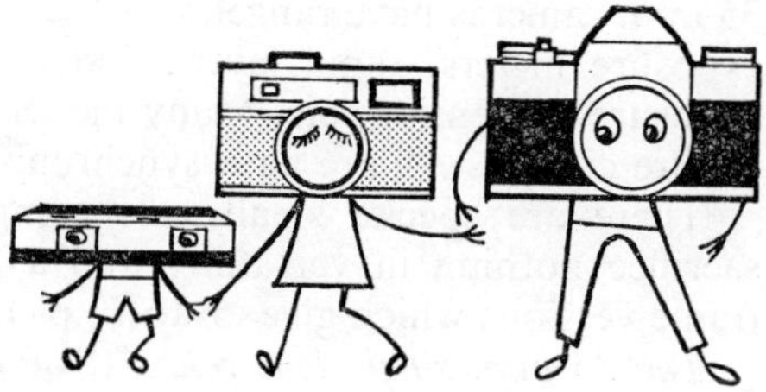

There is no all-round camera which could be guaranteed to deliver nothing but the "best" under all circumstances. Every camera has its advantages and disadvantages.

Cartridge loading cameras are available in two forms—the Instamatic or 126 type and the Pocket Instamatic or 110 type. These use a roll of film preloaded into a cartridge that you just slip into the camera and tip out after all exposures are made. No rewinding is necessary. The 126 type gives 12 or 20 pictures 28 mm. square on black and white, colour negative or colour slide film. The 110 type gives 12 or 20 pictures 13 × 17 mm.

Some of the simplest cameras made are in this category but the 110 range also includes highly sophisticated types with electronic circuitry for automatic exposure control.

The 35 mm. non-reflex camera (so called to distinguish it from the single-lens reflex, see below) has a long history. Starting with the Leica as a high quality product about 50 years ago, it is now available in a wide variety of styles and prices. Nearly all are fixed-lens types giving up to 36 pictures 24 × 36 mm. Only a few interchangeable-lens models remain. After all exposures have been made the film has to be rewound into its container (cassette) because it has no backing paper to protect it from the light.

Apart from the simplest inexpensive models, nearly all 35 mm. cameras have rangefinder focusing facilities, built-in exposure meters, rapid lever wind film transport, double exposure prevention, etc. Many models have automatic exposure control. All are flash synchronised.

There are special small-scale compact versions which sacrifice nothing in versatility and a few remaining half-frame versions which give up to 72 pictures 24 × 18 mm.

The 35 mm. single lens reflex (SLR) is an alternative to other 35 mm. cameras that offers greater versatility in the close-up and long range fields. Its viewfinder shows the image projected by whatever lens is attached to the camera, as nearly all are interchangeable-lens types. This is particularly important in long-range work where the separate viewfinder of the non-reflex can cover a slightly different area. We call this parallax error.

Most SLRs are expensive, some very expensive. They can be fitted with a wide range of lenses and accessories. Exposure meters commonly read through the lens on the camera (TTL metering) and there are increasing numbers of electronically-controlled types providing very sophisticated methods of automatic exposure control.

The rollfilm reflex camera uses the same system of viewfinding as the 35 mm. SLR except in the one or two remaining twin-lens reflexes. These have a separate lens to provide the viewing image and are therefore also subject to parallax error. Only one twin-lens type is made with interchangeable lenses. Picture size varies from the originally most popular 6 × 6 cm. (2¼ in. square) to the 6 × 7 cm. of many current SLRs or 6 × 4½ cm. also beginning to emerge. The film used is standard 120 rollfilm to give 10, 12 or 15 pictures according to size, or size 220 for double loads. These are rather expensive cameras designed for high quality work.

Polaroid cameras are in a category of their own. They are "instant-picture" cameras using film packs containing all the necessary processing chemicals. Black-and-white or colour prints can be produced within 60 seconds or less of pressing the shutter release. Generally, no negative is available, but there are many Polaroid models and with some a negative pack can be used. The cameras do not give colour slides.

On the whole, the choice of camera is a matter of temperament and purse, just as it is with cars, clothes etc.

And How About Automation?

"You press the button, we do the rest" was the slogan of the photographic trade in the 1920's. It was quite justified, because the box camera, then predominantly used by amateurs, was a reasonably automatic instrument.

It had a small lens aperture that could not be altered. So the depth of field was great and no focusing problems arose. It had a single shutter speed, so you could do little about controlling exposure.

Viewfinders were a bit of a hazard. You could assume that you would get any general view that you saw in them, but when it came to close work you had to trust to luck.

Today, we expect very much more from our camera. It should cope with all types of subject in good, indifferent and even the poorest light. To this end, the camera has to have a fast lens, which in turn requires accurate distance setting. It

Camera	*Features*	*Advantages*
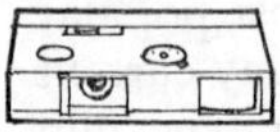 110 type	Range from simple snapshot camera to sophisticated electronically-controlled types. Cartridge loading	Small, genuinely pocketable. Easy loading and unloading
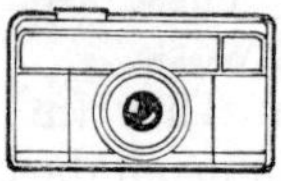 126 type	Larger format version of 110 camera. Smaller range. Cartridge loading	Small, easy handling, loading and uploading
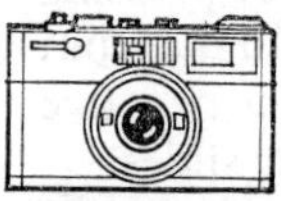 35 mm. non-reflex	Standard 35 mm. camera with separate viewfinder. Wide range of models from snapshot to precision-built types	Easy handling, large film load, rapid focusing. Some advanced models with full automation
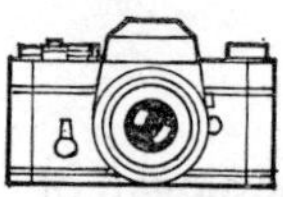 35 mm. reflex	Reflex camera showing image on internal screen viewed through magnifying eyepiece. Extensive accessory range and built in features	Extremely versatile. Parallax-free viewing with any lens. Accessories for all types of photography
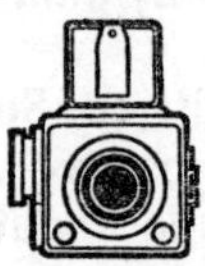 Rollfilm SLR	Large format camera for high-quality work. Reflex viewing and focusing. Various models giving different picture sizes. Interchangeable lenses	Suitable for highest quality results. Accessories for specialised work
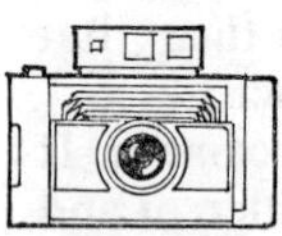 Polaroid	Instant-picture camera in wide range of black-and-white or colour models	Prints available immediately after shooting

Disadvantages	*Film and Picture Size*
Small picture size limits degree of enlargement	No. 110 for 12 or 20 pictures 13 × 17 mm.
Small picture size limits degree of enlargement. Lack of precision for quality results	No. 126 for 12 or 20 pictures 28 × 28 mm.
Limited capabilities at very close or very long range, even with interchangeable lenses. Parallax problems at close range	Standard 35 mm. film for up to 36 pictures 24 × 36 mm. (Half-frames up to 72 pictures 18 × 24 mm.)
High price, bulk and weight compared with many non-reflexes	Standard 35 mm. film for up to 36 pictures 24 × 36 mm.
High price, bulky and heavy. Costly accessories	No. 120 for 12 pictures 6 × 6 cm. or 10 6 × 7 cm. or 15 6 × 4½ cm. according to model. No. 220 film for double loads
Bulky. High cost of film	Range of black-and-white or colour print films in various sizes

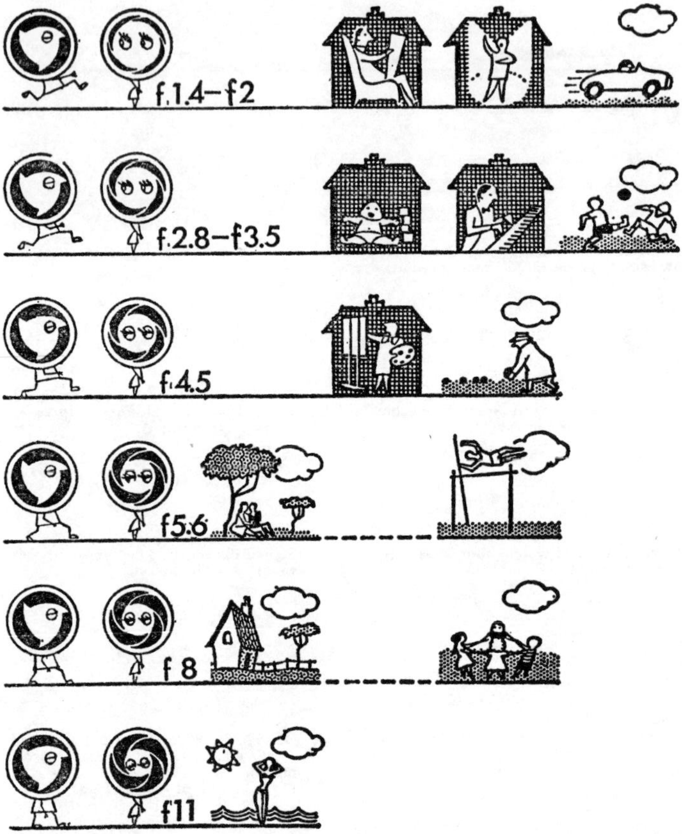

The performance of a camera is to a large extent dependent on its lens. The wider the aperture (=the faster the lens) the wider the scope of the camera. A fast lens enables you to take photographs in poor light conditions and of fast-moving objects. A small aperture (=a slow) lens limits the use of the camera to good light conditions and slow subjects. If you have a fast lens you can afford short shutter speeds. The columns, read horizontally, tell what can be expected from a lens. For example with an *f*2 lens shots of people indoors, fast moving cars as well as stage photographs, can be taken. With an *f*5.6 lens people outdoors under trees as well as not too fast sports pictures (the jump is, at the point shown here, slow) are possible.

In addition you can take pictures indoors with flash with any camera. See page 108.

should also have a variety of speeds to arrest fast movement. Wide-aperture lenses, and a range of shutter speeds, combined with the high sensitivity of modern films and the limited tolerance of colour materials to errors in exposure, have made amateur photography a rather more technical subject.

But camera designers have not been slow in developing instruments to cope with all these problems.

To overcome guessing distances, rangefinders have been built into cameras to measure the distance correctly and set the lens at the same time. Small reflex cameras (35 mm. SLRs) make viewing and focusing easy with any lens or attachment, even at the closest range.

There are various types of automatic exposure control. In some you select a shutter speed and then set the meter needle, usually visible in the viewfinder, to a mark or to line up with a pointer. This automatically sets the aperture to give the correct exposure.

Sometimes you do not even have to line up a needle. You set the shutter speed and the aperture is set automatically when you release the shutter.

Yet another type sets both stop and shutter speed automatically when you press the release, and on some of these you can disconnect the automatic features and use your own judgment by operating the camera manually.

We have come full circle: we have come back to the simplicity in handling of a box camera with all the advantages and extreme versatility you would expect from a modern camera. "You press the button, the camera does the rest."

HINTS AND TIPS

Protect Your Camera

If you value your camera do not drag it about unprotected in city streets or dusty country roads, in woods and fields. A camera is a piece of delicate mechanism and must be protected from dust.

Nor are prolonged air and sunbaths beneficial to its health. The lens will suffer from very long exposure to the sun.

So get a proper case for your camera. Best of all, buy an "every-ready" case which allows you to take a picture without removing your camera from its carrier.

Fine sand is especially dangerous, as it gets through the smallest chinks of the camera, making the shutter grate for weeks. If this happens the camera must be cleaned by an expert.

Like the human eye, an exposure meter cannot bear direct sunlight for long. So do not point it directly at the sun. Whereas the short exposure necessary for making measurements will do no harm, prolonged exposure to direct sunlight may injure the delicate mechanism for good.

About Tripods

Tripods may be had nowadays which fold up small enough to go into a lady's handbag, but which extend to a height of 4 *feet.* (1.2 *m*). *Being made of light metal they are very easy to carry about.*

Exposures of ½ *or even* 1 *second can be made with the help of what is sometimes known as a "chain tripod", though it is not a tripod at all. It consists of a metal screw, fitting the bush in the base of the camera, from which hangs a long chain. You stand on the end of the chain and press the camera firmly upwards. This gives the necessary stability which makes possible the exposures mentioned.*

A string, tied to the camera, can be used as a substitute for the chain, but is not so reliable.

It sometimes happens that the legs of the tripod start to slide apart on the slippery floor, with great risk to the precious camera. To prevent this, stand the tripod on a little mat.

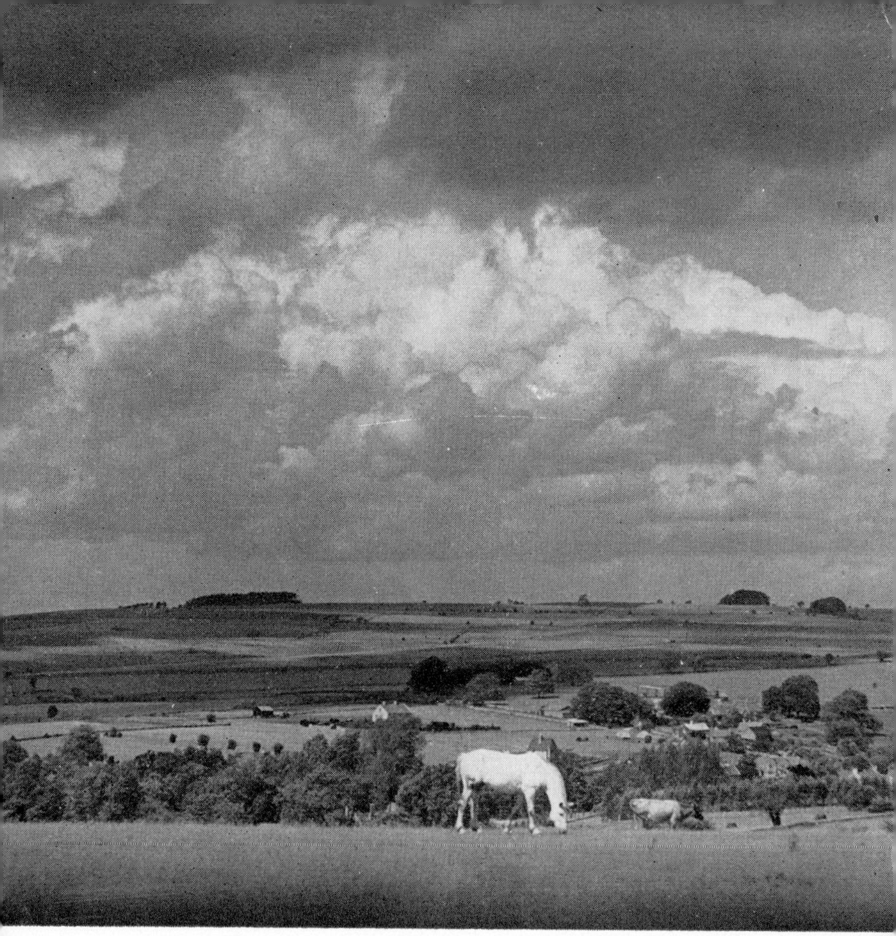

ANY CAMERA can take a picture like this. The lighting conditions are ideal and so any lens will do. There is practically no movement in the scene and so any shutter speed will do. An inexpensive camera can produce almost as good a result as a really costly model. (See pages 20–21.) —Photograph by *H. van Wadenoyen.*

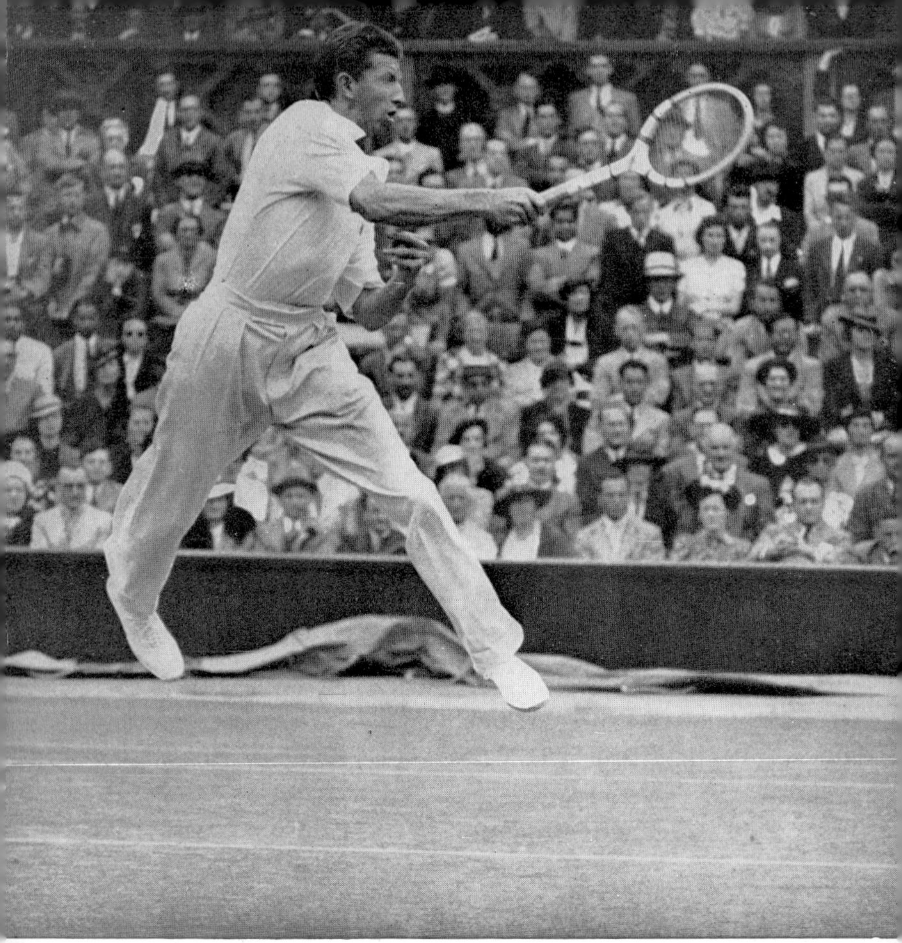

RAPID MOTION of this kind wants a shutter which is able to respond to the fastest speeds. The picture above was taken with 1/1000 of a second. Only focal plane shutters will produce such speeds. They are therefore frequently used in miniature rangefinder and reflex cameras and in many other types. (See page 20–21.)—Photograph by *M. Schirner.*

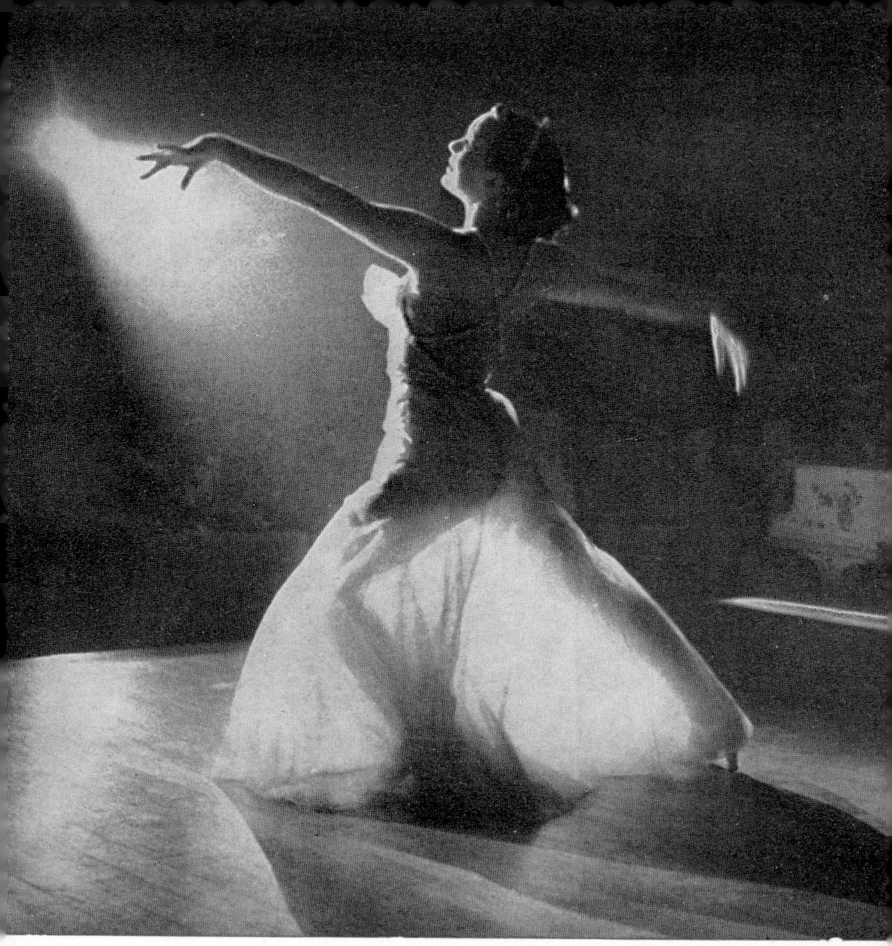

MOTION AND RESTRICTED LIGHT call for a very fast lens. This picture was taken with one of *f* 1.5 aperture, which is almost the fastest that can be found. Lenses like this are usually attached to the modern miniature rangefinder and reflex cameras. They are rarely practicable with larger-sized cameras. (See page 21.)—*Daily Mirror* photograph by *Lancelot Vining*.

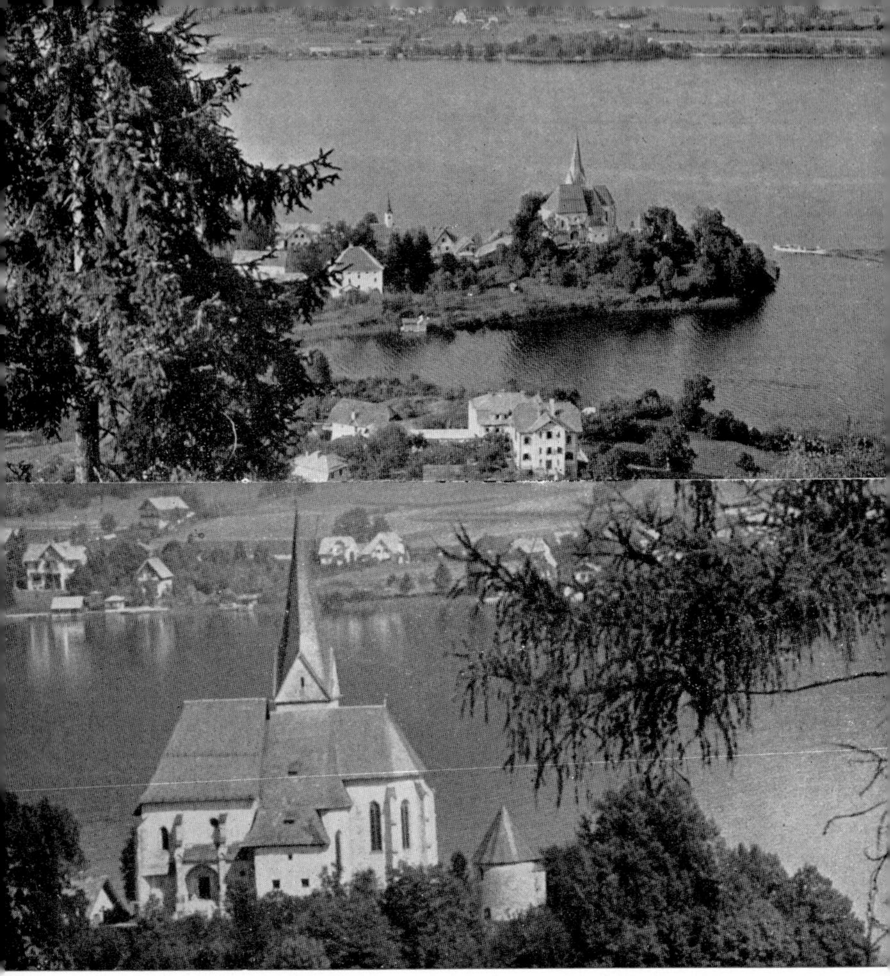

BOTH THESE PICTURES were taken from the same distance and with the same camera, but lenses of different focal length were used. The picture at the top was taken with a 2-inch (5-centimetre) lens, the picture at the bottom with a 7-inch (18-centimetre) lens. Interchangeable lenses add to the versatility of any camera. (See pages 20–21.)—Photograph by *Christopher Croeber*.

TAKING THE PICTURE

Basic rules and individual examples of successful technique

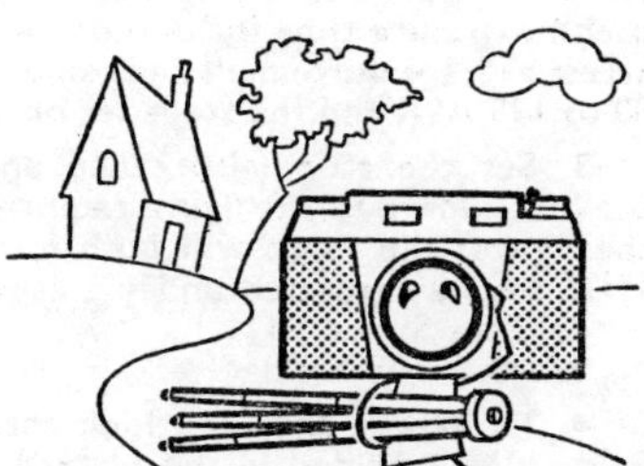

FOR BEGINNERS ONLY

This is All

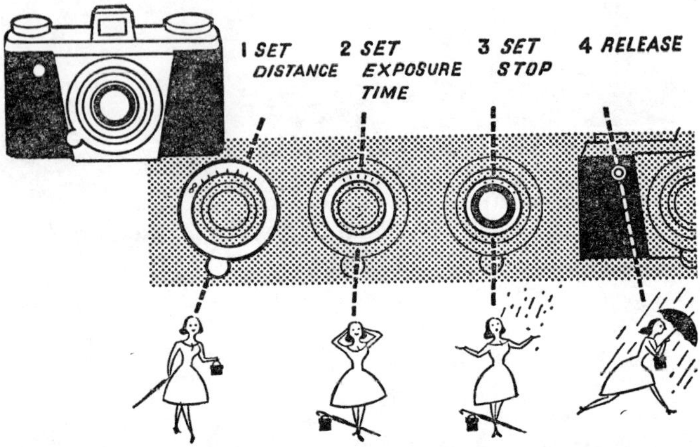

1. Set on the distance scale in feet (or in metres) the distance between the camera and the subject to be photographed. The distance may be guessed, paced out (a normal step being approximately 3 feet), or measured with a rangefinder. If objects both near to the camera and farther away are to be sharp, make use of the zone-focusing explained on p. 46.

2. The exposure time is set by turning the index mark opposite the exposure figures to the speed wanted. The figures 30, 60, 125, etc., stand for fractions of seconds, i.e., 1/30, 1/60, 1/125 sec. The most useful exposure time for outdoor work is 1/125 sec., short enough to arrest average movement and camera shake. With a medium speed film, 80 to 125 ASA and the stops set out under 3, little can go wrong.

3. Set the stop (also called aperture or diaphragm) by moving the index mark to the figure required. The smaller the stop (the higher the figure) the more will both fore and background be sharp. With 1/125 sec. as suggested under 2 use with

Brilliant Sun	*f* 11	Overcast Sky	*f* 5.6
Weak Sun	*f* 8	Dull Day	*f* 4

4. To expose the film, look through the finder to determine the field to be included in the picture and press the release lever gently while holding the camera firmly and still.

After having exposed, wind film on to the next number.

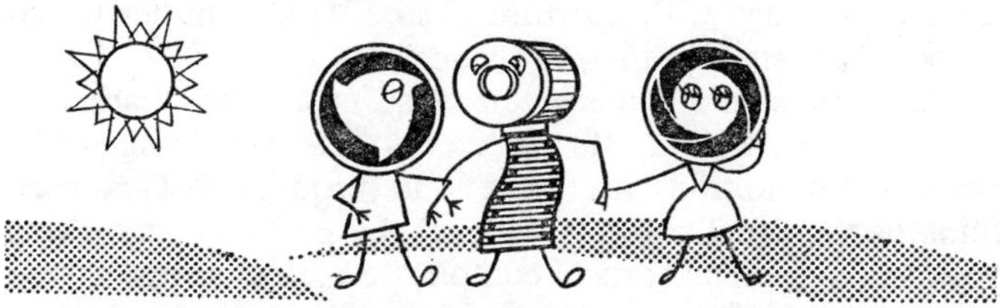

On a sunny day and with a film of 125 ASA in your camera there is nothing to fear. You set the diaphragm (or stop) at 16 and the shutter at 1/125 second and can take home very nice pictures of the usual subjects: Tom and Mary in their hiking outfit, Baby's first steps, Miss So-and-So on the diving board—all without the help of an exposure meter.

So with sunshine, a film of 125 ASA, stop 16, and shutter at 1/125, photography is simplicity itself. You can find dozens of these subjects illustrated in photographic magazines, calendars and similar publications, all taken under these conditions. Sometimes you will see it stated that a film of 100 or 150 ASA has been used, or else that the exposure given was 1/250 instead of 1/125 second. But these variations need not worry anybody. The final result is usually the same, because the lower degree of sensitivity of the film or the shorter exposure has usually been made up for by a larger aperture, 11, for example.

Moreover, modern films possess what is known as *latitude*, which suppresses any small differences of exposure without any difficulty. That is, it is no longer of any great importance if, on many occasions, you give 1/60, where an exposure of a 1/125 second would have done.

So with sunshine, a highly sensitive film, and a medium stop and medium shutter speed, you are fairly safe in dealing with the usual run of subjects. It is no accident that the simple camera, which has neither an adjustable diaphragm nor a variable shutter speed, produces excellent results, even in the hands of the merest tyro. Snapshot cameras are usually provided with aperture 11 and with a shutter which works at about 1/40 to 1/60 second.

But with such a camera you must have good weather or highly sensitive film. If these essentials are fulfilled the necessary conditions are present to produce well-exposed films of the usual subjects without the necessity of racking your brains with all sorts of complicated calculations.

An Easy Way of Focusing

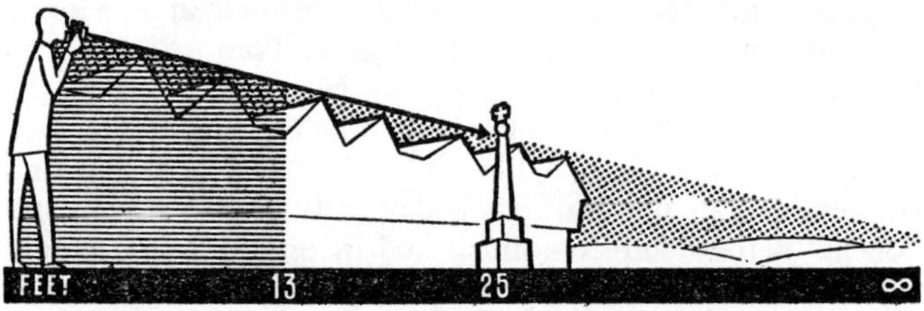

Of course we want our pictures to be sharp.

Now there is a very handy method which enables you to take in objects which are quite near as well as things in the distance. To get all these things sharp on your film you must have a medium-sized aperture, say, 8, one which is quite useful in any case with sunshine and a medium exposure. (See page 41.) This aperture gives you great depth of field, and if the camera is set at 25 feet (7.5 m), the area of sharp definition actually begins at a distance of about 13 feet (4 m) in front of the lens and reaches as far as the horizon. *To infinity* as the experts put it.

Provided, therefore, that an object is not within 12 or 13 feet 3.5 to 4 m of the camera, it will be in focus: the picturesque market-cross, the ivy-covered church tower or the mountain with its pine forests and snow-capped peak. That is to say, this *near to infinity* focusing will give you a picture containing objects in the foreground and objects in the far distance, all of them with almost the same sharpness of definition.

Owing to the great depth of field it provides, this *near to infinity* focusing (focusing at what is called the "hyperfocal distance") is quite useful even for reflex cameras, with which, it is true, you usually focus by means of the ground-glass screen, or with cameras fitted with a focusing scale. But its real usefulness is for the simpler types of apparatus which possess neither ground-glass screen nor focusing scale and are therefore sometimes known—rather unkindly—as "blind" cameras.

The exact figures for various focal lengths for the "near to infinity" setting are:

Focal length	*Camera size*	*Distance-scale setting*	*Stop*	*All sharp from*
3.5 cm. (1⅜ in.)	35 mm.	12 ft. (4 m.)	8	6 ft. (1.8 m.)
4.5–5 cm. (1¾–2 in.)	35 mm.	12 ft. (8 m.)	8	12 ft. (4 m.)
7.5 cm. (3 in.)	V.P., 2¼ × 2¼ in.	25 ft. (8 m.)	8	12 ft. (4 m.)
10.5 cm. (4⅛ in.)	3¼ × 2¼ in.	25 ft. (8 m.)	11	12 ft. (4 m.)

Another Simple Method of Focusing

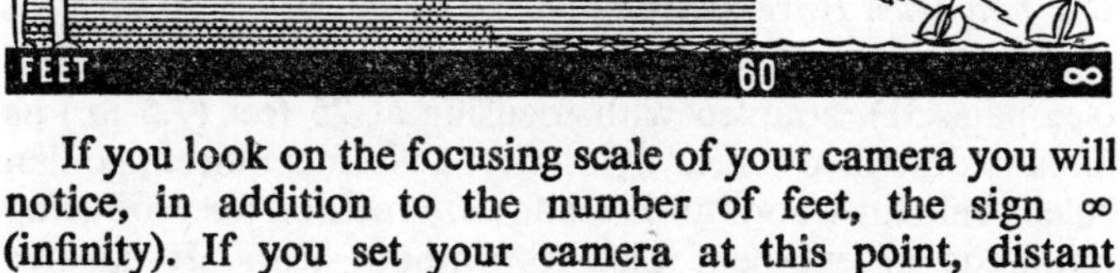

If you look on the focusing scale of your camera you will notice, in addition to the number of feet, the sign ∞ (infinity). If you set your camera at this point, distant objects will be sharply focused and objects near the camera will be out of focus. This differs, therefore, from the previously mentioned "near to infinity" focus which gave sharp definition to both near and distant objects. If you set your camera at infinity, you will get the distance clearly, even with a wide stop, whereas the near to infinity focus needed, you will remember, a medium or even a small aperture.

So, you set your camera at ∞ when there is nothing close to the lens. Landscapes without any foreground, aeroplanes flying in formation against the clouds, and all such distant subjects can best be captured by the *infinity focusing*. It is also useful for pictures taken from a hillside, looking down into the valley, or from the top of a tower, provided that the nearest objects, tree-tops, roofs, etc., are far enough from the lens.

How far away they must be depends on the size of the camera, or, more exactly on the *focal length* of the lens—(this is printed on the lens mount)—and on the size of aperture used.

Focal length	*Camera size*	*Infinity begins for:* Stop 4:	Stop 5.6:
3.5 cm. (1⅜ in.)	35 mm.	33 ft. (10 m.)	22 ft. (7 m.)
4.5–5 cm. (1¾–2 in.)	35 mm.	60 ft. (19 m.)	45 ft. (14 m.)
7.5 cm. (3 in.)	V.P.K., 2¼ × 2¼ in.	60 ft. (19 m.)	45 ft. (14 m.)
10.5 cm. (4⅛ in.)	3¼ × 2¼ in.	90 ft. (28 m.)	65 ft. (20 m.)

So you see that even with focusing to infinity the beginning of the area of sharp definition is fairly near to the camera—nearer, perhaps, than you would expect.

But You Must Have Sunshine

The formula: Sun + 125ASA = stop 16 + 1/125 second (see page 31), coupled with focusing at 25 feet (7.5 m.) as already described ("near to infinity"), is a magnificent golden rule, a rule for woods and meadows, a method for producing hundreds of excellent pictures without tears. It ensures sharp definition for everything farther away from the camera than 13 feet (4 m.), and gives sufficient illumination.

The exposure of 1/125 second is rapid enough for any not too quickly moving objects outside the minimum distance, and if the objects in motion are a long way away from the camera, then even more rapid movements, such as of children at play, animals, cars travelling at a moderate speed, will be quite sharp on the film. You will not need either an exposure meter or a distance meter and you will snap your picture while others are still fumbling and calculating how to do it.

With this amount of information you can trust the veriest beginner with a camera to come home with good pictures, provided he realizes (or at any rate observes) the limitations of the method.

Remember: the area of sharp focus does not begin until the object is at least 13 feet (4 m.) from the camera, and sunshine is essential. If the sky is clouded over you must lengthen the exposure to 1/60 second. But in that case you must make doubly sure that no fast-moving objects come into the picture, as otherwise this relatively slow shutter speed could not cope with them. And hold the camera still!

In any case this handy rule of thumb, with its merely approximate length of exposure, requires suitable compensatory treatment in the dark-room. That is, care must be taken to ensure that the moderately-exposed parts of the picture appear clearly and that the over-exposed parts are damped down. So choose a reliable firm to do your developing.

In Other Cases Use an Exposure Meter

The easy rules we have just described are only applicable to favourable lighting conditions. In cases where these are not present, we must use an aid to correct exposure.

You can obtain exposure tables (see pages 41 and 66) which give you the correct length of exposure for various subjects (landscapes, buildings, portraits) classified according to brightness, and for various times of day and different speeds of film. With these the correct exposure for a given aperture can be worked out, and vice versa. But this requires time on each separate occasion and even then the results are not entirely reliable. That is why you should get hold of an exposure meter. It will soon pay for itself.

The best instruments are the electric exposure meters. They are accurate and need very little previous knowledge to use. You can read off the exposure from them as easily as you tell the time by your watch.

How to Use the Exposure Meter

If you are taking a landscape, the meter should be pointed downwards somewhat so that the reading is not influenced too much by the brightness of the sky. And when you are making a picture of a dark object against a bright background, or of a brightly-lit object against a dark background, the measurement for exposure should be made from a point nearer to the object than the camera. This compensates for the disturbing effect of the highly-contrasted surroundings.

This holds good also for cameras with built-in meter. Where the setting is fully automatic you can sometimes measure the light by pressing the release to its first pressure point. This will hold the setting, then you go back to the actual position and release the shutter fully.

Most exposure meters are fitted with a ready-reckoning scale by means of which the shutter speed can be read off easily for any aperture (or the aperture for any given shutter speed).

If the meter gives an exposure of 1/30 second for stop 8, the scale will tell you that with stop 4 you must give 1/125 second, or that with stop 16 an exposure of 1/8 is required, according to whether the subject in question requires a small aperture and a longer exposure or a large aperture with a correspondingly shorter exposure.

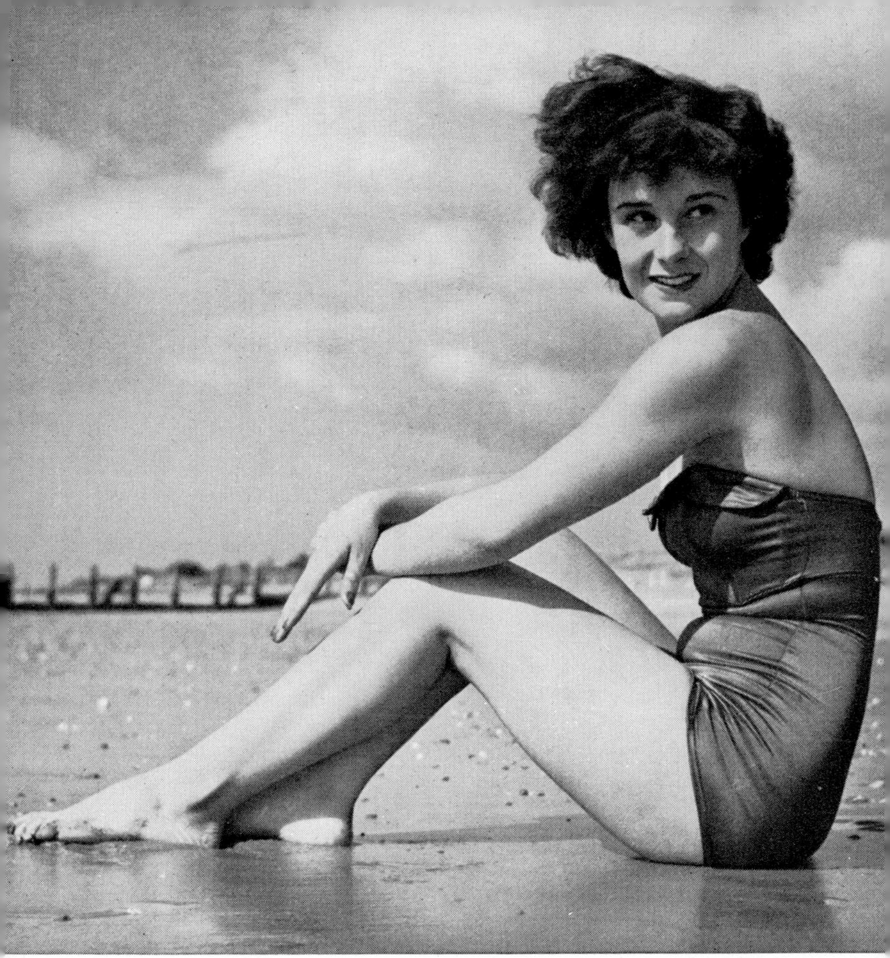

IDEAL CONDITIONS: plenty of sun, the subject is practically motionless and there is a medium fast film in the camera. There is nothing to hinder the photographer from stopping down as far as *f*8. He is quite safe in giving 1/250 second exposure. Even where a very bright sky really called for only 1/500 second, he did not make a real mistake. (See pages 31–32.)—Photograph by *Molly Jones*.

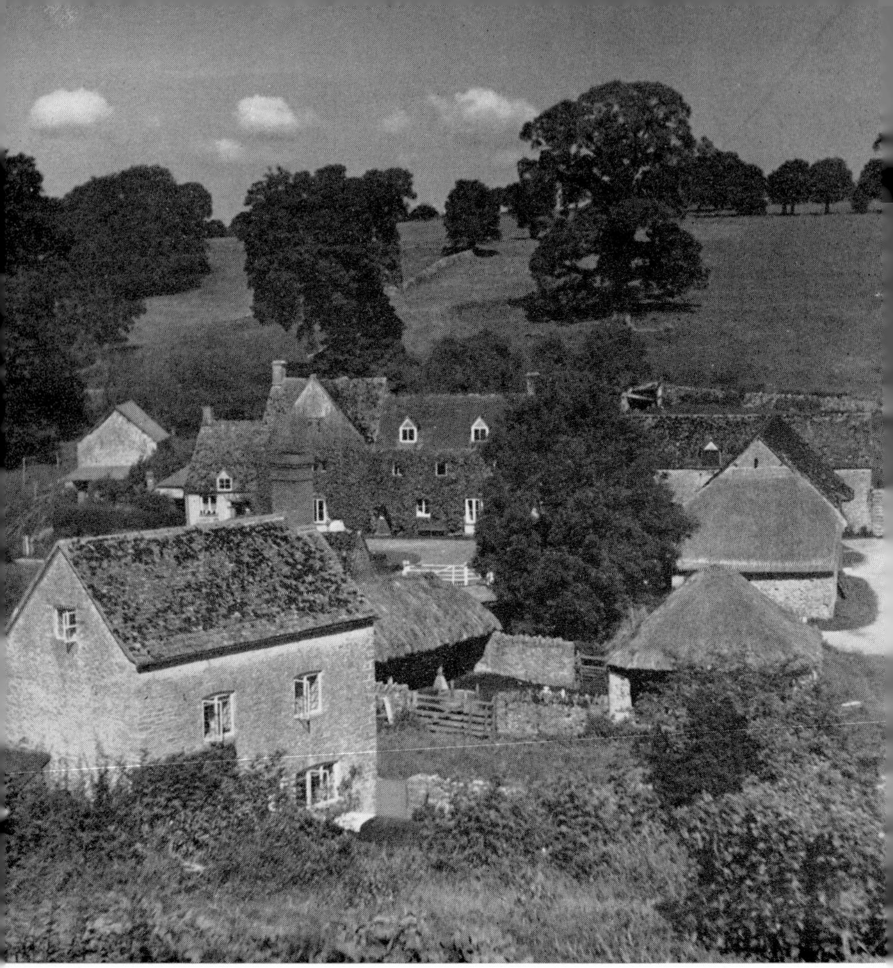

THE FOREGROUND: a group of houses is only a few yards from the camera. The background is quite far away: at infinity. In a case like this the camera is focused at 25 feet and with a stop of 11 it will give a sharp picture over the whole depth of the scene (as described on pages 32 and 33). The exposure was 1/25 second on a slow film.—Photograph by *H. van Wadenoyen.*

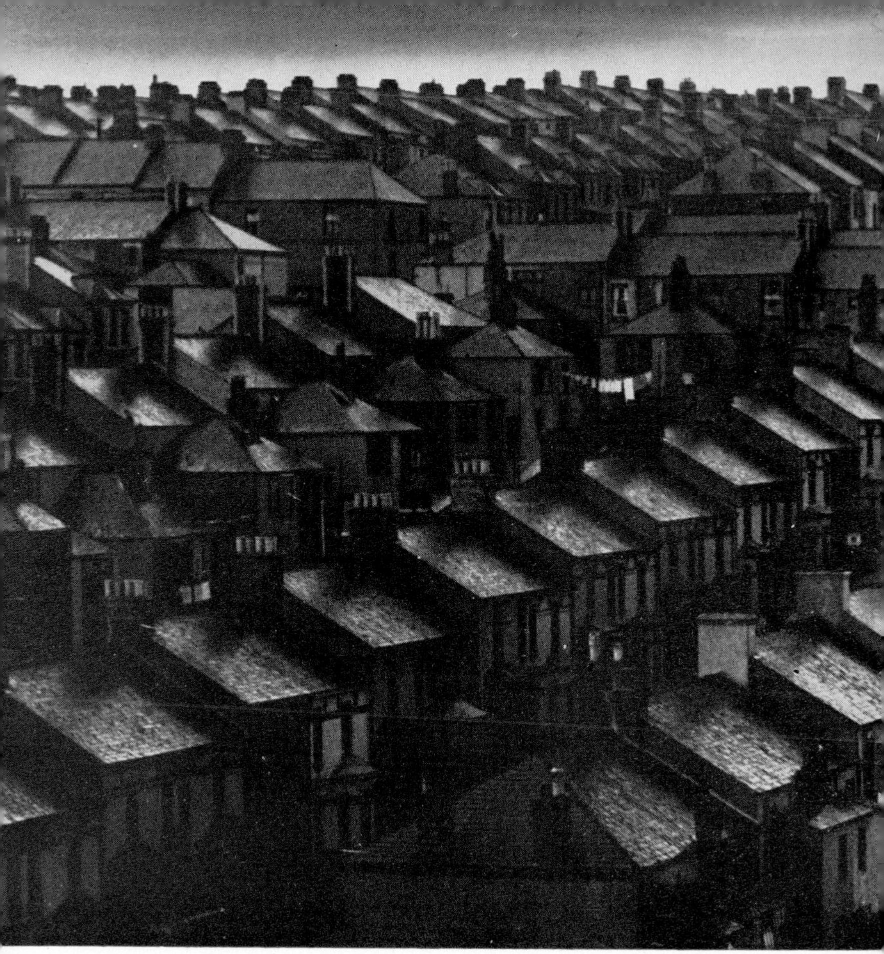

THE SUBJECT OF THIS PICTURE IS AT INFINITY, below and opposite the hill from which it was taken. There is no foreground to be taken into consideration. The infinity focusing (as described on pages 33 and 34) can be applied in this case. The exposure on a slow film was 1/25 second and stop 8.—Photograph by *Bill Brandt*.

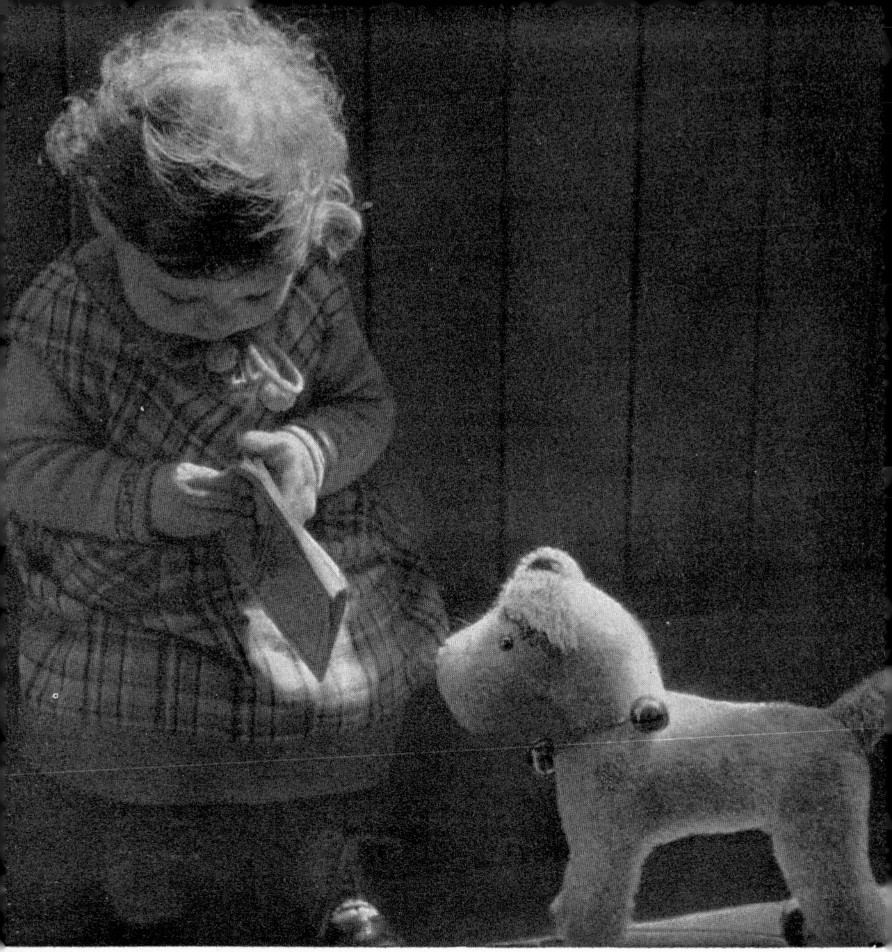

HEAVY SHADOWS are here side by side with brilliant patches of light. No exposure rule of thumb will help us this time. An electric exposure meter should do excellent service if used with care. The exposure was 1/50 second and stop 5.6 was used. (See pages 35, 36, 41.)—Photograph by *G. Gesell*.

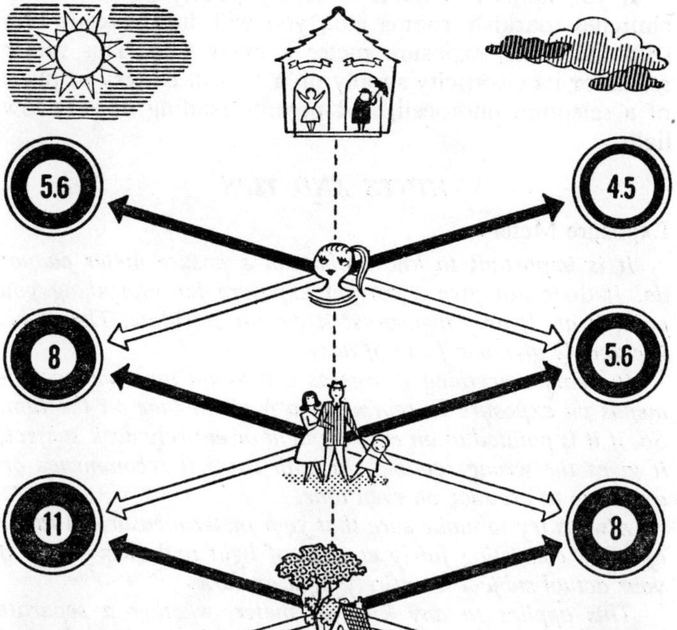

THIS DAYLIGHT EXPOSURE-FINDER assumes the use o a medium speed film of 64–125 ASA, and a shutter speed of 1/125 sec. *The stop* shown at the edges will always secure a satisfactorily exposed picture if you trace the line down through (1) weather condition, (2) subject, (3) tone of subject, i.e., dark or light, to (4) "stop" required.

The left-hand side will guide you in sunny conditions. *The right-hand side* will guide you when the sky is overcast.

Example: If you photograph in sunny weather somebody wearing light clothes at medium distance you may use stop 11—but if the weather is dull and your subject wearing dark clothes close to the camera you need stop 4.5 provided that in both cases medium speed film is used and your shutter speed is 1/125 sec.

If you make it a habit of taking poorly lit subjects in churches, darkish rooms etc., you will find a cadmium sulphide (CdS) exposure meter a great help. This meter relies for its electricity supply on a button battery in place of a selenium photocell, and permits reading of very low light.

HINTS AND TIPS

Exposure Meters

It is important to know what an exposure meter cannot do. It does not *give a correct exposure for everything you point it at. It only measures: it cannot calculate. Therefore, it can only give one form of answer.*

It treats everything it sees as a medium tone and recommends an exposure to reproduce a medium tone on the film. So, if it is pointed at an entirely light or entirely dark subject, it gives the wrong reading. In both cases it recommends an exposure to produce an even tone.

Always try to make sure that your meter measures a range of tones consisting fairly equally of light and dark—even if your actual subject is entirely light or dark.

This applies to any kind of meter, whether a separate instrument or built into the camera, whether it takes an individual reading or reads through the camera lens (TTL meters).

Through-the-lens meters are no different to any other meter, especially when used with a standard focal length lens, when they may even read a wider angle than a separate meter. The so-called "spot" reading types have to be used with extreme care in accordance with the camera instruction manual.

THE PROBLEM OF MOVEMENT

The Importance of Instantaneous Snaps

It is usual to divide the long series of commonly used exposures into two parts. Exposures of 1/60 second and faster belong to the instantaneous group, whereas the slower shutter speeds, such as 1/15 second and longer, count as time exposures, that is those for which the shutter is opened and then closed again after the elapse of the required time.

The 1/30 second shutter speed holds a position mid-way between instantaneous and time exposures, sometimes being counted as one and sometimes the other. If your hand is reasonably steady you will be able to give an exposure of 1/30 without moving the camera. A picture of this kind, made without the help of a tripod or other fixed support, can be counted as a snap—an instantaneous exposure.

On the other hand, there are excitable people who are unable to give an exposure of 1/60 second without wobbling or shaking the camera, with the result that the picture is two-fold or three-fold or merely blurred all over. The result in any case is a failure. Such people should certainly consider 1/30 as being a time exposure and either use a tripod or place the camera on a firm base before pressing the release. Only in this way can they hope to keep the camera perfectly steady and obtain a stable image on the sensitive emulsion of the film inside.

With modern photographic films, the emulsion is so sensitive, that is, the films are so fast, that most pictures taken out-of-doors can be given quite short exposures, even when the sky is overcast or when shadows cast on the model decrease the light value. Even when reckoning with a small aperture the exposure meter will often indicate 1/60 or even 1/125 second, and the question of giving the longer exposures arises only in exceptionally unfavourable lighting conditions such as might occur in the early morning or late evening or with photos taken indoors. But otherwise you can do everything you want with short exposures, and you will find that these instantaneous snaps will be considerably more numerous than time exposures.

Moving Objects Demand Short Exposure

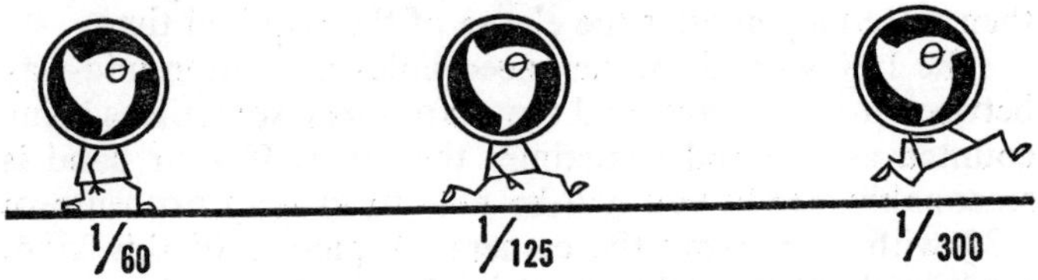

When you take a picture of people or things in motion, the movement in front of the camera is reproduced by the image which is thrown by the lens on to the film. So the image must not be allowed to remain on the film long enough for the movement of arms and legs, cars and other moving vehicles, to result in a visible shifting on the film.

If the movement is moderately rapid, an exposure of 1/30 second will probably be short enough, though, for safety, 1/60 is to be preferred. Even quickly-moving vehicles and so on can be taken at this speed, provided they are at some distance from the camera.

The swifter the movement and the nearer the moving object is to the camera, the shorter the exposure. Photos of sporting events often require a shutter speed of 1/500 second, and even this may be only just short enough. If the object, runner, car, etc., is moving away from or towards the camera, the exposure can be somewhat longer, provided that the snap is taken at an acute angle. For example, a car disappearing into the distance straight in front of you will require a much less rapid exposure than one which is passing in front of you from one side to the other.

In photographing rhythmical movements—such as high-jumps, exercises on the horizontal bar, swings and so on, wait for the *dead point*, that is the moment at which the jumper, for instance, reaches his highest point before starting to come down. If your timing is accurate, the action picture will, in reality, be made from a stationary model. On page 56 a table will be found giving the maximum reliable exposures for various rapid movements.

If the photos are to be enlarged, the original negative must be needle-sharp in every detail, for even the slightest trace of blurring in the film will be plainly visible on the enlargement. And the higher the magnification the more apparent will the defect appear on the enlarged copy.

Since the image is only allowed to remain on the emulsion for a very short time, the diaphragm must be wide open to allow more light to come in. This means that the depth of field is considerably reduced, and this means, of course, that the greatest care must be taken to focus accurately. For it would be useless to avoid a blurred image due to rapid movement, if the picture is going to be spoiled by being out of focus.

Snapshots Must be Snappy!

The technique of snapshotting can only partially be learned. For the rest it is a question of luck and a good nose for any likely subject which may crop up. The genuine snap is neither planned nor posed. It just happens, to-day, next week, here, there, round the next corner.

You must be very quick if you don't want to lose the really good snap. It is now or never. A moment later and you are too late. Press photographers with all their wits about them have shown us what can be done in the way of unpremeditated snaps. But there is no need for the amateur to wait for an aeroplane crash or a street accident. Good snapshots can be quite harmless and pleasant.

When Blackie, the cat, thinking he is quite alone, stands on his hind legs and delicately dips a paw into the bowl of gold fish, or when the girl at the bus stop opens her handbag and begins to renew her war-paint—here is your chance for a snapshot. So out with your camera and snap. The picture must be safely on the film before Blackie, realizing that he has an audience, assumes an innocent pose or makes himself scarce, and before the lady sees her bus coming and pops the mirror and lipstick back into her handbag.

This is where good photographic technique comes in. Of course good lighting is highly desirable. To make sure, see that your camera is loaded with a good, rapid film. Use stop 11 (or 8 if the light is poor) and set the shutter at 1/125 second. There remains the question of focusing. "Near to infinity" will not do here, seeing that the area of sharp definition only begins at thirteen feet in front of the camera. It is no consolation to know that it extends right over the houses on the other side of the street. We need a "snapshot-setting". We do not need sharpness in the distance, so we focus at 13 feet. The area of sharp definition now lies nearer to the camera:

Focal length	*Camera size*	*With Stop 4 sharp*		*With Stop 5.6 sharp*	
		from	*to*	*from*	*to*
3.5 cm. ($1\frac{3}{8}$ in.)	35 mm.	7 ft. (2.1 m.)	∞	7 ft. (2 m.)	∞
4.5–5 cm. ($1\frac{3}{4}$–2 in.)	35 mm.	9 ft. (2.7 m.)	19 ft. (5.8 m.)	8 ft. (2.5 m.)	27 ft. (8 m.)
7.5 cm. (3 in.)	V.P. $2\frac{1}{4} \times 2\frac{1}{4}$ in.	9 ft. (2.7 m.)	19 ft. (5.8 m.)	8 ft. (2.5 m.)	27 ft. (8 m.)
10.5 cm. ($4\frac{1}{8}$ in.)	$3\frac{1}{4} \times 2\frac{1}{4}$ in. (6 × 9 cm.)	10 ft. (3 m.)	17 ft. (5 m.)	9 ft. (2.7 m.)	21 ft. (6.5 m.)

Naturally one can use this snapshot-setting for other subjects, in fact whenever near objects have to be taken quickly, though not with such extreme speed as in the cases mentioned.

Near Views Require Careful Focusing

While it is an easy matter to get distant views sharply in focus by means of the simplest focusing method (page 34), near objects, surprisingly enough, demand much greater care, and the nearer they are, the more care they require. The tree a hundred yards away and the castle on the hill behind it, half a mile away, will both come out sharp on the picture with the same focusing. But the child playing four or five yards away must have a different focusing from the one which will be necessary if he comes up to within two or three yards of the camera.

The ingenious devices with which modern cameras are fitted, such as the ground-glass focusing screen of reflex cameras, or the rangefinders with which others are fitted, are intended chiefly for close-up views. For objects in the distance one could very easily get along without these refinements. But if your camera does not possess any of these things, it is advisable to purchase a separate rangefinder in order to take the guesswork out of estimating distances.

A Small Stop Gives Depth of Field

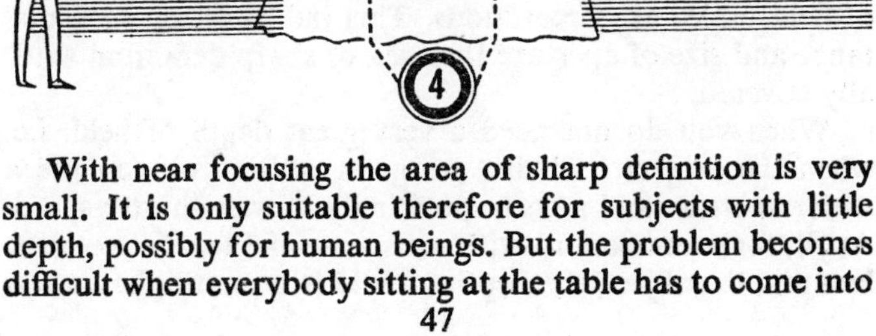

With near focusing the area of sharp definition is very small. It is only suitable therefore for subjects with little depth, possibly for human beings. But the problem becomes difficult when everybody sitting at the table has to come into the picture. However carefully you focus, your belt of sharp definition is too narrow: either the people nearest the camera or those farthest away are out of focus, sometimes neither is properly focused. It's like trying to put a bus into your garage: it simply won't go in.

But the necessary depth of field can be obtained by stopping down, that is, by having a very small aperture. This brings every part of your subject within the area of sharp definition. For this purpose stop 16, which is not much used otherwise, will not be too small. Sometimes, even, there will be a case for a still smaller stop, 22, provided, of course, that the camera in question is fitted with a stop of this size.

But another and less desirable result of these small apertures is the reduction in the amount of light which passes through the lens, with the consequence that the image is faint. To compensate for this you must give a longer exposure, so long that the picture becomes a "time" instead of an "instantaneous" shot. This in its turn means that the camera can no longer be held in the hand, and that even slight movement in the field of vision will result in a blurred image. All very awkward.

If the exposure meter gives an exposure of 1/60 second for stop 8, the adjustment scale will show that for stop 16 the necessary exposure is 1/15 second. So it is inadvisable to stop down to a pin point; one should reduce only as much as is necessary to get the required depth of field. If your camera is provided with a depth of field scale, depth of field tables are superfluous. This indicates for each distance and size of aperture the area of sharp definition actually covered.

When you do not need a very great depth of field, i.e. when the subject itself has no great depth, you can use a wider aperture and a correspondingly shorter shutter speed. At *f*4, for example and with a distance of 3 feet between the lens and the object, the depth of field is no more than a few

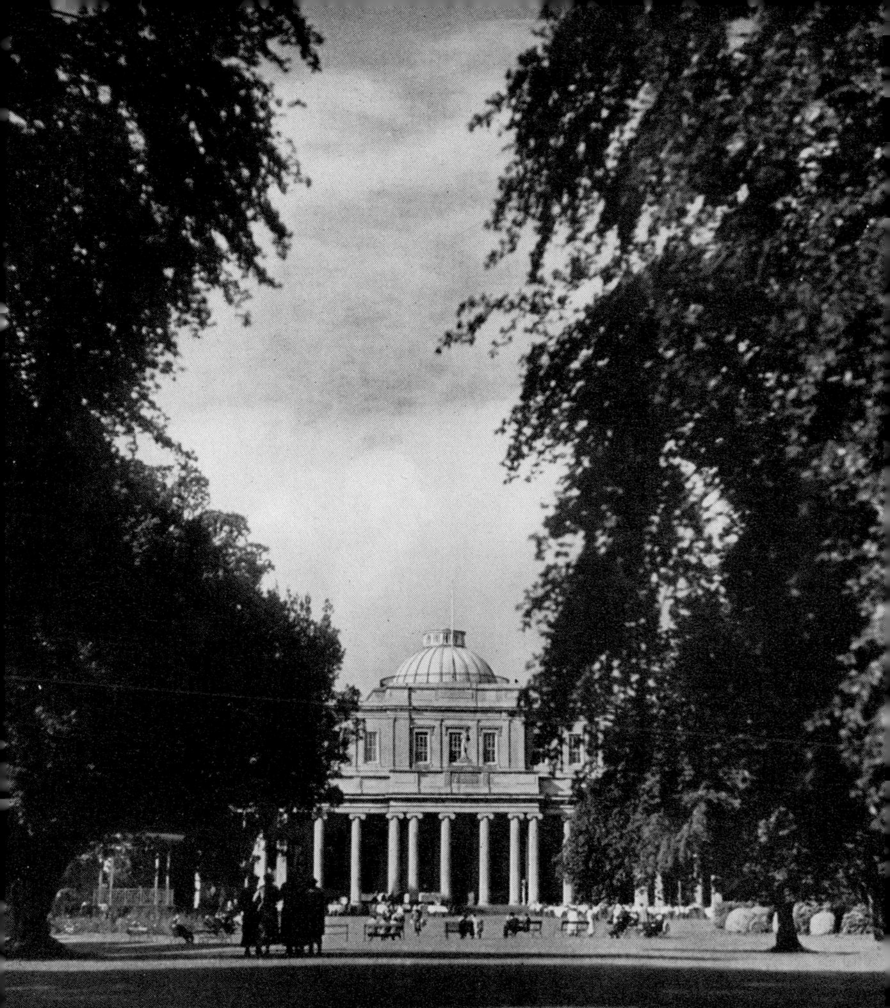

THIS PICTURE OFFERS NO PROBLEM of movement and no problem of focusing either. The choice both of shutter speed and stop is left entirely to the photographer. Here he was using a slow film and chose stop 8 with 1/50 second.—Photograph by *H. van Wadenoyen*.

THE RACING YACHTS (page 50) have their spinnakers out and a shutter speed of 1/300 second was needed to arrest movement of the billowing sails. Bright sunshine made a stop of 16 possible even with a yellow filter to darken the sky.—Photograph by *F. W. Beken*.

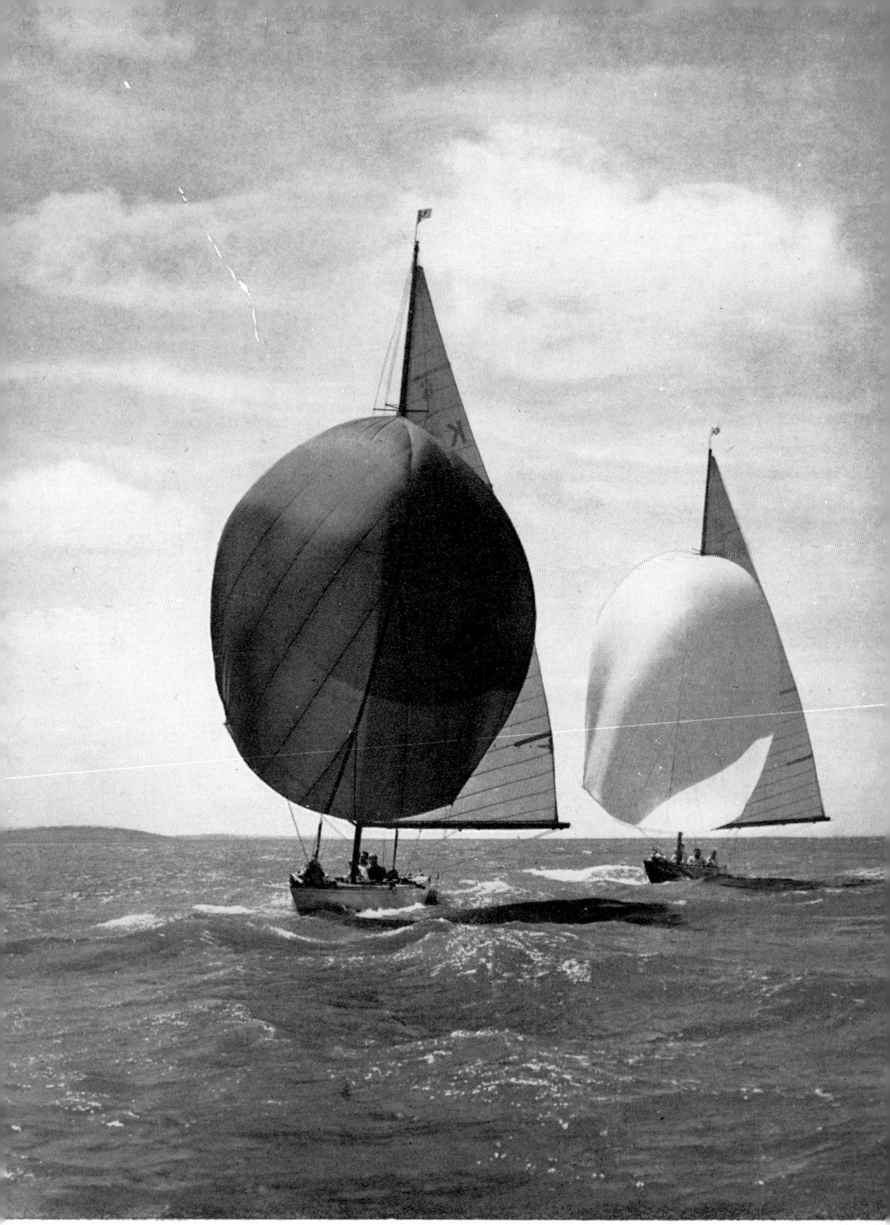

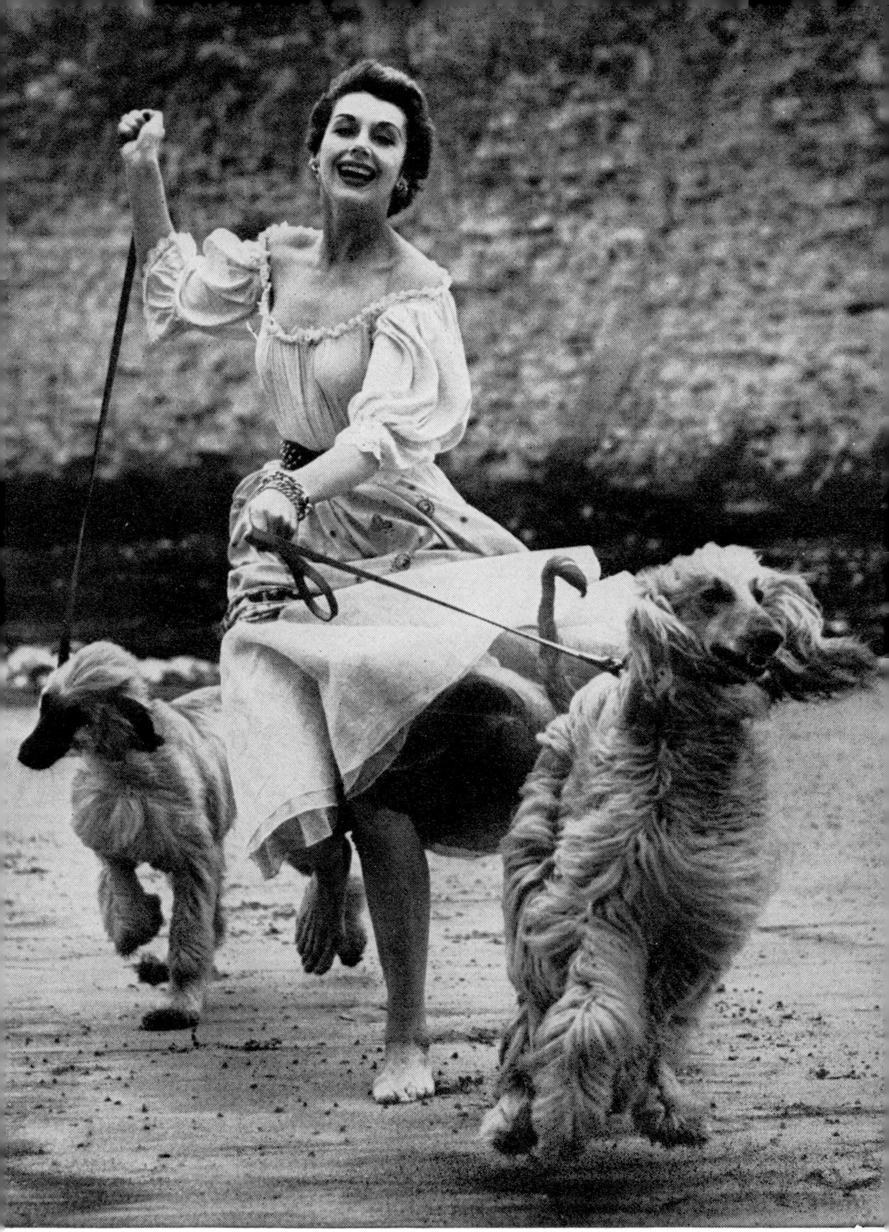

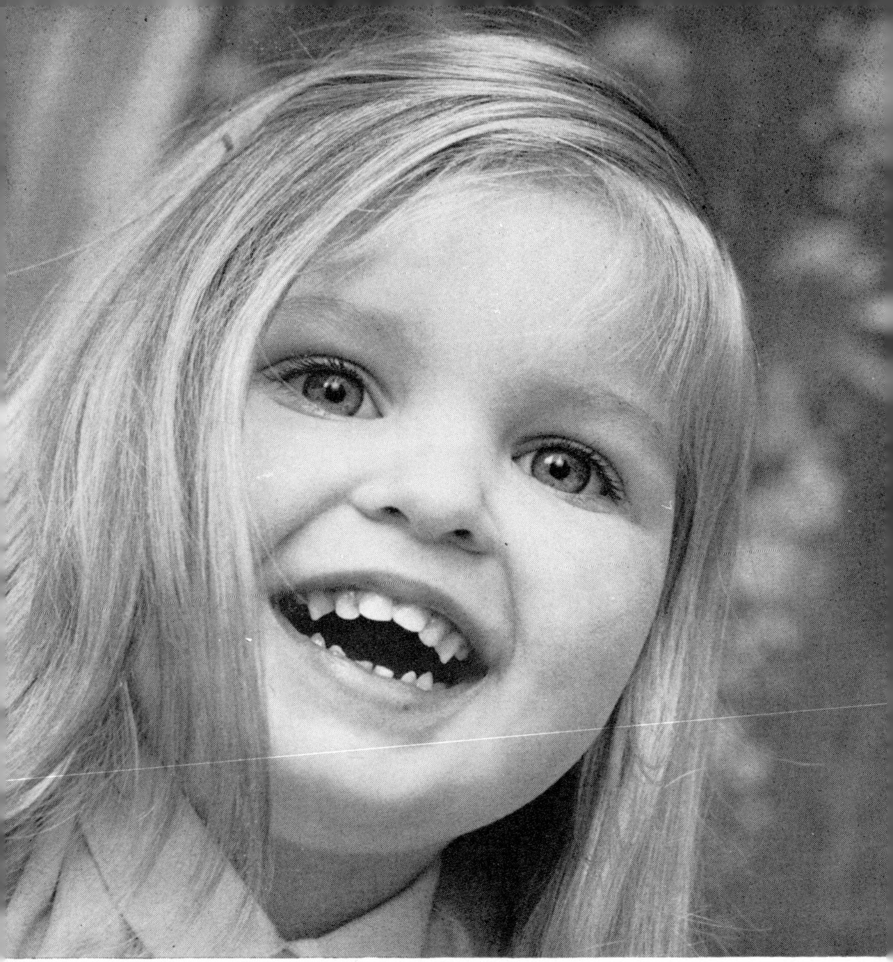

A CLOSE-UP PORTRAIT should be focused carefully and the lens not stopped down more than really necessary. The background should be out of focus, to make the head stand out against it. (See page 53.) Taken in bright, direct sunshine with 1/100 second.—Photograph by *Dixon's Photographic*.

GIRL AND DOGS (page 51) were heading fast towards the camera. A shutter speed of 1/500 second at stop 5.6 has caught them in full cry. The lens was first focused on a certain spot, and the shutter released when they got to it.—Photograph by *Malcolm McNeill*.

inches! And everything outside this small area will, of course, appear blurred on the picture.

A blurred background is usually no disadvantage. On the contrary it is often an advantage for objects in the background to be out of focus, so long as the general effect is not too wild and woolly. When the unimportant bits of the picture are blurred, your eye will pick out the really important things and ignore the rest. But blurred details in the foreground are to be avoided. Everything between the camera and the main object should be left out of the picture unless it is sharply in focus.

HINTS AND TIPS

Snaps of People

To snap a child at play or a character on the market-place, begin by turning your back on your quarry. Then adjust your shutter and aperture at your leisure and set the rangefinder at some suitable distance. Then turn round and discreetly approach the object until the rangefinder images line up—and release the shutter.

Naturally you choose your distance at the beginning so that only one or two paces are necessary to bring the rangefinder to the right distance from the object.

*If you are just walking around the streets or the beach taking pictures of people, it is a good idea not to bother with focusing every time. It slows you down. Set a fairly small stop, say f*8 *or even f*5.6, *and you can get everything sharp over quite a range of distances* (*see page* 46). *Set your distance scale to about* 12*ft* (4 *m.*). *Then you can walk up to your subject until you are anywhere within about* 8–20*ft.* (2,5–6 *m.*) *before bringing the camera quickly up to your eye and shooting. Quite often your subjects will not even know they have been photographed.*

If you intend to snap a quickly-moving object from a fixed point, say a runner on the cinder-track, your camera should be focused beforehand on some point over which the object must pass. The spot should be distinguishable by some detail—a tuft of grass, or a scrap of paper placed there for that purpose—and the shutter is opened when the moving object reaches the spot in question.

Depth of Field

The belt of sharp definition does not extend, as might be expected, equally on both sides of the focusing point. It is always wider beyond the point than on your side of it.

To take a striking example: with the camera focused at 25 *feet* (8 *m.*) *and with a correspondingly small stop* (*page* 33), *the area of sharp definition on the near side of the focusing point is only* 12 *feet* (4 *m.*) *deep, whereas beyond the point, the belt stretches to "infinity"—which is quite a good distance!*

If your camera is fitted with a depth of field scale you should use it. For one thing it gives you the region of sharp definition for every point on the focusing scale and for every aperture and makes a depth of field table superfluous. What is more, it indicates the beginning of the sharp zone for "Distant Focusing" and, in the case of "Near-to-infinity" focusing, the best point on the distance scale for each size of stop.

And, last but not least, with the help of this scale you can discover the largest aperture possible consistent with sharpness of definition for an object of known depth. For there is a limit to the smallness of aperture. Poor light or moving objects may require a comparatively large opening. Our depth of field ring shows us what is possible and what is not, and gives us the correct focusing to ensure the desired depth even with a large aperture.

A Rangefinder

Even "blind" cameras will guarantee sharply focused pictures with the aid of a rangefinder.

A cheap form of "rangefinder" is a metal tape measure that rolls up inside a little round box which fits the waistcoat pocket. But some subjects make the use of a metal rule out of the question. The cat, for instance, nicely perched on the gate-post, would promptly disappear if you thrust a measuring tape under its nose.

A proper rangefinder on the other hand, has the advantage of being unobtrusive and quick in action as well as giving measurements over a whole field from 2 *to* 100 *feet* (0.6–30 *m.*) *—which is more than a pocket-rule can do.*

Supplementary Lenses

For close-up work at shorter distances than are shown by the distance scale of our camera, supplementary lenses may be had. A simple single-glass (meniscus) lens will be found very satisfactory. The table on page 56, *shows the strength of lens in diopters to select to cover a certain distance range. It must be emphasized that, in order to ensure the same quality of definition as the lens would give without a supplementary, one should avoid using the largest stop. No change in exposure time is required.*

Incidentally, if yours is a technical camera with "double extension" you may use a negative supplementary lens which increases the focal length, bringing distant things nearer. Stop down the lens by two stops, and give four times the normal exposure for full double extension; with 50 *per cent increase of extension twice the normal exposure must be given. Should your camera have a sliding extension you may use the "close-up" lens as a "wide-angle" showing more on the picture than the normal lens. But if your camera is of the fixed focus, or one where you move the front-cell of your lens or the complete lens in a helical focusing mount you can use this type of lens for close-up work only.*

USEFUL TABLES

SUPPLEMENTARY LENSES FOR CLOSE-UP WORK

Lens set to	*Distance of object when using lens of diopters:* +0.5	+0.67	+1	+1.25	+1.5	+2	+3
ft. in.	ft. in.	ft. in.	ft. in.	ft. in.	ft. in.	ft. in.	ft. in.
∞	6 6¾	4 10⅝	3 3¼	2 7½	2 2⅛	1 7¾	1 1
48	5 9¼	4 5¼	3 ¾	2 5⅞	2 1⅛	1 7	1 ½
24	5 1¾	4 ¾	2 10⅝	2 4¼	2	1 6⅜	1 ⅛
15	4 6¾	3 8½	2 8¼	2 2¾	1 10¾	1 5¾	1
10	3 11½	3 3¼	2 5⅝	2 ¾	1 9⅜	1 5	11⅞
9	3 9¾	3 2⅛	2 4¾	2 ⅜	1 9⅛	1 4⅝	11½
6	3 1½	2 8¼	2 1⅜	1 9¾	1 7⅛	1 3½	11⅛
5	2 10	2 5⅝	1 11¾	1 9	1 5½	1 2¾	10¾
4 6	2 8	2 3½	1 10⅝	1 8½	1 5¼	1 2⅜	10⅜
3 6	2 3½	1 9½	1 6¾	1 5½	1 4	1 ¾	10

MAXIMUM EXPOSURE TIMES FOR MOVING OBJECTS

Object	*Distance of object*	*Towards or away from camera*	*Obliquely*	*Directly across*
People, animals at normal pace ..	25 ft.	1/60	1/125	1/250
Cyclists, street-traffic	25 ft.	1/125	1/250	1/500
Galloping horse, cycle races, car ..	25 ft.	1/250	1/500	1/500
Trains 30 miles per hour	50 ft.	1/125	1/250	1/500
Trains 60 miles per hour	50 ft.	1/250	1/500	1/1000

If twice the distance, exposure may be doubled. If four times the distance, exposure may be quadrupled. If your shutter does not have some or all the above speeds, set the nearest available speed (e.g., 1/100 for 1/125, 1/300 for 1/250 and so on).

CHOOSING THE RIGHT MATERIAL

There are two basic types of film that you can use in your camera. One takes only black-and-white pictures; the other shows the subject in full colour. The two types of film have very different characteristics so we shall deal with them one at a time—black-and-white first. Colour film is described on page 120.

What Speed of Film Shall I Use?

There is no such thing as a "best" film—a film that is best for any and every kind of picture. It does not follow that the most sensitive, that is, the fastest film, is the best, any more than that the biggest potatoes are always the best or a racing-car the most suitable model for taking out the family.

Before going further you should know that the speed of a film can be expressed in a number of different systems according to the method employed in testing film speeds. Here the ASA system is used because it is the most widely known. The only other system commonly encountered is DIN. The GOST system is occasionally seen on Russian cameras. A comparison of film speed ratings is given on page 66.

The fastest films, with a speed of 1000 ASA or more are to be recommended only for those occasions which cannot dispense with great speed, even at the cost of relatively poor rendering of tone values. The "normal" fast film of about 400 ASA, however, is essential for taking high-speed sporting events, or overcoming unfavourable lighting conditions indoors.

Medium fast films, that is, those with a sensitivity of about 100 to 200 ASA are remarkable for their correct rendering of tone values and for the fineness of their grain. Moreover, they lend themselves splendidly to enlargements and can therefore be considered as the most reliable all-purposes material.

Films below 64 ASA are only suitable for those specialists who make huge enlargements from tiny sections of their negatives. This is possible without producing unpleasant *grain*, that is, visibility of the granular structure of the emulsion, owing to the extremely fine grain and high resolving power. All these advantages are naturally offset by a smaller degree of sensitivity.

But the man who is satisfied with contact prints, that is, with pictures of the same size as his films, or with a very moderate enlargement, would gain nothing by the use of this type of film. For the average amateur the medium fast film is handier from the point of view of exposure and development, and will serve for most purposes.

Panchromatic Film

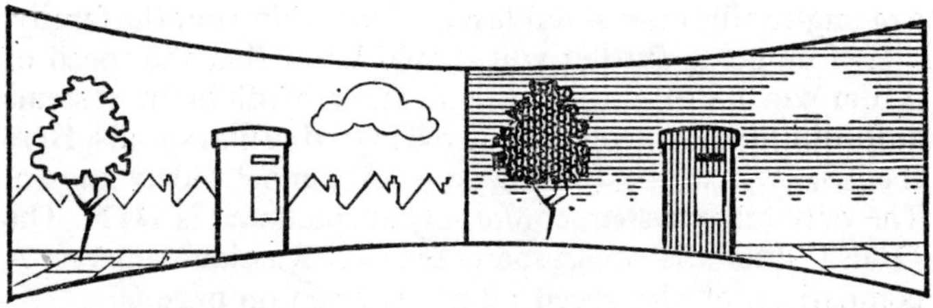

All black-and-white films used by the amateur photographer have what is known as *panchromatic* emulsion. This reproduces the coloured world of nature in black and white, with shades of grey approximating to the brilliance of all colours.

Older films used an orthochromatic emulsion but its disadvantage was that it did not translate colours correctly in black and white tones. For example, red things especially appeared much too dark, whereas red appears to our eye as a bright colour. Orthochromatic films, in other words, are colour-blind so far as red is concerned. Yellow, too, comes out too dark, whereas blue, which appears to us as a rather dark colour, is rendered far too light, or even white. This produces disappointing results.

Panchromatic emulsion acts quite differently. It gives a much more faithful rendering of colours, though not a strictly accurate one. In pictures from panchromatic films, red appears as a medium tone, yellow very light, and blue much darker. Panchromatic films are better, too, for mixed colours which contain red. The tanned faces of bathers at the seaside, for example, would be made nearly black by ortho films, and the difference is most striking when the same picture is made on panchromatic material (which is available in a wide range of speeds).

Orthochromatic film is still available for specialist applications but only as cut or sheet film. There are no 35 mm. or rollfilm versions. It can be useful for various copying purposes and in the darkroom, where it can be handled under safelighting to allow, for example, processing by inspection. Panchromatic film must always be handled in total darkness or, in extreme circumstances, in deep green safelighting for very short periods.

Panchromatic film, being sensitive to light of all colours, makes it easy for you to control the tones of your picture to an infinite degree by the use of filters (see page 68).

The Problems of Grain

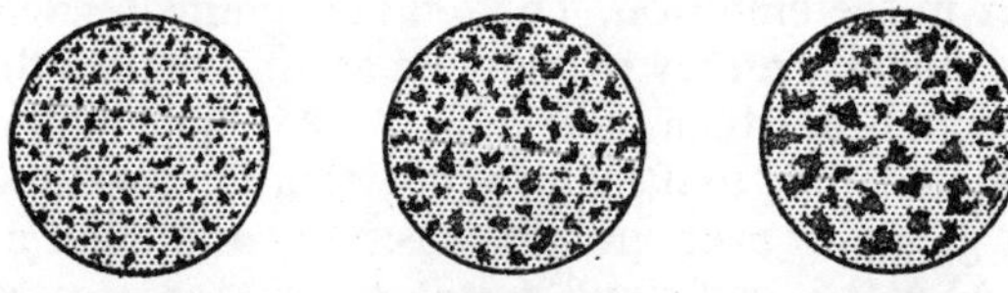

If you look at a crowd of people from the distance, the human mass seems to be so compact that there would not be room for a child to slip through. But when you go close up you find that the crowd is not so dense as you thought and that there is quite a lot of elbow-room between the various individuals who make up the gathering. It is somewhat similar with the silver grains which go to make up the picture on the emulsion. To the naked eye they form a compact, dark mass, but under the magnifying glass, or still better, under the microscope, the separate grains are visible.

Much has been written about this question of grain. Some writers make a hobby of it, which they trot out on every possible occasion. But in point of fact, for many amateurs, indeed for most of them, the question is not very important. The vast army of amateur photographers who content themselves with enprints (fairly small trade-processed enlargements) need not bother their heads about the grain business. Even quite fast film will give them reasonably good pictures. Even people who limit themselves to moderate-sized enlargements need not worry too much about fineness of grain. Provided they do not use super-sensitive film, that is, over 400 ASA, any coarseness in the grain will not be enough to spoil the picture.

Grain has, in fact, ceased to be a problem to any but the most careless of photographers. It used to be true that only the slow (40–50 ASA) films could give really big enlargements without the grain becoming objectionable. Fast films (320 ASA and faster) derived their extra speed from larger grains of silver in the emulsion. These larger grains tended to become visible when they overlapped at different depths in the thicker emulsions then used.

Now, the film makers produce thinner emulsions with smaller grains of even greater sensitivity and there are films of 400 ASA that can stand quite extensive enlargement.

Problems of grain are, in fact, so lightly regarded by the manufacturers that they now concentrate on different aspects. Modern medium-speed films are designed to produce *edge-contrast*, i.e. a sharp distinction between adjacent areas of different tone, rather than a gradual shading from one tone

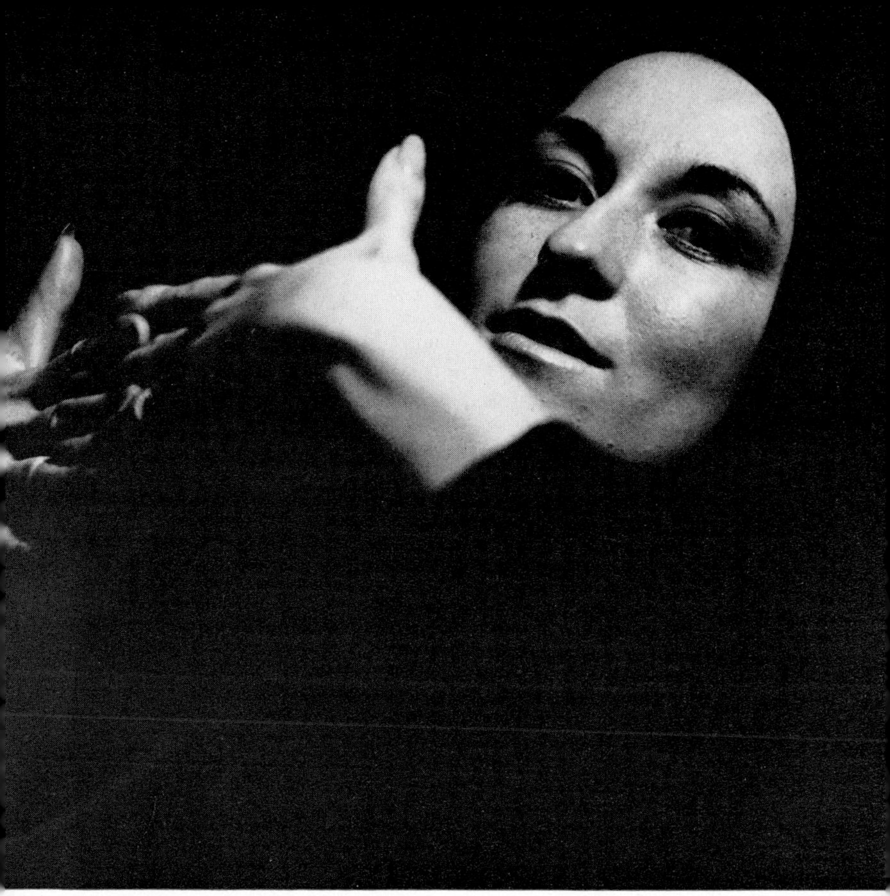

LOW-LIGHT photography calls for a fast film or longish exposures. Where there is no movement or a pose can be held, there is no point in using high-speed films. Where action is involved or the sitter cannot pose effectively the fast film may enable you to retain life in the picture. Exposure is often a compromise, dictated by the slowest shutter speed the movement will allow.—Photograph by *Stephen Young*.

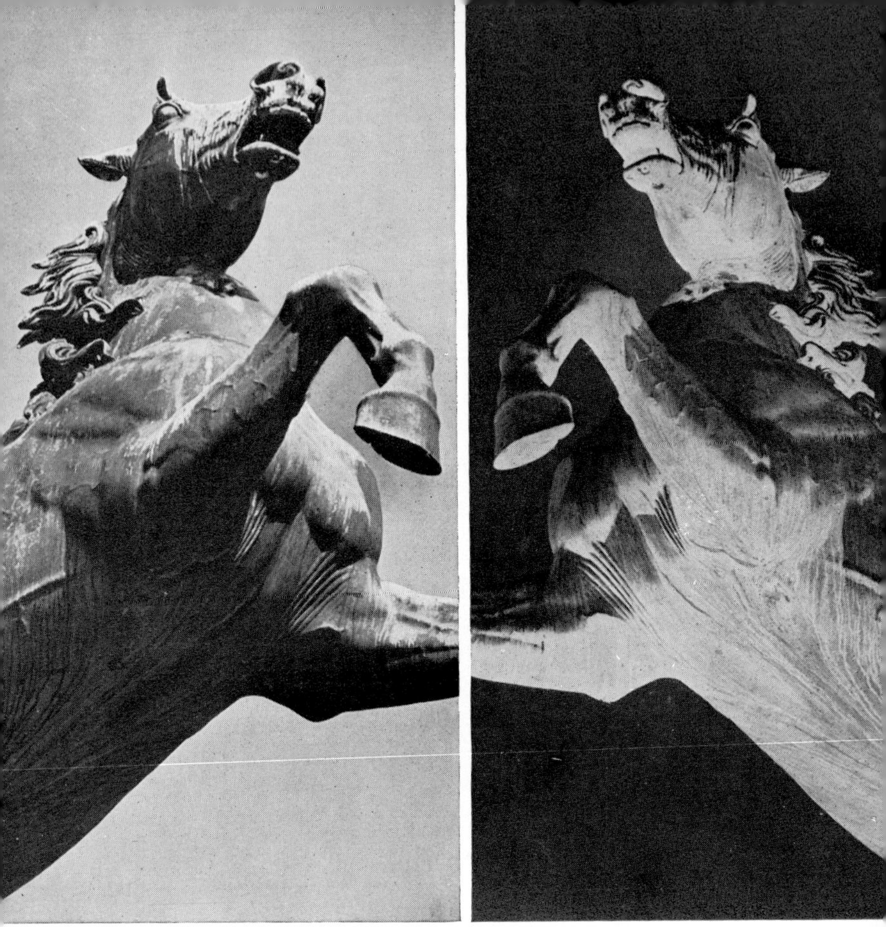

THE RIGHT EXPOSURE results in a satisfactory negative, as shown above on the right, which again helps to get a satisfactory positive, as shown above on the left. Both negative and positive show complete details in the shadows as well as in the light parts of the picture.—Photograph by *H. Gorny*.

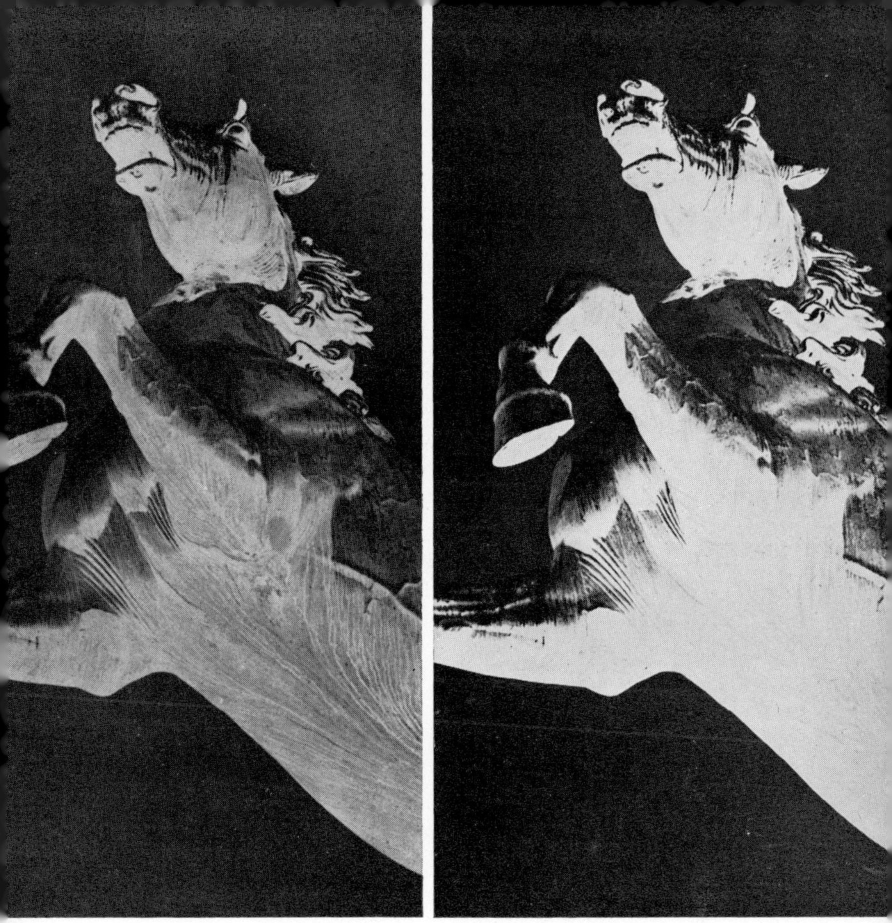

THE WRONG EXPOSURE leads to one of the effects shown above. The negative on the left is over-exposed: the shadows are veiled. This negative can be saved, however. (See page 226.) The negative on the right is under-exposed, showing violent contrasts between the light parts and the shadows. It is hard. This negative is practically lost. (See page 225.)—Photograph by *H. Gorny*.

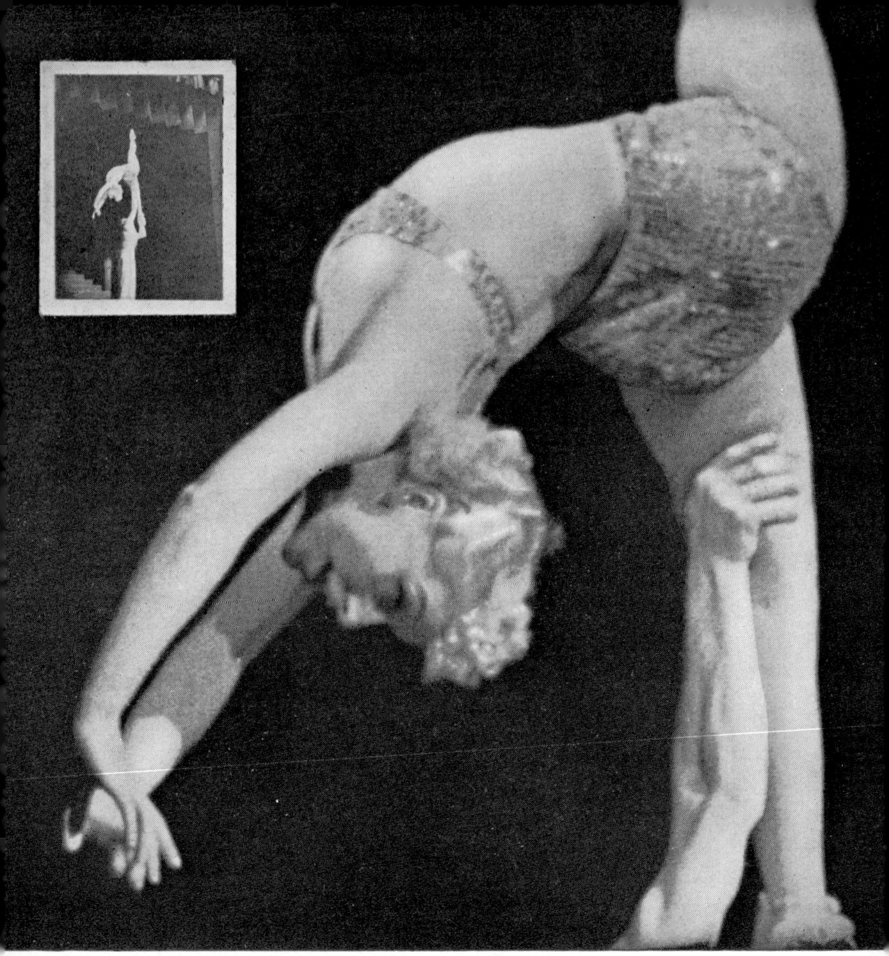

THE EFFECT OF GRAIN can be observed on the picture above; an enlargement of a small section of the original negative, as shown in the left top corner. It should be noted, however, that this photograph had to be taken on the older type of fast film. With most modern films, problems with grain arise only when processing is careless. (See page 64.)—Photograph by *Lancelot Vining*.

to another. Even the developers designed for use with them are vigorous types that do not produce particularly fine grain. These are the so-called acutance developers.

The theory behind this reasoning is that an image looks sharper to the eye when its granular structure is regular and the edges of the grains are sharper than when the grains are irregular in size and the edges are less well defined. As traditional fine-grain developers often contained a solvent which tended to soften the grain edges, the later process represents quite a radical change of technique.

HINTS AND TIPS

The Question of Exposure

So long as you do not under-expose, you need not be too anxious about the exact degree of accuracy. Modern films have enough "latitude" to compensate for the little extra light. But this must not lead to systematic over-exposure.

There is so little difference in light values between stop 4 *and* 4.5, *or* 5.6 *and* 6.3 *and so on, that they can be considered as interchangeable. If, for example, the exposure meter indicates stop* 9 *you need have no hesitation in giving stop* 8. *Any reasonable emulsion can get over bigger differences than these. (The same thing applies to the depth of field given by aperture* 4 *and* 4.5, *for example.)*

Film Speed Ratings Compared

The emulsion speed of the negative material may be expressed according to different methods of testing for film speeds. While a scientifically correct conversion cannot be made, the list on next page gives the practical relationship.

FILM SPEED SYSTEMS

ASA	DIN	GOST*	ASA	DIN	GOST*
25	15	22	200	24	180
32	16	32	250	25	250
40	17	32	320	26	250
50	18	45	400	27	350
64	19	65	500	28	500
80	20	65	650	29	500
100	21	90	800	30	700
125	22	130	1000	31	1000
160	23	130	1250	32	1000

* Approximate.

EXPOSURE TABLE FOR DAYLIGHT

Add the respective figures in Tables 1, 2 and 3. The sum is the exposure value to be set on the shutter which can be set directly on many camera shutters. For models without exposure value scale convert the exposure value to apertures and speeds with Table 4. (Set the shutter to the nearest marked speed if necessary—e.g. 1/25 for 1/30, and so on.)

1. *Subject and Weather*

Subject	*Clear*	*Cloudy Light*	*Cloudy Medium*	*Dull*
Distant landscape, no foreground ..	13	12	11	10
Landscape, light foreground	12	11	10	9
Open streets, light buildings	11	10	9	8
Figures and groups in the open ..	10	9	8	7
Figures and groups in the shade ..	9	8	7	6
Average interiors	3	2	1	0

2. *Month and Time*

A.M.		*P.M.*	*April to Aug.*	*Sept. Oct. Feb. March*	*Nov. to Jan.*
11	to	2	3	3	2
9–11		2–4	3	2	1
7–9		4–6	2	0	—

3. *Film Speed*

ASA	
10–12	−2
20–32	−1
40–64	0
80–120	+1
160–250	+2
320–500	+3

4. *Exposure Values (Sum of Tables 1+2+3) and Exposures in Seconds*

Exposure Value	f2.8	f4	f5.6	f8	f11	f16	f22
1	4s.	8s.	15s.	30s.	60s.	2min.	4min.
2	2s.	4s.	8s.	15s.	30s.	60s.	2min.
3	1	2s.	4s.	8s.	15s.	30s.	60s.
4	1/2	1	2s.	4s.	8s.	15s.	30s.
5	1/4	1/2	1	2s.	4s.	8s.	15s.
6	1/8	1/4	1/2	1	2s.	4s.	8s.
7	1/15	1/8	1/4	1/2	1	2s.	4s.
8	1/30	1/15	1/8	1/4	1/2	1	2s.
9	1/60	1/30	1/15	1/8	1/4	1/2	1
10	1/125	1/60	1/30	1/15	1/8	1/4	1/2
11	1/250	1/125	1/60	1/30	1/15	1/8	1/4
12	1/500	1/250	1/125	1/60	1/30	1/15	1/8
13	1/1000	1/500	1/250	1/125	1/60	1/30	1/15
14	—	1/1000	1/500	1/250	1/125	1/60	1/30
15	—	—	1/1000	1/500	1/250	1/125	1/60
16	—	—	—	1/1000	1/500	1/250	1/125
17	—	—	—	—	1/1000	1/500	1/250
18	—	—	—	—	—	1/1000	1/500

FILTERS HELP THE FILM

Filters Give Correction

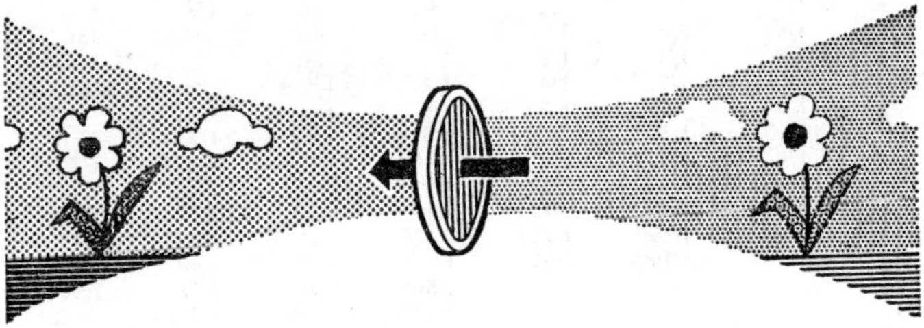

Black-and-white film (for filters for colour film, see page 126) does not always render colours in their true tone-values, so that the photograph often looks disappointing as compared with the real scene with all its vivid colours.

For example, we want to get a picture of some white flowers standing against a dark-blue background. We get the finished print, and what do we see? The dark-blue sky is almost white, and the white blossoms merge limply and disappointingly into it. Nor does the picture of the country scene show much trace of those beautiful cottony fine-weather clouds above the fields, while the blue hills in the distance are hardly visible. For blue, which to our eye appears dark, is rendered rather lighter by the pan film, so that all distinction between white and blue disappears.

There is, fortunately, a means of improving colour reproduction. In practice a yellow filter placed in front of the lens will help considerably. This allows the red, yellow and green rays to pass, but subdues the blue ones. So the somewhat "pushing" blue light can no longer have such a powerful effect on the emulsion, and everything blue in the scene will now appear darker. Which is just what is wanted. But even green and yellow are improved to some extent by the filter. The yellow flowers now appear really bright and stand out clearly against the darker green of the grass.

There are suitable filters for a wide variety of purposes. The question is dealt with in detail on page 70 of this book.

Making Up for the Loss of Light

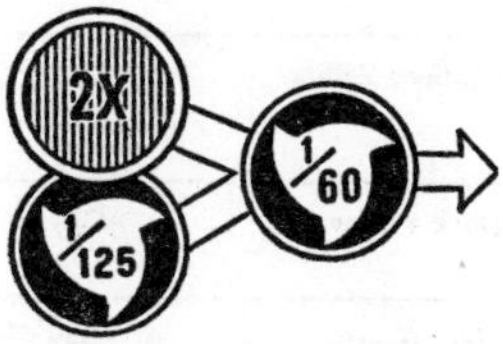

The improvement in the tone values which accompanies the use of a filter is not obtained without cost. Since the filter subdues certain important elements in the light which falls upon it, the consequent weakening of the image must be made up for in one way or another. Otherwise the result will be under-exposed pictures.

There are two ways of doing this: either the image can be allowed to remain for a longer time on the emulsion of the film, or else more light can be allowed into the camera. In the first case this means a lengthening of the exposure, and in the second a widening of the aperture. The result in both cases is to strengthen the image on the film.

If great depth of focus is considered desirable, in the case of near views, for example, then a longer exposure is indicated. If, however, a short exposure is essential, for example, if the object is in rapid motion, the extra light must be provided by a wider stop.

If a medium yellow filter is used with a pan film it is usually sufficient to double the time of exposure, or to use the next bigger stop. For example, instead of giving an exposure of 1/125 second, one would give 1/60 second, or, using the second method, stop 5.6 would be used instead

FILTERS, THEIR EFFECT AND USE ON BLACK-AND-WHITE PANCHROMATIC FILM

Filter Colour	*Light*	*Factor*	*Blue Objects Appear*	*Green Objects Appear*
None	Day	1×	Light	Dark
Light Yellow	Day	1.5×	Light	Rather dark
Medium Yellow	Day	2×	Normal	Normal
Dark Yellow	Day	3.5×	Dark	Light
Light Green	Day	3×	Normal	Normal
Dark Green	Day	4×	Rather dark	Light
Light Orange	Day	4×	Dark	Normal
Orange	Day	5×	Dark	Dark
Red	Day	8×	Very dark	Very dark
Blue	Day	1.5×	Light	Normal
None	Half-watt	1×	Normal	Rather dark
Green	Half-watt	4×	Normal	Normal
Blue	Half-watt	1.5×	Normal	Rather dark

This table intends to give a generalized survey of the various filters for the amateur as more often than not, a certain "effect" is aimed at instead of a true rendering.

Yellow Objects Appear	*Red Objects Appear*	*Field of Application of the Filter*	*Remarks*
Normal	Normal	—	Under corrected
Normal	Normal	To eliminate haze, to improve colour rendering	Slightly under corrected
Normal	Light	To produce colour-correct pictures of flowers, landscapes, cloud-effects, distant work	Correct
Light	Very light	For heavy clouds, darkish sky, etc.	Over corrected
Normal	Normal	For true colour rendering, including red	Correct
Normal	Dark	As "Light Green", but emphasizes blue and red	Over corrected
Normal	Light	Effect filter, rendering sky darkish, emphasizes clouds and far distance	Over corrected
Normal	Very light	As "Light Orange", but slightly increased effect	Over corrected
Normal	Very light	For dramatic effects: almost black sky, moon-effects in daylight	Over corrected
Rather dark	Rather dark	To make blue sky print as white. Makes pan-film behave like non-colour sensitive material	Under corrected
Normal	Light	Good corrected	—
Normal	Normal	Gives fullest possible colour correction	Correct
Normal	Normal	Gives almost full colour correction with minimum of exposure increase	Correct

The fact that a filter is termed "Correct" does not mean it is the most useful one of colour-values in black and white.

of 8. The *multiplying* or filter factor, which in this case is 2, will be considerably bigger if a darker filter is used.

Exact figures can only be given for each particular case, that is for the particular film used, for the exposure ratio depends not only on the nature of the filter but on the speed of the film as well. Although some photographic manufacturers give the multiplication factors for their filters with great accuracy, and speak of 1.3 and 1.7 times the exposure, we can cheerfully ignore the fractions and read the next whole number. For in the first place it is difficult to calculate with fractions and, secondly, the latitude possessed by any modern film is quite able to cope with any small degree of over-exposure which may result from our approximation.

Using a Contrast Filter

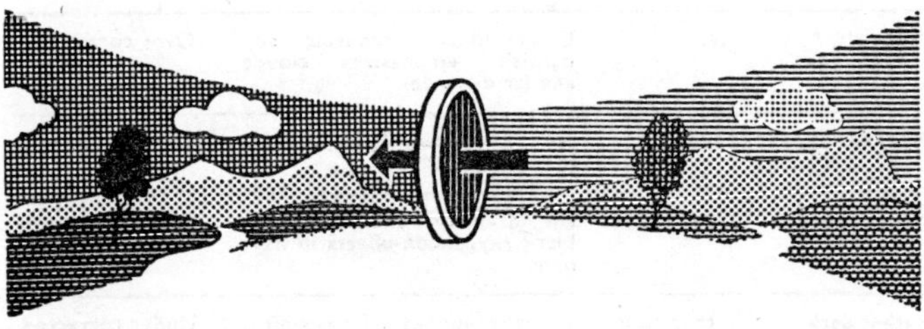

When photographing a landscape in black-and-white, it often happens that the bright blue light which comes streaming in from the space between the foreground and the sunny distant scene is scattered by the solid particles in the air and prevents objects in the distance from being seen clearly in the picture. The outlines are there all right, but they are smothered by the lively blue rays of light. Where our eye could see land distinctly in the distance, the finished print shows nothing there but a white haze.

Now if we put an orange filter, or, for an even stronger effect, a red filter in front of the lens, this blue light can no longer find its way into the camera. These filters let through only red, or at the most, orange light. The result is that distant hills and rocks and snowy mountains which would otherwise have been lost in the mist are clearly reproduced in the photograph.

Of course this improvement in the distant view has to be paid for, and paid for dearly. A red filter requires a six- or ten-fold exposure, or a correspondingly larger aperture. So if your exposure meter gives you 1/250 second for a given stop, you must, if you are using a red filter, allow 1/30 second even in the most favourable circumstances. Or else you must make a corresponding increase in the size of aperture, using, that is to say, stop 4 instead of 11.

Even an orange filter requires three to four times the normal exposure to be given (or an equal compensation from the size of aperture). For in either case, you are trying to make do with the light rays which remain over after the filter has taken its share.

By giving a considerably longer exposure, say, four times the normal time, or by using an aperture only two sizes bigger, one can obtain with panchromatic material and a red filter sham moonlight effects in broad daylight: an inky-black sky, walls of a ghostly white, and heavy, velvety shadows. If you decide to try these artificial night effects, see that the sky is cloudless and that the usually welcome figures in the foreground, people, cars, dogs and so on, are conspicuous by their absence. They would spoil the midnight atmosphere.

We started off this chapter saying that it refers to black and white film; let us finish by re-stating it. Filters for colour-photography are discussed on page 138.

SOME TECHNICAL REFINEMENTS

Pictures Against the Light are Effective

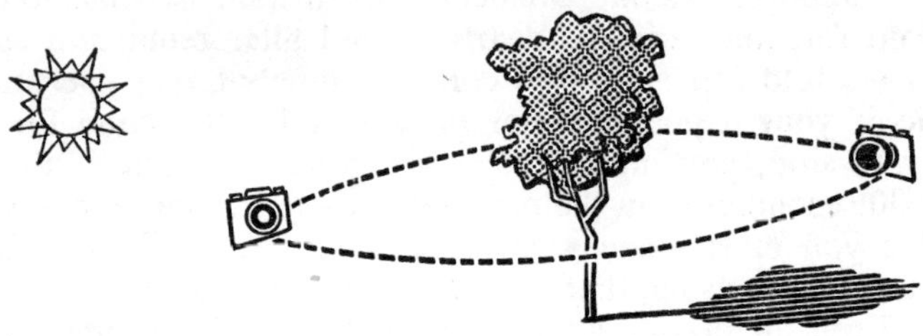

An important point to be considered is the position of the sun in relation to the camera.

If it shines from directly behind the photographer's back, objects are illuminated bang in front, and the result is a flat, shadowless picture which is rarely pleasing. Black and white representation of objects depends for its effectiveness on the interplay of light and shade.

Even side lighting gives better results, for it casts powerful shadows and gives things depth and "body". Foreground and background which, with back lighting, seemed to lie on top of each other, are now clearly separated.

But the most beautiful effects of all are produced by taking the picture against the sun, that is, with the sun in front and to one side, or even right in front of the camera. Of course, one must not exaggerate and allow the light to shine straight into the lens. This would only produce ugly halation effects on the emulsion of the film and details would be blotted out by unwanted circles.

But apart from this extreme case, against-the-light methods give excellent results. Long shadows lie alongside patches of brilliant sunshine. Everything is beautified by a shining halo round its edges. Sometimes the light between the near foreground and the distance, with its millions of light-reflecting dust particles, seems so solid that one could grasp it. It is remarkable how the most unpromising subjects—depressing suburban streets, for example—can be transformed and beautified by working against the sun. Then there are other subjects, such as the maze of tree trunks and masses of foliage in a forest which are simply unthinkable as photographs by any other than against-the-light methods.

Since the light comes at such an acute angle from in front of the camera, it is essential to use a *lens-hood.* It is fixed on to the camera in front of the lens, which it protects from the glare of the sun, just as we protect our eyes by shading them with one hand. The lens-hood also serves as a protection against the bright glare from things in the foreground. If there is a shady spot handy, such as a doorway or arch, under which you can stand while you are taking the picture, you can, of course, dispense with the lens-hood; your surroundings are acting as a protection for the lens.

Expose Accordingly

Since in against-the-light pictures things are attacked from their shady side, the exposure must be full. Otherwise the shadows will be pitch-black and show no detail at all. In cases like this the exposure meter, usually so reliable, must be used with great caution. It is apt to take its cue from the brightest rays of light which sneak past the dark shadows, and indicate an exposure which would be far too short for the shadows. So the meter must be pointed towards the shadow, and the effect of the bright sky must be reduced by shading the instrument with one hand while taking the reading but don't overdo it and measure only the shadow.

Another necessary precaution is to take the exposure measurement nearer to the object than to the camera, in order to avoid a falsification of the result by one or two bright spots. The reading obtained in this way is usually from 1/60 to 1/125 second with stop 5.6, using a film with a speed of about 50 ASA. Judged by the effect produced on the naked eye, the figures seem rather high, but in fact they are fully justified by the actual conditions.

Of course it is quite a different matter if no detail at all is required in the shadows in the foreground. In this case the exposure is measured from the brightly-lit background. The meter will show an exposure of 1/125 or 1/250 second, and this with stop 8. In the finished picture the foreground will be dark and devoid of detail and behind it the landscape or cloudy sky is brightly-lit and rich in detail. An inn sign, seen from the street below, or a monument standing in a sunny street, or a cross such as one sees sometimes in the fields in France, outlined against the line of blue hills—these and similar subjects are ideally suited for against-the-sun silhouettes.

A small aperture, together with focusing at 25 feet (7.5 m.), gives you "near to infinity" (see page 33) and ensures a sharp definition from the near, dark foreground right up to the bright distance, should this depth of field be required.

The method already described can also be used for colour snaps (page 125) for which against-the-sun methods are otherwise of little use. Here again the foreground is taken in silhouette. The exposure time is measured from the brightly-lit parts beyond. In the picture the foreground stands out dark and sharply outlined against the correctly exposed colour in the distance.

Soft Outlines

The lens maker has taken a great amount of trouble to ensure that his lenses produce an image which is as sharply defined as it possibly can be. Needle sharpness is not always required, however. It is occasionally preferable to produce

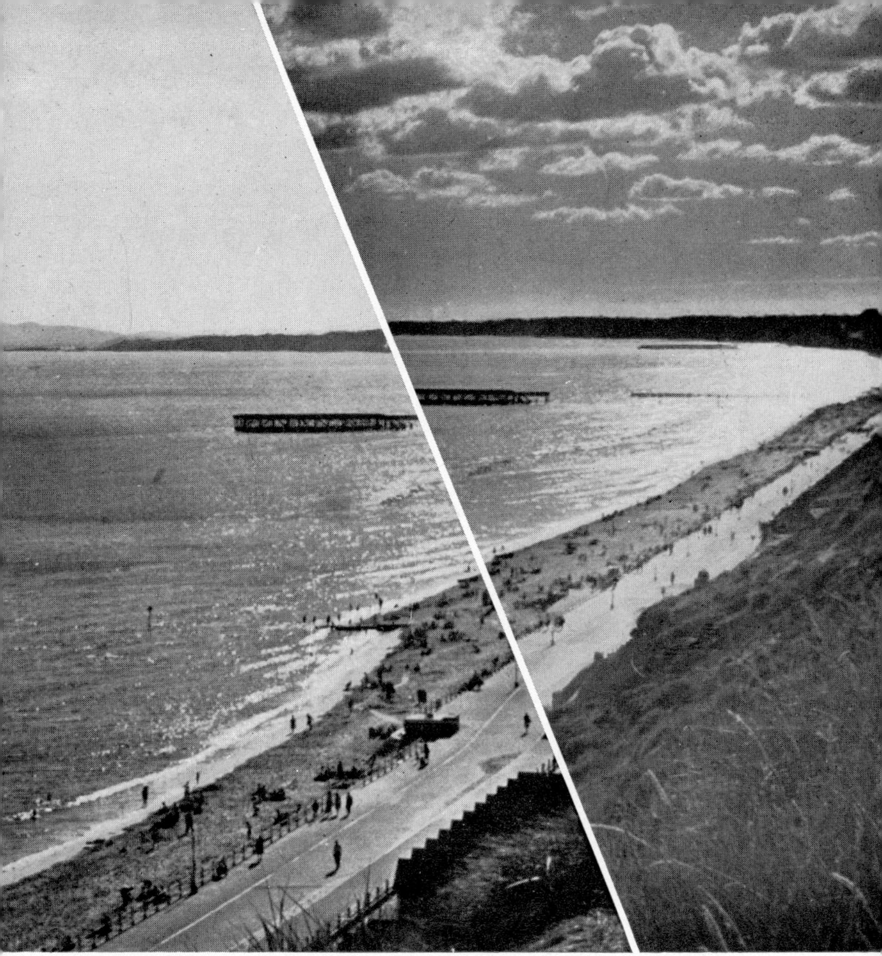

THE EFFECT OF A FILTER: the photograph on the left was taken on a pan film and shows an almost empty sky—the photograph on the right was taken immediately afterwards under exactly the same light conditions but with a medium yellow filter. (See pages 68–70.) On the left: the stop was *f* 12.5. On the right: *f* 9. The exposure time on both occasions was 1/50 sec.—Photographs by *W. D. Emanuel*.

A DEEP ORANGE FILTER (page 78) has produced a particularly striking effect. (See pages 72–73.) The exposure was 1/25 second, although normally without a filter, using the same pan film, only 1/200 second would have been required.—Photograph by *H. van Wadenoyen*.

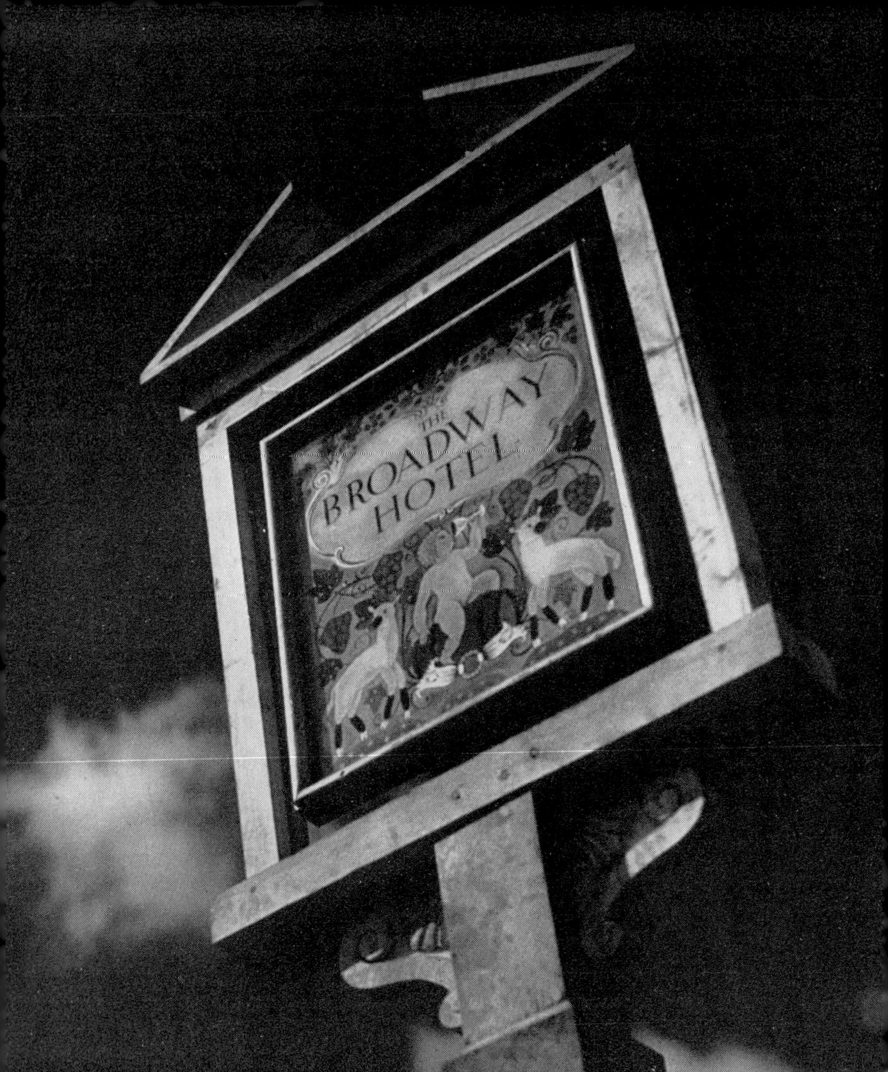
THE
BROADWAY
HOTEL

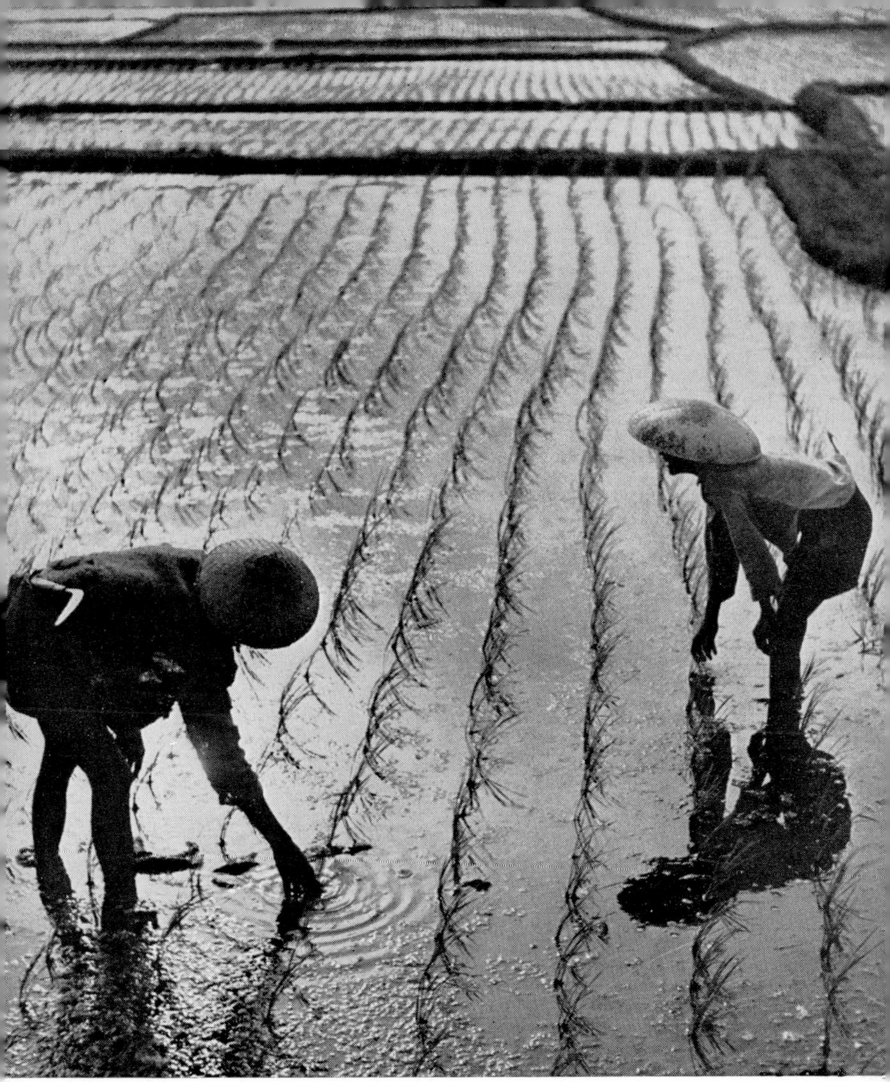

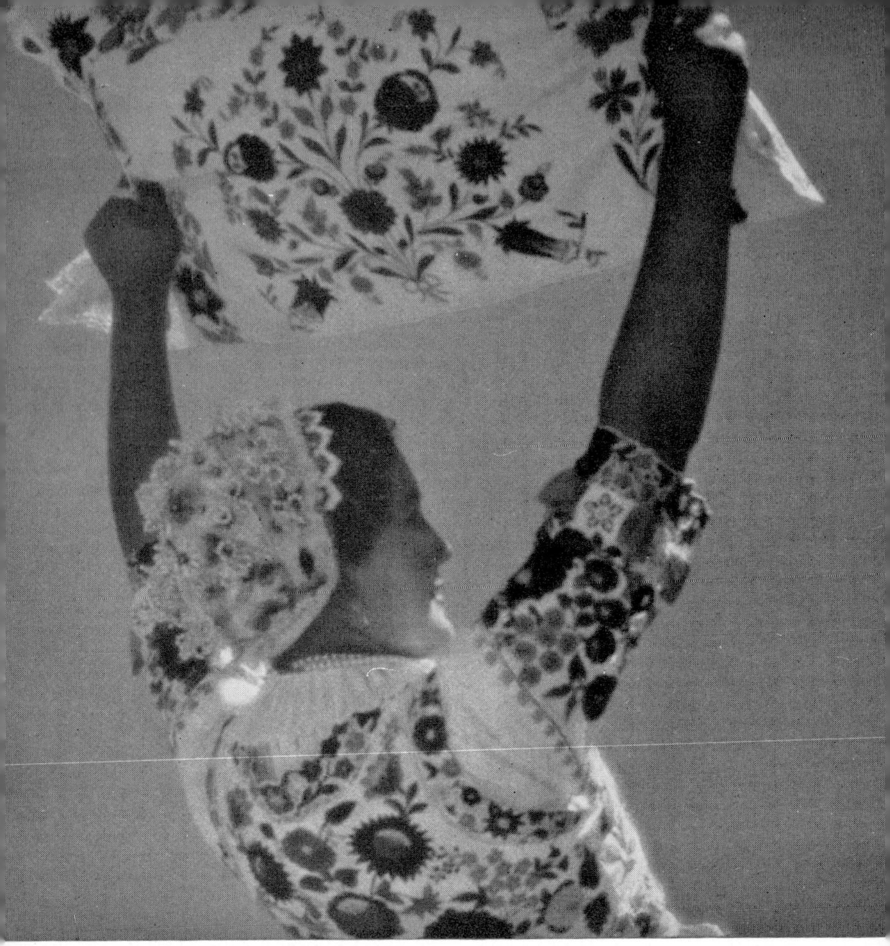

THE SOFT OUTLINES of the composition have been achieved by using a soft focus attachment. The effects can be clearly observed, especially by the way the lights are spread, giving a peculiar sparkle. Note how the highlights stand out. (See pages 76–82.)—Stop 4.5, 1/25 second.—Photograph by *G. Ramhab*.

AGAINST THE LIGHT (page 79). The deep shadows pointing towards the camera, the glittering catchlights on the water, the lively contrast between black and white create the depth and special charm of this picture. (See pages 74–76.) It was taken with stop 8 and 1/100 second.

soft pictures. This is especially true where "atmosphere" is wanted.

Now "soft" must not be confused with "out of focus". You will never get the softness of outline and the gentle merging of tones by focusing your camera inaccurately. There have been some specialist "soft-focus" lenses, which, with a large aperture, give soft pictures without any further ado, but these are not worth while for the average amateur photographer.

There are, however, simple appliances which can be fixed in front of the lens and which produce the same result. That is, they soften the hardness of outlines and tone down extremes of light contrast by diverting to some extent the path of the rays which fall upon the lens. There is, for example, a lens which consists of a flat glass disc bearing concentric rings. Light falling in the flat parts of the disc is undisturbed, and goes to form a sharply-defined image on the film. But the light rays which come into contact with the fluted portion are diverted from their direct path. The result is two images very close together. The second one, produced by the rays of light which have been pushed aside by the raised portions of the glass disc, is less sharp than the first. Together they form a well-defined, yet softened image of the model, in which the edges of the dark portions are lit by the neighbouring bright areas. The whole picture is diffused with a soft radiance. Common things are transformed and beautified in this bath of light. Sun-bathed landscapes taken against the light with the help of such a lens give pictures of real beauty.

When the subject is poorly lit a soft focus attachment is not a practical proposition, since it has the effect of toning down light contrasts. In any case it is a thing to be used sparingly and with discretion.

When using such a soft focus device, it must be borne in mind that its effect is lessened by reducing the size of aperture, the reason being that the fluting exerts less influence on the image if the stop is small. The aperture should not be smaller, therefore, than 5.6. If a very pronounced degree of softening is required even the 4.5 stop is not too large, even if light conditions would otherwise justify a smaller aperture.

HINTS AND TIPS

The Lens-hood

Most lens hoods are rigid metal tubular or conical constructions but there are some rectangular or square models supplied for specific lenses. There are also collapsible rubber types which can be folded flat for easy transport and storage.

If you have forgotten the lens-hood, you can easily make one from a bit of cardboard shaped into a tube and stuck down the side. But the length must be carefully calculated or the view will be blocked.

Soft Focus

Caution is advisable when using soft focus effects. When special soft focus lenses are employed at full aperture, you run the risk of getting a woolly picture.

If cross-patterned gauze is stretched across the lens, to produce soft focus effects, then any source of light appearing on the photo will show cross- or star-shaped light-patterns. This might be amusing once in a while, for instance above the candles of a Christmas tree, but it never looks natural.

If desired, you can add soft focus effects subsequently, i.e., when enlarging, by stretching the soft focus agent across the enlarging lens. This, however, is apt to produce a somewhat depressed effect, as against the cheerful soft focus of the actual snap. The snap shows the bright over-tones of the highlights, while the enlargement stresses the preponderance of the shadows.

COMPOSING THE PICTURE

Upright or Oblong?

The quickest answer to the question is to recommend the square shape. For one thing you no longer have to decide whether to hold the camera upright or on its side, since both dimensions are equal, and secondly, the choice as between an upright and an oblong picture can be made subsequently, and the desired section cut out, that is, if you decide not to keep the original square. This square shape, which used to be considered entirely impossible, has now become quite familiar, thanks to rollfilm reflex cameras and cartridge-loading types.

The case is altered if your camera is rectangular. Here you must examine your subject carefully before deciding whether it will make a better photo, whether it will fit in better, in one way or the other. This is true especially for the smaller, handier sizes of camera, when enlargement is not contemplated. If the prints were to be reduced in size by cutting out a section of the required shape, the result would be too much like a postage stamp.

Some subjects immediately suggest the shape of the picture: a person, a tower and similar subjects will be taken with the camera in an upright position; a group of people or a landscape will suggest the oblong shape.

Sometimes, as far as the view itself is concerned, there is nothing to choose between the two shapes. The question then arises as to what particular aspect of the scene is to be emphasized. Let us imagine that we are taking a picture of a lake. Do we want to fix on the paper the picture of the great expanse of water, with its sailing boats on the surface and the long line of hills on the opposite bank, or are we chiefly interested in the sky with its masses of cloud towering above the shimmering water? In the first case we choose an oblong; in the second, an upright picture to give the desired effect. And so it is with a great number of subjects: it is less a question of mere reproduction, it is a matter of interpretation, too.

Tilting the Camera

Tilting the camera must not be confused with holding it crooked. Twisting it round its longer axis will have the result of making the horizon look crooked and water flow uphill. It will make towers lean to one side, although they are in London or New York and not in Pisa. Now this is a serious matter if you are going to make contact prints from your negatives. But if you are going to make enlargements, the defect can be partly remedied and leaning towers will regain their equilibrium.

But by tilting the camera we mean pointing the lens upwards towards the sky or downwards towards the ground. If we say the camera is crooked, we mean that it is by inadvertence. If we say it is tilted upwards or downwards we mean that we do it on purpose.

In bygone years every self-respecting camera used to be provided with a spirit level. This appliance was as indispensable to the camera's equipment as the trenching tool is to the kit of the infantry soldier. One used to gaze earnestly through the glass cover at the fidgety little air bubble until it settled down exactly in the middle of its oil bath, in order to be quite sure that the camera was perfectly level. Nowadays spirit levels have all but disappeared from cameras, and so has the fear of pictures taken at an unusual angle.

The modern photographer has no scruples about tilting his camera upwards or downwards just as it suits him, without worrying about the slight degree of distortion it causes. If necessary he will get down on his knees so that his model stands well above his lens. The background, with

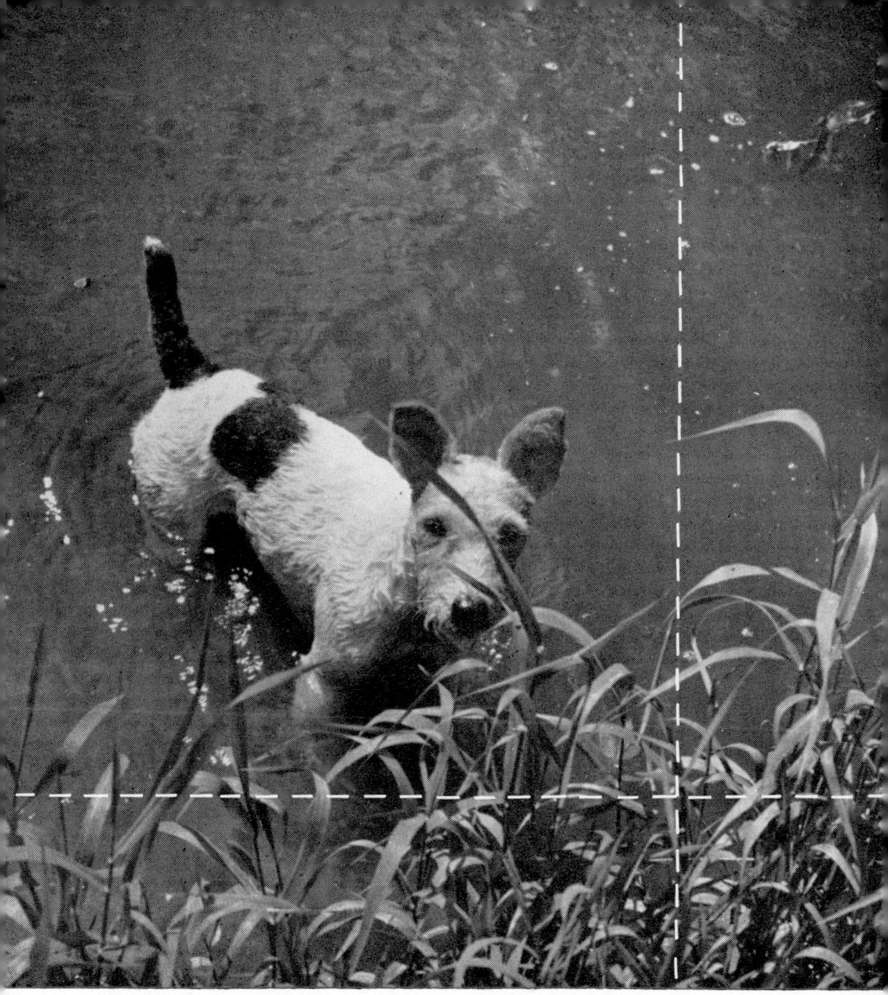

A SQUARE PHOTOGRAPH can easily be turned into an upright or an oblong one, as is shown in the picture above. How different shape and contents of an upright and an oblong picture can be, although taken of the same scene, will be seen by covering a part of the whole once along the vertical and then along the horizontal white line. (See page 83.)—Photograph by *P. Wolff*.

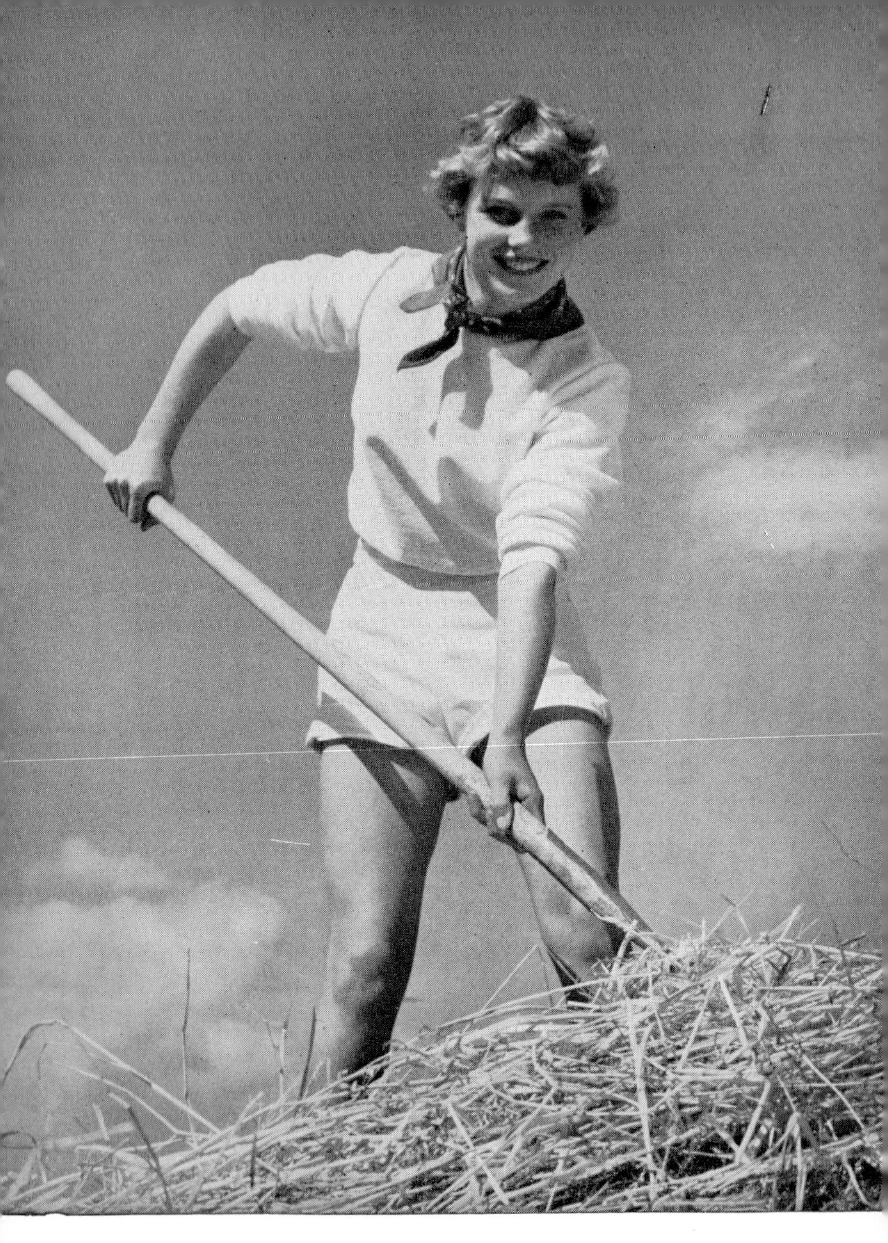

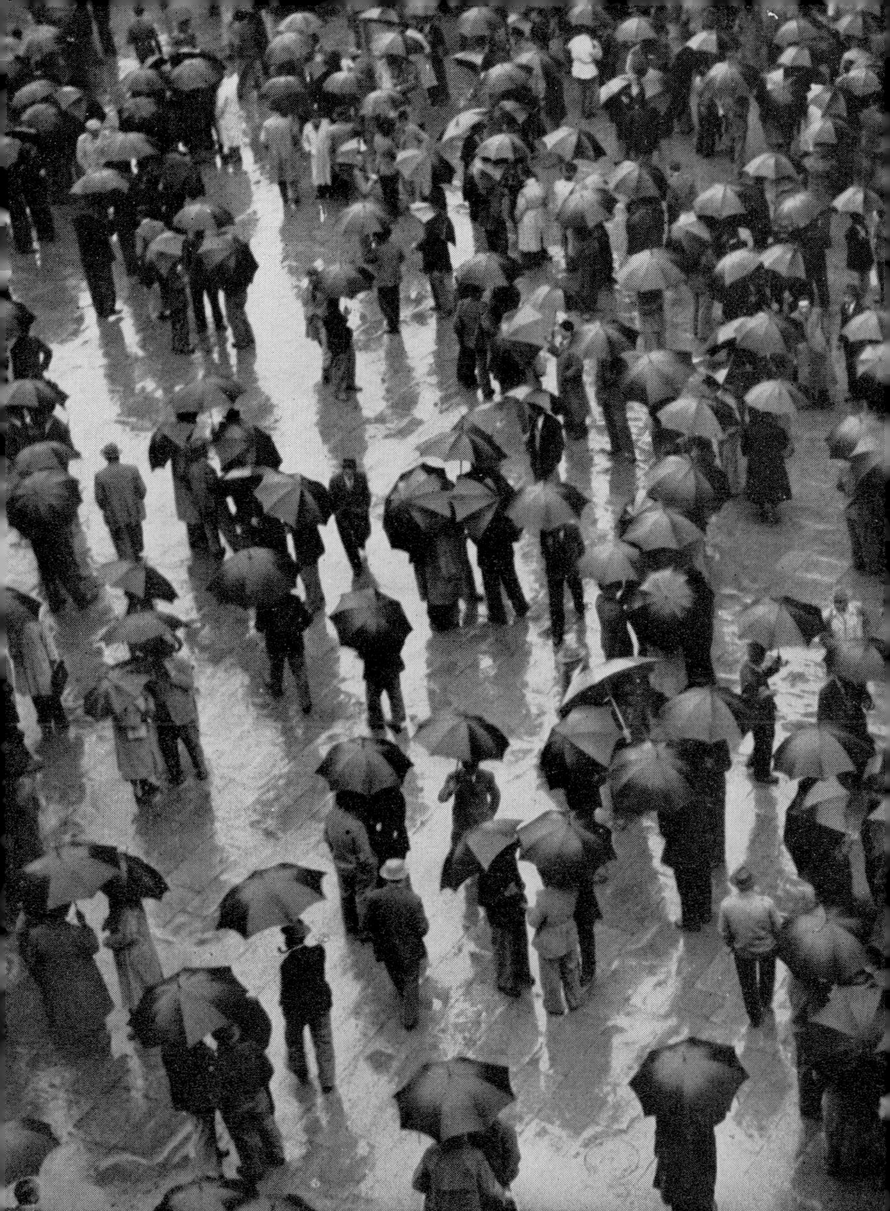

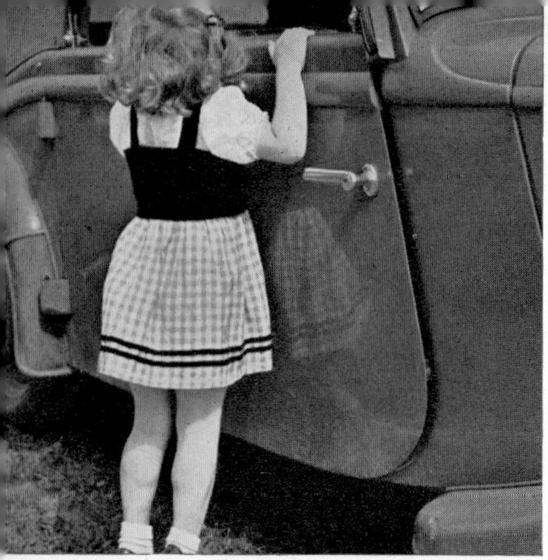

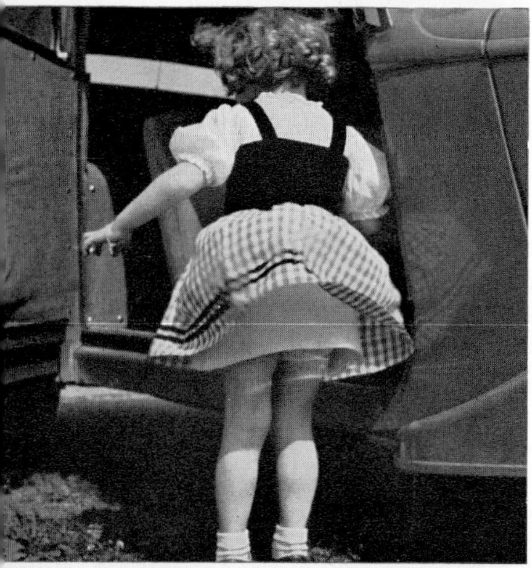

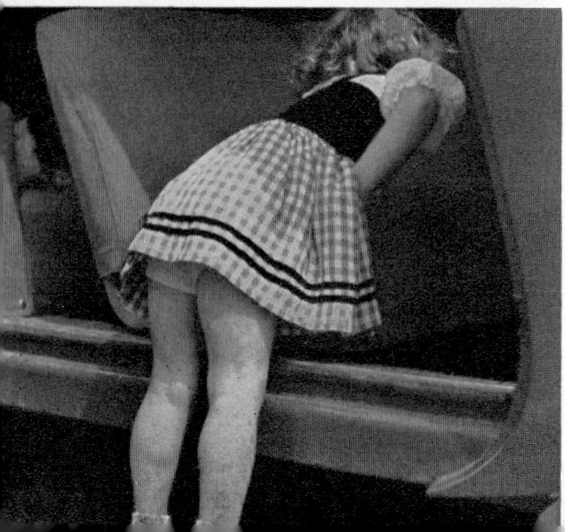

SHOOTING A WHOLE SERIES of pictures of some amusing situation, especially of children or animals, enables practically everybody to make photo-stories of the type nowadays so popular with the illustrated magazines. (See pages 92–93.) These pictures were taken on panchromatic film with stop 5.6 and 1/50 second.—Photographs by *G. Gesell.*

A LOW VIEWPOINT (page 86) is ideal for the informal portrait. A yellow filter darkens the sky and makes the subject stand out clearly with nothing else to distract the attention. A medium speed pan film was used with 1/25 second at stop 16.—Photograph by *Ilford Ltd.*

A HIGH VIEWPOINT (page 87) gives the camera a wide outlook over masses of people or things. The subject is dwarfed, and main emphasis falls on shapes and patterns. Taken on a dull, rainy afternoon the exposure was 1/50 second at stop 6.3 with medium speed pan film.—Photograph by *Ludwig Windstosser.*

all its disturbing and distracting details, sinks out of sight, while the principal subject of the picture remains in undisputed possession of the field of view. That market-cross or equestrian statue, that rather ordinary group of tourists, the physical-culture expert doing a hand-stand on the parallel bars—all of them will gain in impressiveness when they are made to stand out against the sky. If there are some handsome clouds in the sky, they will be a welcome addition to the picture. If, on the other hand, the sky is cloudless, whether brilliantly blue or uniformly grey, it will be just as effective as a background. In the latter case the person looking at the picture may not even realize that it is the sky.

This makes a yellow filter (with black and white film) indispensable, in order that the sky may not appear as a monotonous expanse of white, but has a good "solid" grey tone. In using the exposure meter you must be careful not to measure the bright light coming from the sky which would give a wrong reading, but the light reflected from the principal object in the picture, which is much darker in tone.

When the camera is tilted in front of buildings the resulting picture will show what are known as "converging verticals". These serve excellently to emphasize the powerful upward sweep of the architectural feature. But if correct perspective is required and these lines are not wanted, they can in many cases be corrected subsequently during the enlarging process by the method described later on in this book. (Page 213.)

The Bird's-Eye View

Extensive subjects containing a mass of detail, such as a beach with its merry host of holiday-makers, a town-square with its traffic, a flock of grazing sheep, and so on, are best taken from above. People and things which, seen from the same level, would present the appearance of a confused mass, now sort themselves out into small individual groups and can be much more easily recognized. The observer's eye wanders pleasantly from detail to detail, covering the whole ground progressively.

So shots from above are the exact opposite to shots from below, not only in the method employed, but in the results obtained. Whereas the upwards tilt purposely isolates single individuals or solitary objects by taking them out of their immediate surroundings, the view from above, the bird's-eye view, deliberately includes a multitude of things in the picture.

If you think of getting a picture of the crowded street scene, choose your perch on the top of a building or tower. The village with its few score houses clustering round the church can best be taken from a neighbouring hill-top. For other objects a doorstep, a park seat, or a table will give the desired viewpoint.

Exposure is an easy matter, since the sky and distance, which, as a rule, are much brighter than the subject itself, are automatically cut out from the picture by pointing the camera downwards. The field of view therefore is uniformly illuminated, so that the photographer can get an accurate estimate of the lighting from his exposure meter without any further trouble. Moreover, the depth of the field required is far less than in the case of pictures including near objects and a distant background, both of which should be more or less sharply defined.

Here, as in other things, we must not exaggerate. It is true that people and vehicles taken almost vertically from above may sometimes look quite amusing owing to the foreshortening which takes place. And if long shadows are present, as happens in the early part of the morning or late in the evening, the results can be most effective, sometimes even, grotesque. But apart from such exceptional cases a moderately-tilted camera is to be preferred over a violently-titled one.

Small Section—Big Effect

Every photograph we take should fix an impression we have had of a particular thing at a particular time. To-day it may be the face of a friend, another day it may be a child at play, or a country scene that attracted us on our holidays. When, days or weeks or months later, we pick up the photograph and look at it, it should immediately—if only temporarily—take complete possession of our imagination, dismiss from our mind all thoughts of unpaid bills and other daily worries, and re-create for us the reality of yesterday. More than this, our photographs should be able to convey even to a stranger something of what we have felt and experienced.

But a magnetic influence of this kind can only proceed from a clear representation of the object, be it animal, person or place, which once gripped our imagination. "Clear" implies in this connection that the main feature fills the picture, that it is as big as possible, and that all useless frills, which would otherwise take up space, are left out. This small selection from the object should not include more than is necessary to suggest the real thing in an unmistakable manner.

The easiest way of emphasizing the importance of the object is to go close up to it. The closer your camera is to the object, the bigger the picture of it will be, and the better the use made of the available space.

But we cannot always go up as close as we would like to the thing we want to take. There may be a fence or a moat in the way. Or if we are stalking people or animals, the former are apt to get self-conscious and the latter frightened or over-interested in the camera if we go up too close to them.

If our camera is adapted for interchangeable lenses we can substitute a long-focus lens or a *telephoto* lens for the one we use in the ordinary way. This will bring things nearer without our having to go up closer to them. With double the focal length any given object, taken from the same spot, will be twice as big on the film. But this extremely helpful piece of apparatus can be used not only to bring distant objects nearer, but, even more frequently, to get a larger image than would be possible with an ordinary lens of things which are comparatively near.

It is true that a long focus lens makes the camera rather more difficult to use. Even the slightest movement, which would not hurt a picture taken with a lens of normal focal length, is plainly perceptible on the enlarged image. It is therefore inadvisable, if the camera is held in the hands, to make snaps with a long-focus lens at a longer exposure than 1/125 second. Moreover, it is more important to measure the distance very accurately than when using a lens with normal focal length, because the area of sharp definition is much shallower when a long-focus lens is used.

There is yet another way of securing the maximum effect. This is to enlarge one small portion of the negative only, showing just that part of the whole which is wanted and no more. The greater the amount of unnecessary detail that can be cut out, the greater the effect of the small remaining section.

A Series of Pictures

If you possess a miniature camera you will be sure to want to make a series of photos. Since you have twenty or even more exposures in one roll of film, and since each shot only costs a matter of pence, you will feel less inclined to be too economical. One or two exposures more or less do not make any great difference, so you can afford to use up several on the same subject. It often happens that the miniature film is almost completely exposed and you feel like finishing it off so that you can see the results. In this case you will be more than ready to try a new method which involves the sacrifice of several exposures.

If the worst comes to the worst you can always choose the best negative for enlargement and throw the others away. But it is often worth while to place several snaps of the same subject next to each other. This is especially true for portraits of people or animals. The result is a kind of movie show, although perhaps not so dramatically alive as a cinema film. Only slight changes in expression or attitude are necessary to make another and different picture. And with three or four snaps you have your photo-serial.

The Question of Aperture

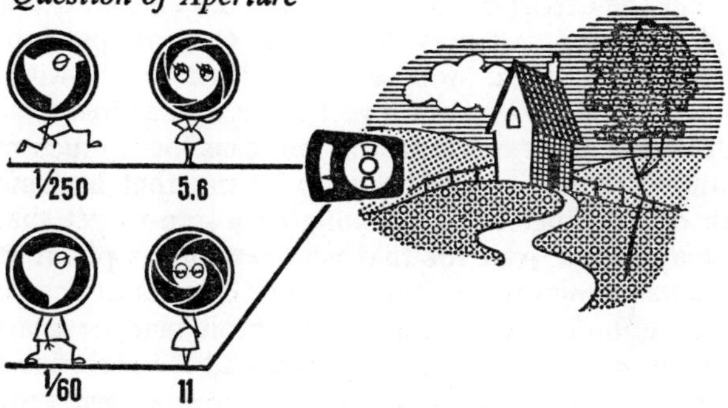

One difference among many between the novice and the expert is the way in which they choose their size of aperture, or stop. The novice, who in many respects is fully entitled to the honourable name of photographer, stops down as far as he can go even if there is nothing to be gained from great depth of field. For him no diaphragm can have a small enough aperture. When reading his exposure meter he always chooses the very smallest stop consistent with the longest safe exposure. His reward is to get an image on his film which is sharp from just in front of the camera right up to the distant background. He is insured against indistinctness—a danger for which he has a wholesome respect—and attains sharpness of definition even of the most insignificant, if not positively disturbing details. One is inclined to ask why he bought himself a camera with a *f*2 lens if he was never going to open his diaphragm wider than stop 11.

The expert goes about things in quite another way. Where depth of field is essential, he, too, must use a small stop. In all other cases, however, he uses a wide stop and profits by the improved lighting conditions to give a short exposure. If the two of them, the novice and the expert, are standing in front of the same object, the needle of their respective exposure meters will both of them tell the same tale. Yet the expert chooses, say, stop 5.6 and an exposure of 1/125 second, whereas the novice, with his passion for great depth of field, stops down at least to 11, with the result that he is obliged to give 1/30 second exposure.

Of course, the expert must in that case focus much more accurately than his neighbour, to ensure that his smaller depth of field includes everything he wants to get sharply into his picture. And for that very reason his pictures are more interesting owing to the various degrees of sharpness they contain. The essential feature, be it man or beast or inanimate object, is clear and sharp, and the mere incidentals, the tedious details in the background are suitably subdued. Whereas the novice gets everything that happens to come within the range of his lens indiscriminately distinct, the expert chooses just what he wants and leaves out the rest.

To sum up, it is often advisable to choose a larger aperture, although its use entails extra care.

DOING WITHOUT SUNSHINE

When the Sky is Overcast

A great number of amateurs never, on principle, use their cameras in bad weather. They must have a clear blue sky and lots of sunshine. And if into the bargain they can limit their working hours to the period between 11 a.m. and 2 p.m. they are completely happy. And, of course, they make their unfortunate model, whether it is little Betty or old Uncle Charles, pose in full sunshine. Otherwise they would think that they were wasting good daylight. In fact, they go about their photography as if they were living in the year 1900.

But photography has made considerable progress since those days. For one thing films are very much faster than they used to be. The most sensitive emulsion then produced would probably be estimated nowadays at something like 4–8 ASA, whereas modern films are up to two hundred times as fast. (Every doubling of the ASA speed represents double the degree of sensitivity.)

These modern films make it possible to take snaps, even if the sky is overcast, at 1/60 or even 1/125 second with an aperture which need be no larger than 5.6 or 8. And the pictures show better values than photos made in full sunlight. For not only is the exposure meter reading more reliable when the sky is overcast than when bright sunshine and dark shadows lie side by side (with the result that the meter is tricked by the bright portions into recommending too short an exposure), but the emulsion is better able to cope with relatively subdued light than with the violent contrasts of light and shade. The negative will be better balanced and will give a better positive whether it is put into the printing frame to make a contact print or whether an enlargement is made from it.

But the sun should not be completely hidden behind clouds. When the model is small enough, when, for example, you are photographing a person, the shadow of a wall or a house will be quite enough to soften the extremes of light contrasts. In any case, whether the subject is in the shade or whether the sky is overcast, the fact remains that the photo is taken out of the sun, and that it comes out.

Even bad weather, with rain or snowstorms, will sometimes produce interesting pictures of objects which, on a bright sunny day, would not be worth taking. If, owing to the comparatively lengthy exposure, say, 1/30 or even 1/15 second, the falling snowflakes or rain-drops, as the case may be, appear on the photograph like continuous streaks or lines, it is all to the good. It makes the picture all the more effective.

The Advantages of a Misty Day

In many respects mist produces ideal conditions for photography. For one thing it destroys the colours, so that there is no necessity for filters designed to aid such colour sensitivity, in order to reproduce the varied tones of nature in their correct black and white values. Nature, shrouded in mist, is already reduced to the required study in black and white. It shows a wide range of greys which can be faithfully captured without any difficulty.

Even the everlasting conflict between foreground and background which, in clear weather conditions, often spoils a good picture, is quickly settled in misty weather. The middle distance and, especially, the far distance, step back of their own accord, since the farther things are away, the more densely are they shrouded in mist. So you focus on the objects in the foreground and you can dispense with great depth. This means that a large aperture can be used. And if the distance is somewhat hazy this will not be attributed to faulty focusing but to the influence of the mist. It

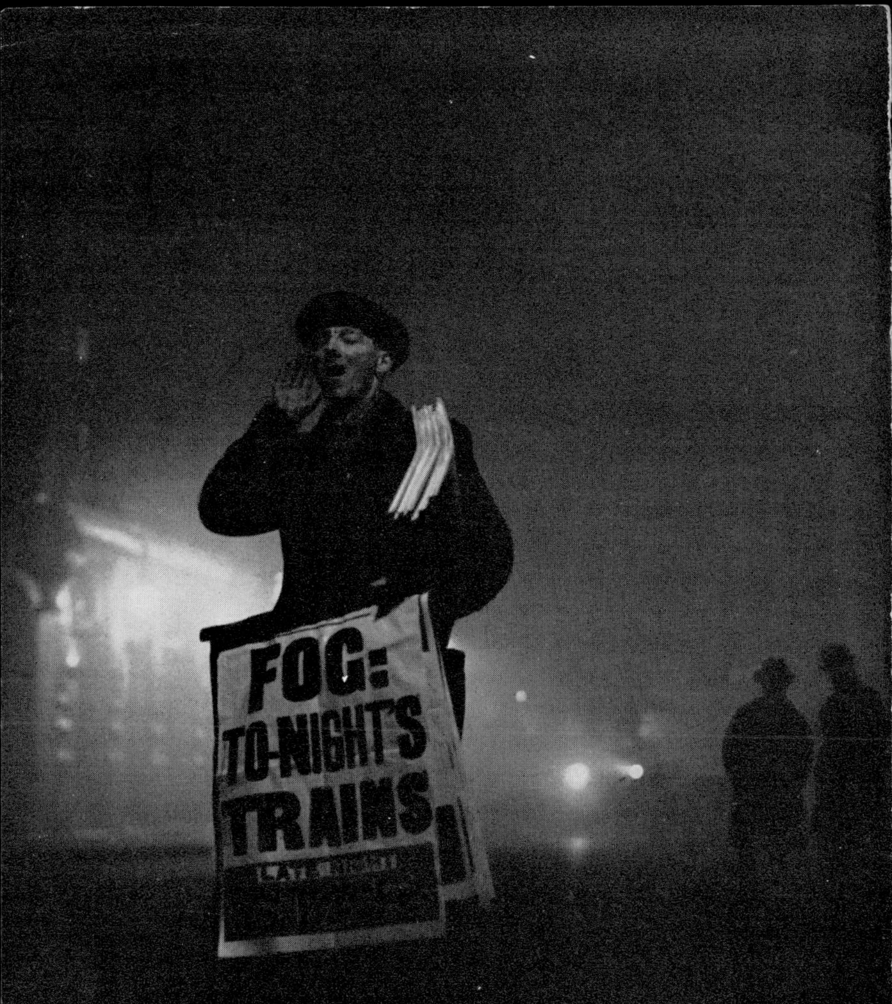

EVEN THE WORST WEATHER is no excuse for leaving the camera behind. When the light is very poor, a posed shot of a few seconds should still be possible. The placard makes this more than a picture of fog, it underlines the meaning of a fog in a big city. (See page 96.) Stop 3.5 and 3 seconds. Photograph by *R. Saidman*.

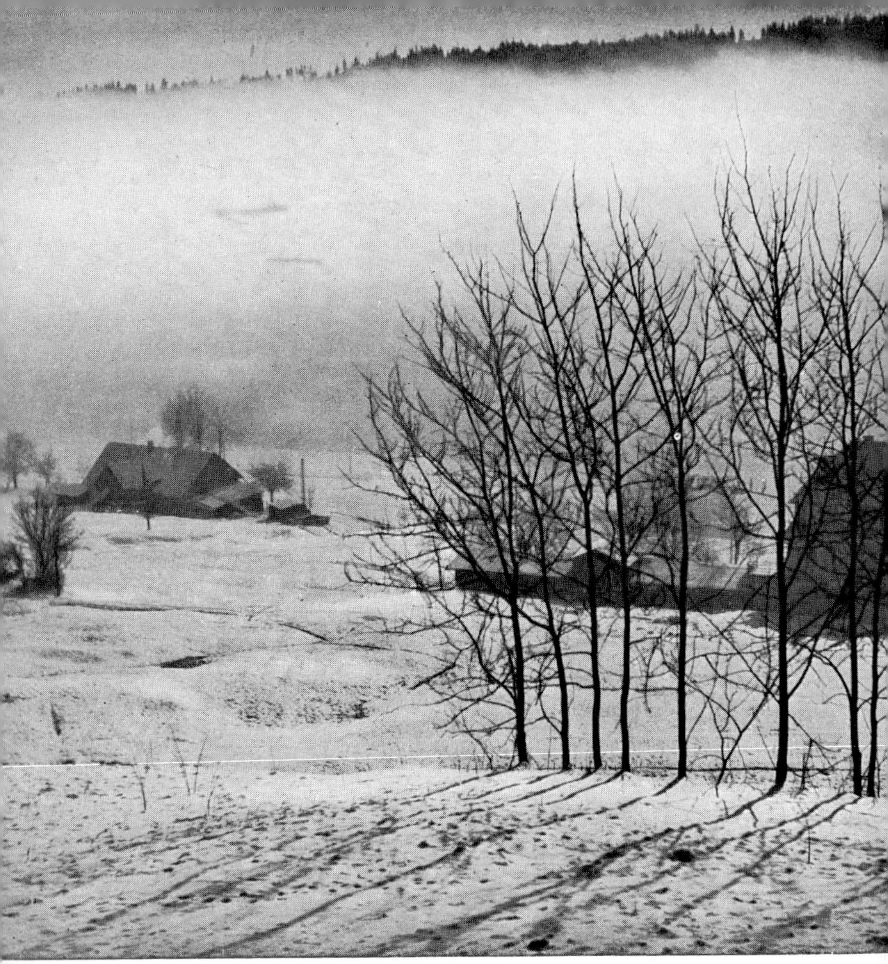

MIST AND FOG give things a mysterious, dramatic appearance, but demand a fairly long exposure. At stop 6.3 this picture was exposed $\frac{1}{2}$ second, with the camera fixed on a tripod.—Photograph by *O. R. Croy*.

NO LIGHT IS TOO WEAK if the scene itself is motionless (*opposite*). This moonlight picture was exposed for 10 minutes at stop 8 to gain plenty of depth of field. (See page 102.)—Photograph by *Bill Brandt*.

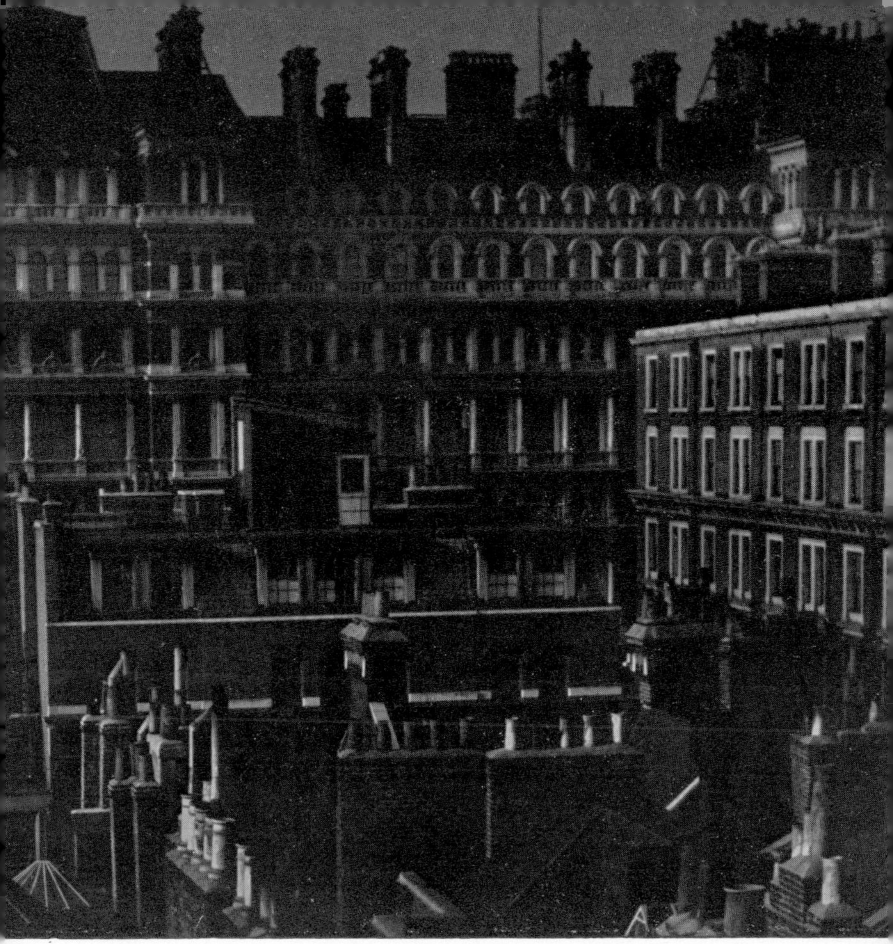

FLOODLIGHTING on Big Ben (page 100) and the street lights on Westminster Bridge provided the only illumination for this picture. Even with fast pan film an exposure of 1 minute was needed (see pages 102–103). Stop 8 was used to give sufficient depth of field. With such a lengthy exposure the camera had to be supported by a firm tripod. —Photograph by *John Gay*.

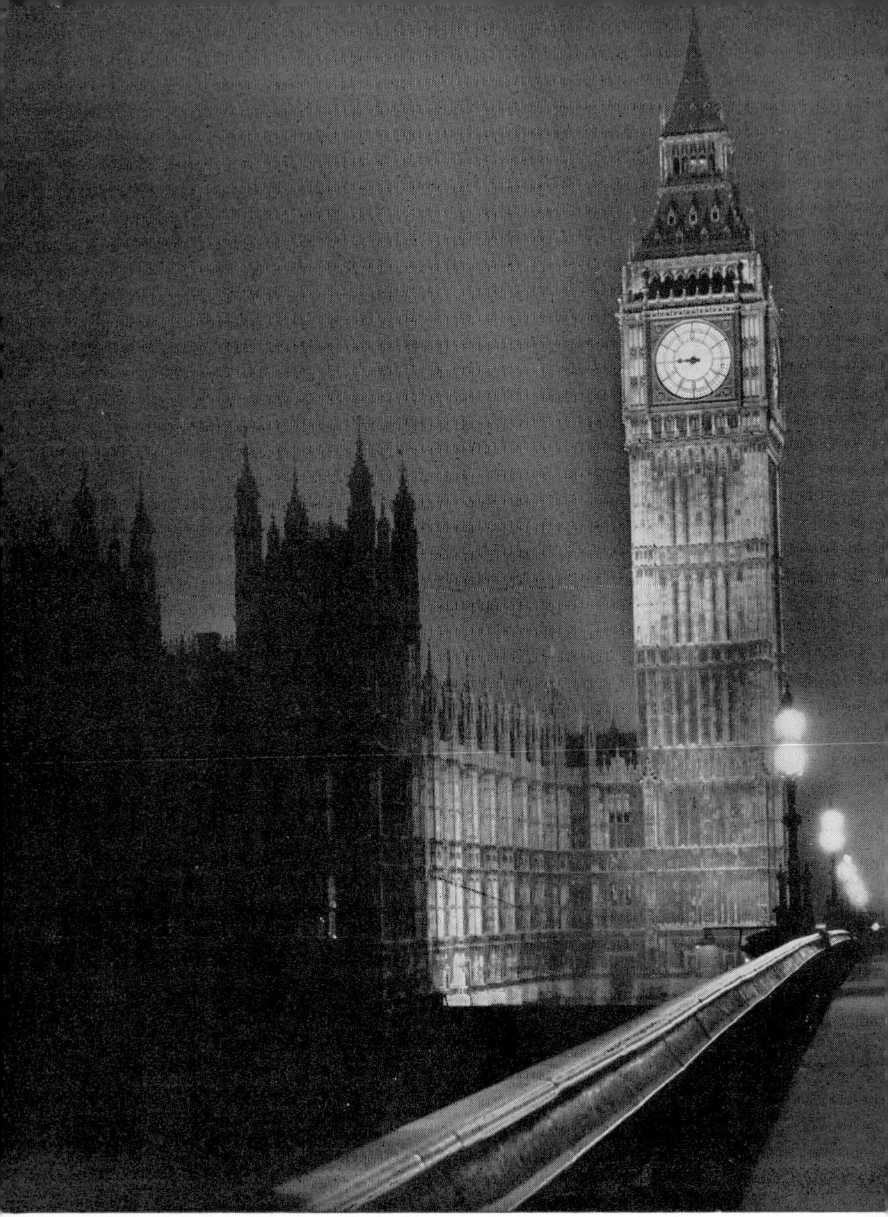

is, however, important to have some suitable objects, such as trees, persons, vehicles, in the foreground to emphasize the stereoscopic effect between the clear details near the camera and the gradually receding distance.

Pictures of misty scenes are especially effective if they are taken against the light, for colours are then entirely suppressed. The resulting silhouette effect combined with the various tones of grey produces a sense of distance such as no other method can give. Moreover, thanks to the mist, harsh reproduction and halation from direct light on the lens, which are common dangers with against-the-light pictures, are excluded.

Exposure for Misty Scenes

Exposure meters are not very reliable at the extreme ends of their scales. Nor are they easy to use where extreme contrasts are present. Their task is made much easier by the lack of contrast which prevails on a misty day. Contrary to the usual practice, exposure must now be reckoned, not from the shadows, as in sunny weather, but from the lighter background. This makes the nearest objects very dark, in fact, under-exposed, but this is just how we see things with our eyes, the light curtain of mist in the background causing things close to us to look black by comparison.

Any attempt to make a hill exposure for detail in the darker objects tends to destroy the mist effect by over-exposure without the compensation of any significant increase in clarity or definition.

Pictures taken in the mist at night are especially beautiful. The very atmosphere is luminous in the light from shop fronts or street lamps. People and things loom up black against the white wall of mist.

Where movement is involved, fast films and large-aperture lenses are necessary. Even then, exposures of up to $\frac{1}{2}$ second may be necessary but, with care, the blurring can be kept to no more than might be expected in the misty conditions.

Time Exposures by Night

There are hundreds of opportunities for making this kind of picture. It may be the town, blazing with street lamps, and electric signs, or a village, dimly lit by the feeble gleam of an old-fashioned gas lamp. Both provide excellent material. Tomorrow, perhaps, or next week, some public building will be all lit up in honour of some civic celebrations, or a famous monument will be floodlit. Subjects of this kind sometimes give amazingly beautiful pictures. So it is well worth while taking out your camera sometimes even at night, for the technique is not so difficult as might appear at first sight.

If the subject of the picture is fairly extensive, it will rarely be illuminated brightly enough to allow of an instantaneous snap. You will need a tripod—and a little patience. The former can occasionally be dispensed with, that is, if there happens to be a convenient wall, or other firm support, on which the camera can be rested.

A large aperture is not important, since the exposure can be as long as is required. Even the simplest camera, therefore, will produce pictures by night provided its shutter can be held open. Nor need the film be extra fast.

Exposure Latitude at Night

As for exposure, one can vary it within very wide limits. At the most over-exposure will alter the character of the picture. If the length of exposure is greatly exaggerated, the night effect is lost; the picture might just as well have been taken in broad daylight. Too short an exposure, on the other hand, will produce all night and no picture. On page 107 the reader will find a table giving suitable exposures for photos by night.

If you possess a lens-hood you should by all means use it. For lens-hoods are not only for protection against the sun, but are useful in all cases where bright lights and dark shadows are found side by side. People passing in front of the camera will do no harm, if the exposure runs to more than 30 seconds, because their impression on the emulsion in the short time it takes them to pass the camera is too weak to be visible.

The lights of passing cars or bicycles, however, are dangerous. The remedy is to put your hat over the lens to protect it until the vehicle has passed. In doing so, you must be careful, of course, not to move the camera.

And Now Snaps by Night

High-speed film (500–800 ASA), and the widest possible stop (2.8 at least) are, of course, desirable. The high sensitivity entails a certain amount of grain in the negative, but it can't be helped. And the wide stop—and here one is even more helpless—is bound up with small depth of field.

But in any case, modern miniature cameras take in a deeper belt of sharp definition than others, and are therefore specially suited to work of this kind. Another of their advantages is that they often have a built-in rangefinder which at any rate enables you to get all the available sharp definition area where you want it most. You naturally focus on the objects nearest to the camera, because they, at all costs, must be sharp. The fact that the background will then be out of focus is even less objectionable in this case than in daylight pictures. In fact it adds valuable "atmosphere".

Despite the wide aperture and high-speed film, you must be prepared to give a relatively long exposure: 1/30 or even 1/15 second, which means that the picture does not strictly belong to the "instantaneous" class, in which the slowest shutter speed is really 1/60 of a second.

It is, therefore, out of the question for most people to hold the camera still without help of some kind. What is sometimes known as a *chest-pod* (or *neck-strap*) will overcome this difficulty. With the help of this device it is possible to keep the camera steady for exposures up to one second, provided the photographer is not an abnormally excitable person. But, besides this, there is often the possibility of steadying the elbows on some convenient railing or balustrade. It may not be considered elegant but it is quite an effective way of keeping the camera steady. Or else, you stand up with your back to the wall (literally), quite stiff, as if you were a human camera stand, press your elbows and your camera close to your body and open the shutter while you hold your breath.

Of course you must wait until any mobile elements in the field of view are as still as possible, so that the long exposure will not entail blurred outlines. In this way you will be able to create faithful "documentary" pictures of the streets by night, lit with the glare of street lamps, shop windows and electric advertising signs. Even if your first experiments result in failure, they will teach you enough to make subsequent attempts completely successful.

To make pictures in the theatre, the music-hall or the circus you must observe the same rules as for night photography outside. As the exposure must be short, you must compensate for it in other ways. The fastest film possible and a wide aperture are more than ever essential, because the movements on the stage, especially in the music-hall or in the ring, are apt to be pretty rapid, so that a longer exposure than 1/60 or 1/125 second is out of the question. In all places of public entertainment, however, you must either obtain special permission to take photographs or ensure beforehand that photography is allowed. Even where permission is granted, be careful not to disturb the audience.

Night photography is a matter of experience. Photographers producing brilliant pictures of night scenes are mostly very well acquainted with the lighting conditions of the place in question. So do not expect to succeed in this field at the first shot.

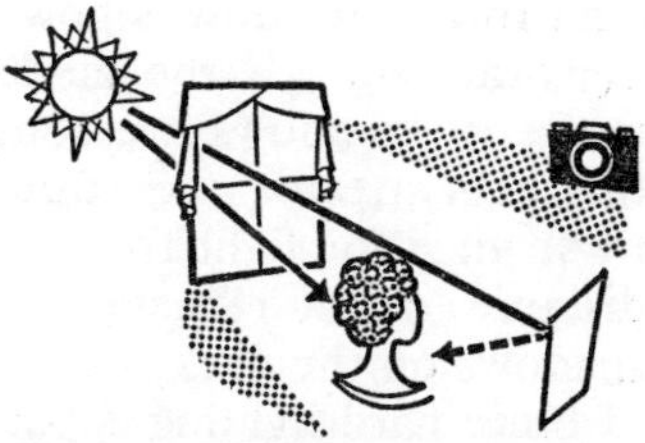

Even the brightest room is considerably darker than one would at first imagine. When we come in from the outside our eyes, though dazzled by the sunshine, soon adjust themselves to the inner gloom, so that we see things much more brightly illuminated than they really are. Our brain comes to the help of our eyes. Yet incorruptible devices for measuring light have proved that only one three-hundredth part of the brilliance outside gets into the middle of a normal living-room.

If the photograph is of the room itself or of motionless objects in the room this meagre illumination will be quite sufficient. You can stop down as much as you like, to get the required depth of field, for if the camera is supported by a tripod or a table, all you have to do is to leave the shutter open long enough to allow the weak rays of light to influence the emulsion of the film in your camera. As to how long to leave the shutter open, your exposure meter will tell you. On page 120 we explain a little subterfuge designed to help the exposure meter to do its work, even under the unfavourable conditions prevailing in a (photographically speaking) badly-lit room.

Near the window the light is much more intense, eight to ten times as strong, in fact, as in the middle of the room. So portraits should be made with the model near the window. This position will allow of an exposure somewhere between 1/30 and 1/2 second, for as no great depth of field is required, a larger aperture can be utilized.

One problem raised by portraits taken near the bright light from a window is how to relieve the dark shadows on the other side. If the model can be placed in a window recess the shadows are considerably lightened by the fact that light streams in on three sides. It may even be possible to arrange for light from a second window, even at some distance, or the reflection from a white wall to relieve the shadows on the dark side.

Since hard lighting is particularly unsuitable for faces it is a good plan to arrange things so that a book or a white tablecloth acts as a reflector and helps to illuminate the dark side of the sitter's features. Or finally, as shown in the diagram, a screen can be erected at some distance from the model—a large white cloth, for example—to provide the highly desirable, in fact essential, lighting for the shady side.

HINTS AND TIPS

An Aid to Focusing

Correct focusing is often difficult under bad weather conditions or in a dim room, whether your camera is fitted with a ground-glass screen or a rangefinder. A leaf from a tear-off calendar with large figures, held or stuck up at the correct distance, will help you to focus exactly.

A Use for your Umbrella

You may not like carrying an umbrella about with you, but it is a very useful article for snaps taken in the rain. Not so much because it keeps you dry, but because it protects the lens in the absence of a lens-hood.

If you have a companion with you who is kind enough to hold the umbrella, leaving both your hands free to hold the camera, by all means accept her kind offer of help.

Night

You need not necessarily wait until it is pitch dark. Dusk is a more comfortable time of day and will give you night effects without necessitating a too lengthy exposure.

Effective studies of picturesque corners and narrow streets can be made by using the headlights of your car as illumination. The exposure, with a small stop, will require from 2 to 4 minutes.

If you are not sure of the state of your battery, keep your engine running at a fast idling speed or you may be stuck there for the rest of the night. Of course, you must not rest the camera on the trembling bonnet of the car. In fact, your tripod should be well away from the effect of the vibration.

A USEFUL TABLE

EXPOSURE TABLE FOR NIGHT PHOTOGRAPHS

Subject	*Pan Film Speed ASA*	Aperture 2 or 2.5	3.2 or 3.5	4 or 4.5	5.6 or 6.3	8 or 9	11 or 12.5
Moderate Lighting: e.g. Provincial town with street lights	250–500	1 sec.	2 sec.	4 sec.	8 sec.	16 sec.	30 sec.
	100	2 sec.	4 sec.	8 sec.	16 sec.	30 sec.	1 min.
Better Lighting: e.g. Station, Factory in night shift, etc.	250–500	½ sec.	1 sec.	2 sec.	4 sec.	8 sec.	15 sec.
	100	1 sec.	2 sec.	4 sec.	8 sec.	16 sec.	30 sec.
Bright Lighting: e.g. Well-lit city streets with electric advertisements	250–500	¼ sec.	½ sec.	1 sec.	2 sec.	4 sec.	8 sec.
	100	½ sec.	1 sec.	2 sec.	4 sec.	8 sec.	16 sec.
Brilliant Lighting: e.g. Floodlit building, *lighted shop windows*, etc.	250–500	1/30 sec.	1/15 sec.	1/8 sec.	1/4 sec.	½ sec.	1 sec.
	100	1/15 sec.	1/8 sec.	1/4 sec.	½ sec.	1 sec.	2 sec.

Half the exposure time given in this table is needed on wet or snow-covered ground.

ARTIFICIAL LIGHT

Flashlight

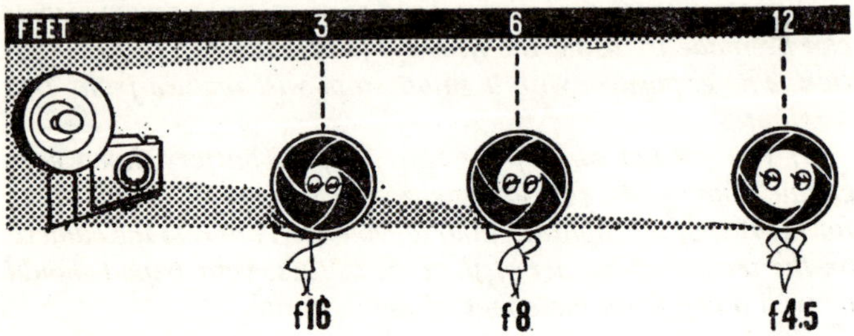

The flash bulb is used in a flash gun and current from a battery is used to set off the bulb. A reflector behind the bulb ensures that all the light is directed towards the subject. The light is strong enough to allow medium to small apertures to be used for the exposure. Flashcubes contain four bulbs each with its own reflector set into each side of the cube. The flash cube holder, either built into the camera top or available separately, facilitates turning of the cube, so that four flash exposures can be made in quick succession. Batteries for the flashcube are usually contained in the camera body. A flash bulb can be fired once only.

A recent variation of the flashcube is the Magicube, which is ignited by a 'striking' system, and needs no battery. Magicubes can only be used in flash units designed for them.

Another type of flash is the electronic flash unit. This creates a flash when the discharge of a high-tension capacitor is put through a gas-filled flash tube. The power is derived from a battery or the mains electricity supply. Anything from 10,000 to 25,000 flashes are obtained from one tube. The light output of small, popular units is less than that of a flash bulb but the flash itself is extremely short (1/700 to 1/2000 second) so it will arrest the fastest movements.

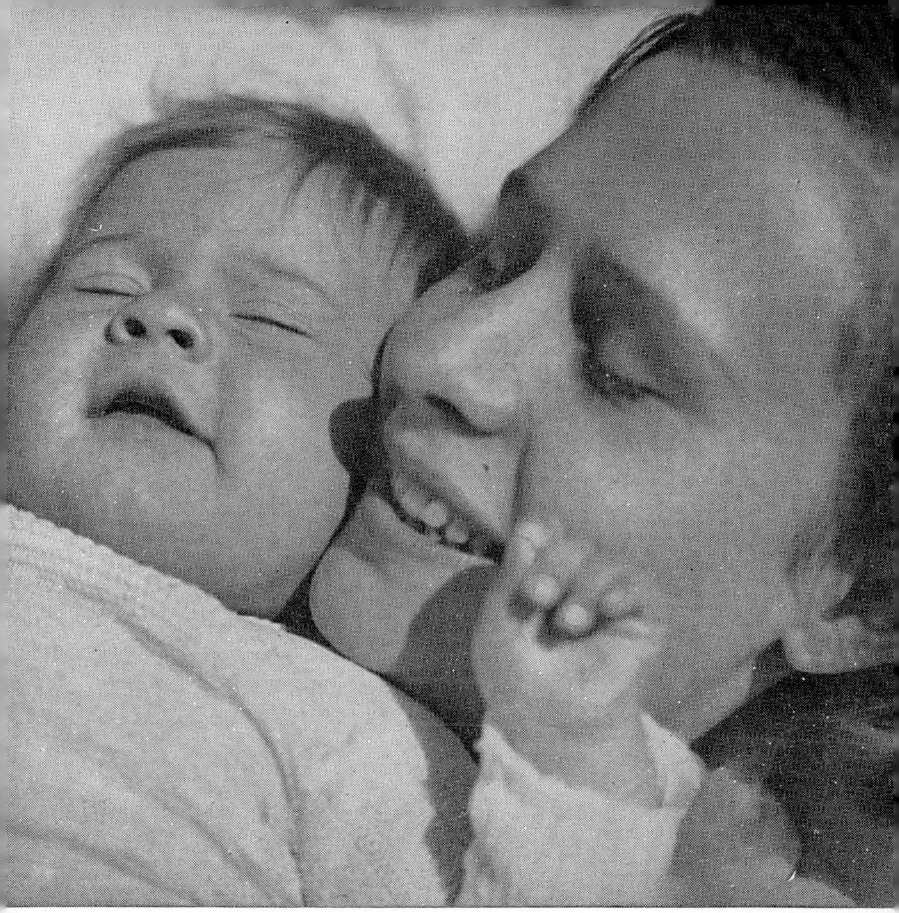

SUNSHINE INDOORS, a quiet corner, and a pleasantly restful picture. The white background and clothing helped a lot to spread light all over the scene. (See page 105.) The shot was taken at stop 9 with 1/100 second.—Photograph by *K. Hutton*.

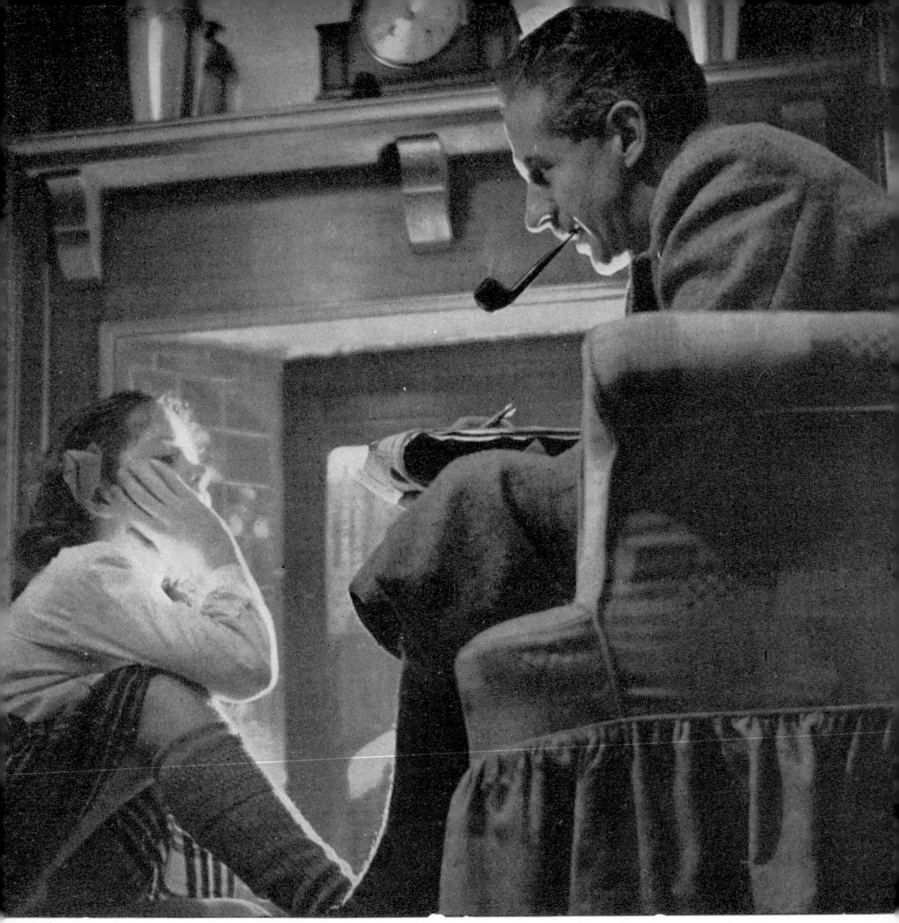

TWO PHOTOFLOOD LAMPS, one placed *in* the fireplace and hidden by the easy chair to create the impression of a burning fire and give contrasting outlines to the figures, the other placed to the left of the camera to illuminate foreground detail. The camera was held in a very low position to emphasize the group against its surroundings.—Photograph by *W. E. B. Ring.*

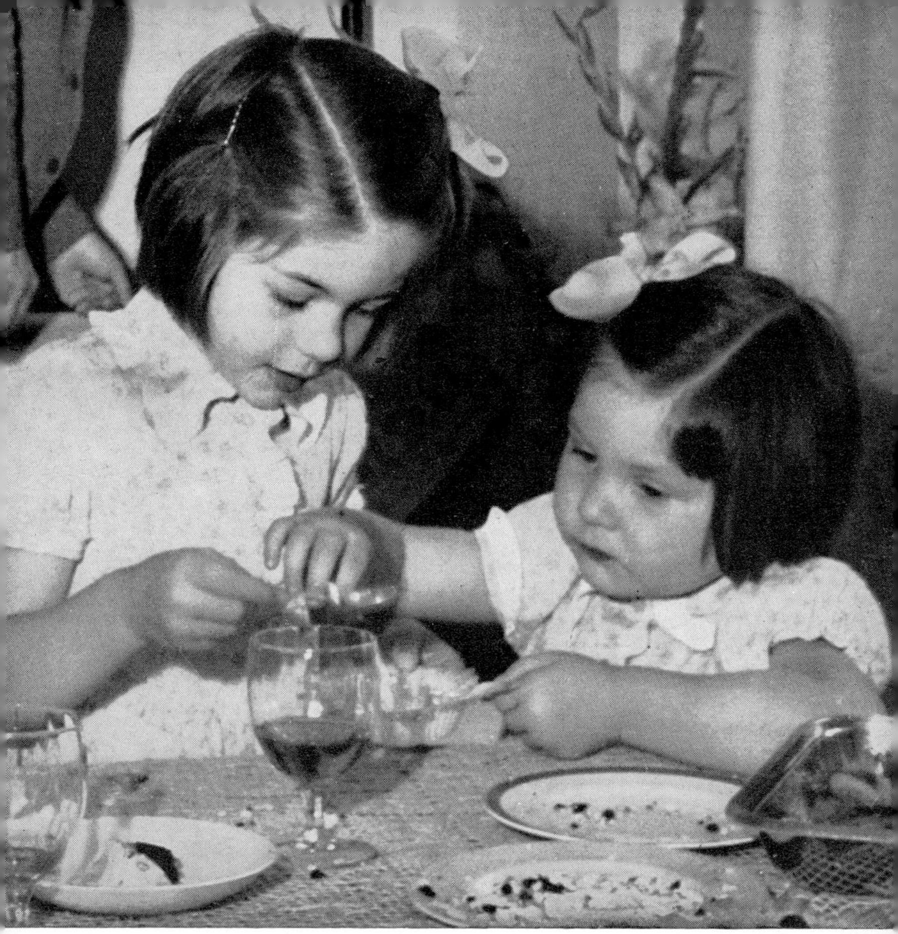

A FLASH BULB helped to capture this completely natural and candid party shot. The light surroundings and clothing helped to soften the light. The short duration of the flash avoided any need for posing, and even managed to cope with a certain amount of movement. A fast pan film was used. Stop 5 6. —Photograph by *Douglas Fulford.*

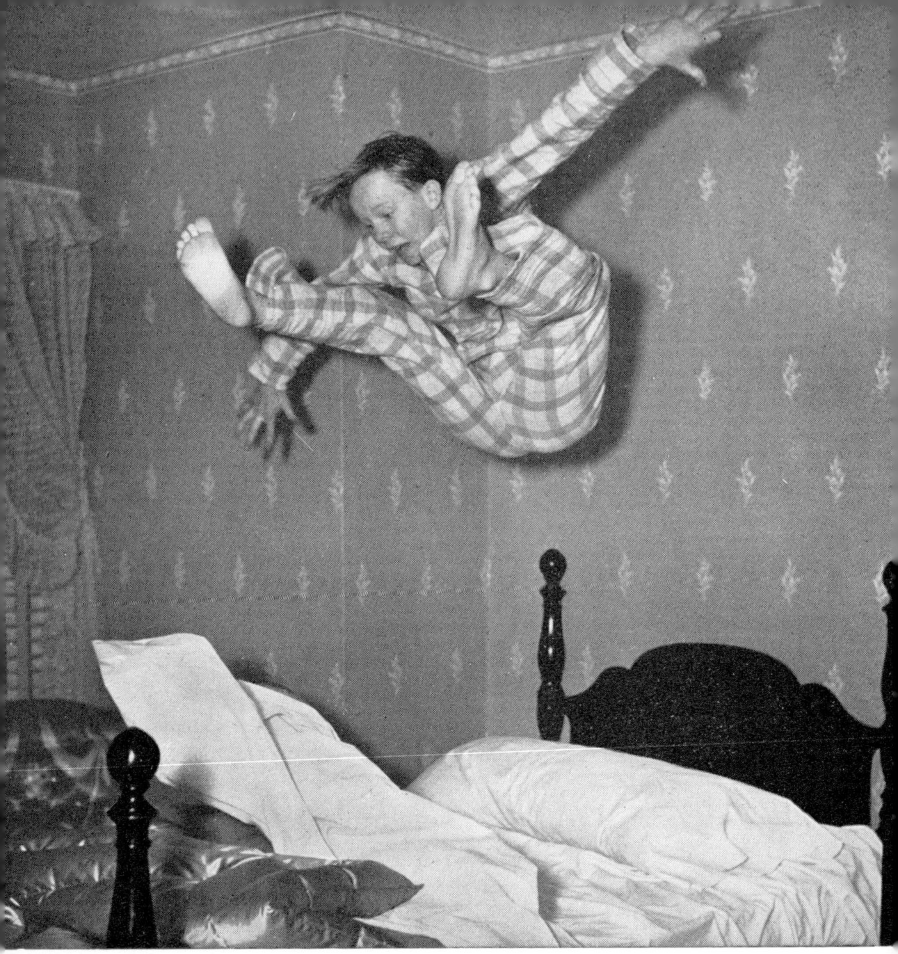

HIGH-SPEED FLASH and real timing on the release button! Stopping fast movement needs high shutter speeds, and an accurate flash synchroniser to make sure that the shutter and flash go off together. This shot at 1/1000 second catches all the excitement of bouncing on the bed, yet shows the subject perfectly sharp. The exposure was made on fast pan film at stop 11.—Photograph by *Harold M. Lambert.*

Most modern camera shutters are flash synchronized, which means they are fitted with flash contacts. You connect the flash attachment to the flash socket. Some cameras have a flash gun built in, which is then permanently connected. On releasing the shutter an electrical circuit is automatically closed when the shutter is fully open, setting off the flash bulb at this very moment. Blade shutters so synchronized should be used at speeds of about 1/30 second (or 1/25 second on some models) to ensure that the full illumination coincides with the full opening of the shutter. The reason for this is that the normal flash bulbs take some 20 milliseconds (1/50 second) to reach the peak of their brilliance. If you used a faster shutter speed the shutter would have closed before this peak brilliance occurred.

Electronic flash has no firing delay and can be used with any shutter speed, except with focal plane shutters (see below).

Speed Synchronized Shutters

Some shutters are speed synchronized for using flash bulbs at even the fastest speeds. These shutters have an adjustable flash contact with two settings marked X and M. The X-setting is like the one described above and is intended to be used for electronic flash. But if you want you can use bulbs at speeds not faster than 1/30 second. For flash bulbs generally, however, you should use the M-setting. This allows for the delay in the bulb reaching peak brilliance and you can safely use any shutter speed. Electronic flash should not be used at the M-setting.

Focal Plane Synchronization

Cameras with focal plane shutters behave somewhat differently. The blinds must be fully apart when the flash lights up. This generally occurs only at shutter speeds of 1/60 second and slower but varies considerably according to make of camera. The next slower speed has to be used with flash to allow the bulb time to ignite. A slow shutter speed, however, need not be a disadvantage. It is the short duration of the flash that serves to arrest movement, not the shutter speed.

Cameras with a second flash socket (marked FP) can be used at higher shutter speeds with special focal plane bulbs.

Flash Exposure

As the duration of the flash from a bulb is only in the region of 1/50 second, the shutter speed setting up to 1/30 second does not influence the exposure. This is regulated by setting the aperture. For any particular speed of film and size of bulb the aperture is adjusted according to the distance between the subject and the bulb. Exposure tables are usually printed on the flash bulb packet, but for your guidance we list here the apertures to use with an efficient reflector, in a room of average brightness with shutter speeds up to 1/50 second, and a film speed of 100–125 ASA.

APERTURES AND FLASH BULBS

Distance (ft)	PFIB, AGIB M2B and other No I or Type I	PF5B, No 5B M5B, Press 25B etc.	PF60/97 No 22, Type 22 etc
5	25	45	—
6	22	32	45
8	16	25	32
10	12.5	22	25
12	11	16	22
15	9	12.5	16
20	6.3	11	12.5
25	5.6	8	11
30	4.5	6.3	8

The figures 6.3, 9, 12.5 etc. are used to denote half-stop positions. Many lenses have click-stop positions for half-stop setting. On most others, the aperture control ring can be set mid-way between marked settings.

In bright rooms (kitchen, bathroom), or with 160–200 ASA film, use next smaller aperture. With 320–500 ASA film use 2 stops smaller. In very large rooms, at night outdoors, or with 64 ASA film, use next larger stop.

Guide Numbers

A convenient way of working out exposures with flash is by means of a guide number. When you buy flash bulbs you will find the guide numbers for any speed of film printed on the packet.

To find the correct aperture to use, divide the guide number by the distance between the flash and the subject. For instance, suppose you find that the guide number of the bulb for the speed of the film in use is 160. If you then want to take a photograph at a distance of 10 ft. from the subject, divide 160 by 10: the result is 16. Therefore the correct aperture to use is *f* 16. Alternatively, if you want to use an aperture of *f* 8 for some reason, then the correct flash distance is 160 divided by 8 = 20. So the flash must be 20 ft. from the subject.

So far we have assumed that the exposures apply to average shots without much subject movement. For these a shutter speed of 1/30 second is long enough to utilize all the light from the bulb. On the other hand, to arrest fast movements a faster shutter speed is required such as 1/125 or even 1/300 second. With each of these faster speeds a different guide number is needed (usually printed on the flash bulb packing) to determine the correct exposure. They allow for a wider aperture to compensate for the fact that at a fast shutter speed some of the light emitted from the bulb is lost.

Special Applications

Bounce Flash—is recommended for photographing subjects indoors. It avoids the unpleasant hard shadows you would have to accept with the flash pointed straight at the subject. All you have to do is direct the flash upwards to the white or light coloured ceiling; the reflected light will be soft and diffused, resulting in an almost shadowless picture.

To determine the correct aperture for bounce flash, use (in place of the direct flash to subject distance) the distance from flash to ceiling plus ceiling to subject. Then set the lens to one stop larger to compensate for the loss of light on reflection from the ceiling.

A white umbrella is a useful bouncing surface for flash—portable, folding and, obviously, dual purpose, although prolonged exposure to bad weather may not be advisable. It gives a soft lighting effect particularly suitable for colour work and can help to avoid unwanted colours being reflected from walls, ceilings, etc. Special umbrellas produced for photographic use have attachments for connecting to a tripod and to a flashgun.

Fill-in Flash is used in daylight to lighten the deep shadows frequently cast by the sun, particularly in against-the-light portraits. The subject is given normal exposure as calculated or metered for the sunlit parts. Then the shadows are filled in with a moderate flash exposure so that they still remain as shadows but with considerable less density. The usual method is to give about one-quarter of a normal flash exposure.

Where you have only X-synchronization, or are using electronic flash with a focal plane shutter, you have to use the appropriate shutter speed, which may be 1/30 second or slower. That makes things difficult with normal black-and-white films and flashbulbs because even the smallest flashbulb has a guide number of 130 with 100–125 ASA film. To give only one-quarter of a normal exposure, you have to double that, giving a guide number of 260. Additionally, at 1/30 second you have no aperture small enough to give correct exposure.

So, in black-and-white, you have to use a slow film and/or a low-power flash such as one of the small, pocketable electronic units.

The exposure calculation is as follows:

Normal sunlight aperture setting at 1/30 sec.—*f*16
Guide number for flash (AG1, 1/30 sec. 40–50 ASA)—85
Guide number doubled—170
Guide number divided by aperture—170/16=11

Thus, the flash should be placed 11ft. (3.3 m.) from the subject. If the flash is on the camera, you have to shoot from

10–11ft. (3–3.3 m.). Otherwise you can use an extension cable to the flashgun to enable you to shoot from closer in. If the flash cannot be removed from the camera or you have no extension cable, you can reduce the power of the flash by draping a handkerchief over it.

M-synchronization allows you to use medium-speed film and faster shutter speeds but makes little difference otherwise.

Normal sunlight aperture setting at 1/250 sec.—*f*8

Guide number for flash (AG1, 1/250 sec. 125 ASA)—60

Guide number doubled—120

Guide number divided by aperture 120/8=15

The flash has to be 15ft. (4.5 m.) from the subject, which is still rather excessive but at least the faster shutter speed allows some movement in your subject. At the slower speeds, the subject must remain completely still or the daylight exposure will record the movement as a blur.

The slower colour films are easier to use with fill-in flash because the guide number is lower and colour film can use a stronger fill-in. It may, in fact, demand an almost full flash exposure to avoid colour distortion from underexposure.

With colour films, you must use electronic flash or blue-tinted bulbs.

Continuous Light

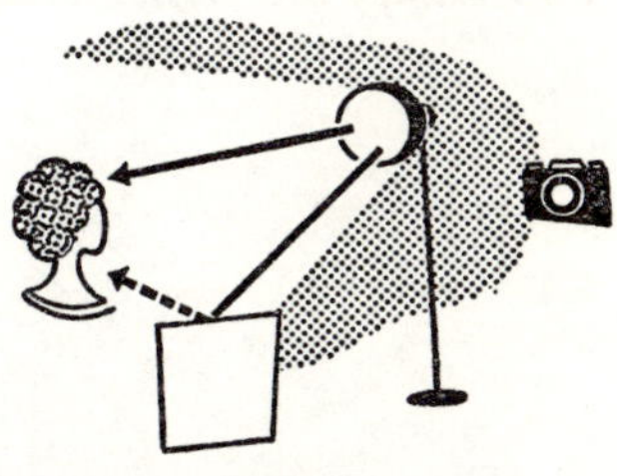

Wherever electric current is available, artificial light can be used for interiors. The ordinary room lamp is rather too weak, however, for this purpose, and requires a correspondingly lengthy exposure. (See page 120.) So we use special photographic lamps known as photofloods. A quite inexpensive variety can be used in metal reflectors or more expensive types are available with built-in reflectors. The No. 1 photoflood gives the equivalent of about 800 watts while consuming only 275 watts. This enables the whole force of the light to be concentrated in a powerful beam which can be directed on to the object to be photographed.

This type of bulb does not give such a brilliant light as flash bulbs. On the other hand it can be tried out in advance. But it is not wise to give way to the temptation of bringing the light close up to the sitter's face, for this would result in unpleasantly harsh lighting. The source of light should be placed at least five feet from the sitter, and not too much to the side of the camera. Otherwise dark shadows will be cast over the field of view. In every case a screen to reflect light on the darker side of the object is strongly recommended. (See page 106.)

The procedure to be followed differs from that required for flashlight pictures. First of all the light is switched on, the ordinary room lighting being retained. The shutter opens for the necessary time and closes again. Lastly the light is switched off.

Two Lamps are Better Than One

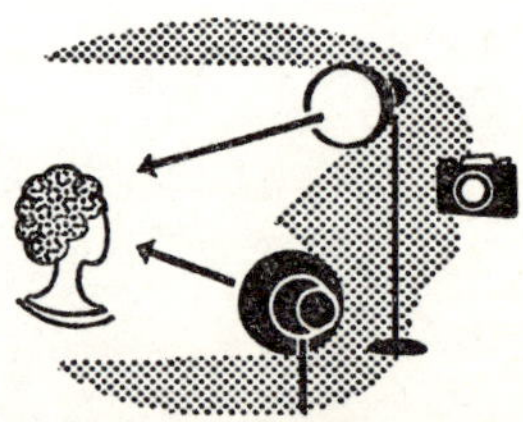

Indoor portraits made in the light of one lamp are in reality only half a job. One side of the sitter's face is too strongly lit, while the other half lies in the shadow. The white screen improves the situation only to some extent.

It is far better to replace the screen by a second lamp. It should be placed farther away from the model than the first lamp, for its purpose is merely to dispel unwanted shadows. The other lamp provides the main lighting.

The relative positions of the two lamps can be changed *ad infinitum*: one can be placed lower than the other; the two lights can be set at any acute angle to each other. A different lighting effect will result from every new arrangement.

HINTS AND TIPS

Flashlight

It is quite possible to place several flash bulbs all connected together in various parts of a large room, and to fire them simultaneously by means of a master switch. In some cases you can have extension units which you connect to the main flash gun. On taking the picture, all the bulbs are then synchronized to the main one. But be careful how you position them. They should not generally be visible and certainly should not fire direct into the camera lens.

A more sophisticated method of firing two or more flashes is to use a slave unit, containing a light-sensitive material connected to a switch. When the main flash fires, the switch of the slave unit closes and the second flash fires almost simultaneously. This cuts out the need for trailing cables. The slave unit needs no connection with either camera or main flashgun.

Electronic flash units, particularly the larger types with non-waterproof cases, should be kept as dry as possible. Moist surfaces are good conductors of electricity and can cause dangerous short-circuiting. Flashbulbs rarely use more than 30 *volts, but few electronic flash tubes fire on less than* 300 *volts.*

The flash guide number has to be adjusted for outdoor work. The normal guide number is calculated for average indoor work in relatively small rooms with good reflecting surfaces. Out-

doors, there are often no reflecting surfaces and the guide number should be taken as no more than half the normal figure. This means that you give two stops more exposure than you would in normal circumstances.

Electric Light

Before using any electrical apparatus, make sure that it is the right voltage for your district. It makes no difference with light bulbs whether you are A.C. or D.C., but it does make a difference—and a costly one at that!—if you join 110-*volt apparatus to a* 250-*volt circuit.*

Pictures can be made even with the help of an ordinary table-lamp, provided the exposure is long enough to allow the feeble light rays to make an impression on the emulsion. And if you replace your 60 *watt bulb by a stronger one, say, a* 100 *or* 200 *watt lamp, the time can be cut down considerably.*

For a really short exposure (1/4 *to* 1/30 *second*) *a* 275 *watt or* 500 *watt photoflood bulb can be substituted, provided the heat is not too much for your lamp-shade. People taken by the light of their usual reading lamp feel more at home.*

For all photos taken by artificial light the distance between the camera and the object has no effect on the illumination. The distance between the light and object matters.

Exposure meter readings can be misleading if the light is rather dim. The more sensitive cadmium sulphide (*CdS*) *meter may help but even that may need some artificial assistance. A useful method is to take a reading from a white card or sheet of paper placed as near as possible to the subject and facing the camera. The exposure recommended by the meter should then be multiplied by about six.*

A camera fitted with a fast lens at least 2.8, *or better,* 2 *or* 1.5, *enables you to take "candid" snapshots in ordinary well-lit rooms, restaurants, hotel halls, etc. By using an ultra fast film an exposure time of* 1/4 *to* 1/60 *second—according to the brightness of the light—should prove sufficient.*

CARE OF THE CAMERA

Storage

When not in use, the camera should be protected from damp and dust, preferably in its case and, as an additional precaution, inserted into a polythene bag.

Care should be taken to see that the camera is not kept in abnormally high or low temperatures—normal room temperature is best.

Take the precaution of removing any batteries because, however well made these may be, there is always a risk of deterioration and corrosion.

Exercise

Cameras (like most mechanical instruments) need to be exercised regularly to keep them in good condition. Store your camera where you can get at it easily and put it through its normal operations at least once a month:

1. Set the shutter release and fire several times.
2. Turn to a slow shutter speed and again set the shutter release and fire. Also operate delayed action device.
3. Examine the exposure meter for correct operation.
4. Check film transport.
5. Check the rangefinder or pentaprism viewfinder.

These exercises will keep the mechanism in good order, retaining the natural qualities of the lubricant—thus ensuring the camera is ready for instant use when required.

Running Test After Storage

Before embarking on a holiday where your camera will be your constant companion or, on an important assignment, make a few trial exposures. It is advisable to test the camera at least four weeks prior to your departure to give time for a test film to be exposed and processed. This will avoid a possibly spoiled holiday record.

Keeping the Interior Clean

When your camera is used on the beach, or other conditions where dust or sand can easily infiltrate into the mechanism, take the precaution of putting the instrument with its case into a polythene or other container so that flying dust, sand, etc. particles are prevented from entering the camera. This applies particularly, of course, if it is laid down on a sandy beach. Furthermore, avoid leaving the camera in such a position that direct sunlight is allowed to fall upon it. This could ruin a camera.

Small chips of film can easily damage the mechanism, therefore always make sure that the inside of your camera is spotless. Check your camera every time it is loaded with film.

Treating the Camera With Care

Your camera is a fine, precision instrument. It has been produced with great care and attention to detail. Do not allow it to be swung by its shoulder strap, thrown into the back of a car, nor treat as if it were as robust as a battleship. If you protect the camera against possible damage due to a knock, you will be amply repaid by years of excellent and trouble-free service. See also page 192, 'Coping with Tropical Conditions'.

AND NOW FOR COLOUR

Photography in colour is here and is possible with every camera. It takes an ever-increasing share among amateur pictures.

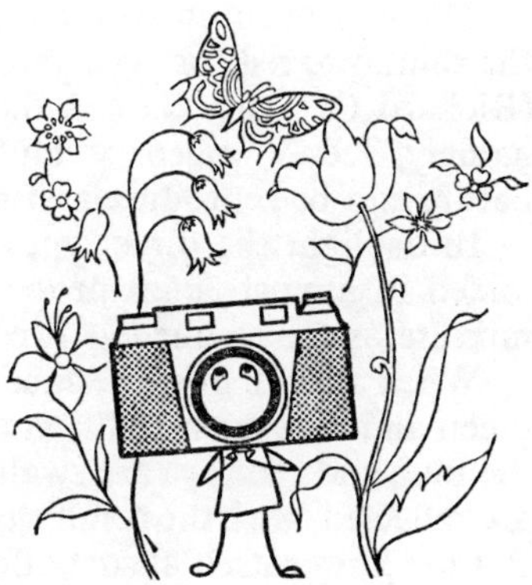

TAKING COLOUR

How it Works

So far, we have dealt almost exclusively with black-and-white photography, which is much easier if you develop and print your own pictures. If you are content to leave these tasks to the specialists, you may find colour photography more interesting.

The science of colour is a fascinating study with many branches and a thorough familiarity with it would require a wide knowledge of physiology and psychology, as well as a considerable acquaintance with astronomy, organic chemistry and the structure of the atom.

Now it would be a poor look-out for colour photography if its adepts needed to know even a fraction of all these matters. But it is fortunately possible to be a radio fan without knowing anything about the complicated process by which the sound travels from the transmitting station, via your receiving set, to your ear. In the same way you can make excellent colour photos without knowing much about the theory of colour.

There is no need to remember all the seven colours of the rainbow: red, orange, yellow, green, blue, indigo, violet (Richard Of York Gained Battles in Vain). Three will do, namely, red × green × blue. All the myriad colours of nature can be reproduced with the aid of these three tones.

In daylight the three types of light rays are inextricably mixed in almost equal proportions. And the result of the mixture as far as our eye is concerned is—white.

When a beam of white sunlight—that is, a mixture of red, green and blue rays—falls on the leaves of, say, a sunflower, the blue and red rays are swallowed up. Only the green rays are reflected, with the result that the leaf appears to us green. But the flower itself absorbs the blue rays and reflects the red and green elements of the sun's light. The mixture of red and green rays produces the sensation which we call "yellow".

Such are the basic principles applied in the process of colour photography in order to capture and reproduce all the hundreds and thousands of shades of natural objects, using only the three primary colours.

The Scope for Colour Photography

There is no lack of subjects for the amateur colour photographer. Almost anything that can be taken in monochrome can also be snapped in colour. First of all you will naturally choose the people around you, grown-ups as well as children, at work, at play and on the sports ground.

If you have a garden you will need no encouragement to reproduce its beauties in colour. The glorious red of your dahlias and the luminous yellow of the king-cups on the lily pond simply cry out for colour films. And of course you will put a colour film in your camera before you set out on your walks and excursions, for you can take all your favourite scenery with the additional advantage of having it in its natural colours. Animals make excellent studies for colour photography too.

In addition to all this there is a wide field of worth-while photography for people with hobbies of all kinds. One man will want to produce a picture in colour of some particularly fine specimens in his stamp album. The naturalist will make pictures of his butterflies and moths, or catalogue the flora of his district by means of a series of photographs showing the flowers in their natural colours. The microscopist will want colour pictures of his specimens. And so on in many other domains, in all of which, with the help of colour films, one can secure original and valuable photographs. In this way a hobby may develop into a real achievement, something which, besides amusing the author of the work, makes a contribution to the whole community.

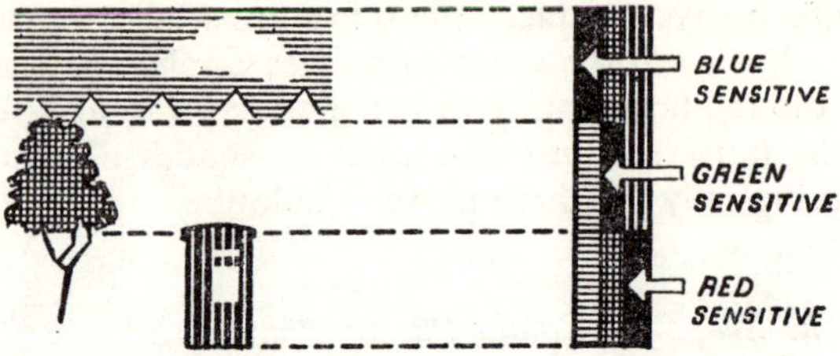

But how does colour film produce a colour picture?

Most colour films carry three light-sensitive layers. Each layer is sensitive to one colour only: the top layer records the blue parts of the image, the middle one the green, and the lowest layer the red. It is the combination of these three images which produces the picture in natural colours.

There are two types of colour film: they are "reversal" and "negative".

Reversal films (often referred to as "colour-slide film" listed under this heading in the colour film data table on page 137), produce, when processed, a colour transparency or colour slide. If you hold such a transparency to the light, you will see a positive image with all parts of the subject in their original colours. You can view it in a transparency viewer of pocket size, generally with a magnifier built in; you can project it in a slide projector to give a large and brilliant picture on a screen or you can project it in a table viewer with a built-in screen, similar in appearance to a television set.

There is little doubt that the projected image is the most natural and satisfactory way of showing colour transparencies.

Further, you can make from your colour transparencies: duplicate positive colour transparencies; a black-and-white negative which can be used to produce black-and-white prints or enlargements; direct colour enlargements on colour reversal material (expensive); separation colour prints or enlargements on paper by a colour separation process (difficult and expensive). You could also make a colour negative for making colour prints and enlargements as from colour negative film (described below). Colour prints on paper invariably show a loss of colour quality as compared with the original positive transparency.

Negative films, now often referred to as colour print film (listed under this heading in the colour film data table on page 137), produce, when processed, a colour negative which shows you a negative image of the subject in its complementary colours, e.g. blue appears yellow, red appears blue and so on.

The main purpose of the colour negative is the production of colour prints on paper. The quality is generally higher than that obtained from a positive transparency. From the colour negative you can also make: direct black-and-white prints or enlargements in the same way as from a black-and-white negative; positive colour transparencies for viewing or projection (expensive).

Making Your Choice

The choice between reversal or negative film remains an individual question in spite of the various uses that can be made of either type of material. First, there is the way you want to see the result—as a colour transparency or as a colour print. The print has, no doubt, much to commend it; it is easily shown, stored and carried about. The transparency calls for the aid of a viewer or projector. But the cost of a colour print is about three times that of a transparency; this may be at times mitigated by the fact that you do not need to make prints from unsuitable negatives. The transparency user, however, has additional outlay in the form of a viewer or projector with screen (in most cases both).

The final point to consider is the quality. The transparency will record each colour and its brilliancy in full. Held to the light or projected on a screen, the brightness range (it may be 100 to 1) is fully, or almost fully retained. It shows colours brilliantly, with great depth and realism. The colour print can, at its best, only show four-fifths of the light falling on it, and its full brightness range is no more than about 16 to 1. While the colour print is by necessity duller than the transparency, it is only fair to say that the eye soon adjusts itself to the reduced brightness range and subjects without very great contrast will be very satisfying.

In recent years the colour print film demand has overtaken that for colour slide films.

Speed

In comparison with black-and-white film, colour films are somewhat slower and can be used in simple cameras only in good lighting conditions.

The table on page 137 gives the film speed in the ASA rating system.

Use a reliable meter to determine the exposure time when using colour film, as the exposure latitude is rather less than that of black-and-white material.

If you have no exposure meter, consult the exposure table which is generally printed in the instruction leaflet with each film. These tables are invariably a good guide to correct exposure.

We give such a table below which is suitable for Kodachrome 25 (25 ASA).

COLOUR FILM EXPOSURES

Subject	*Bright Direct Sun*	*Hazy Sun*	*Overcast Bright Day*	*In Shade, Bright Day*
Light colours } with front lighting	1/60; *f*16	1/60; *f*11	1/60; *f*8	1/60; *f*5.6
Dark colours } with front lighting	1/60; *f*11	1/60; *f*8	1/60; *f*5.6	1/60; *f*4.5
Subjects in side light	1/60; *f*11	1/60; *f*8	—	—
Subjects against the light	1/60; *f*8	1/60; *f*5.6	—	—

This table is valid for mid-March to mid-September, from 9 a.m. to 3 p.m. In the winter months use the next larger aperture.

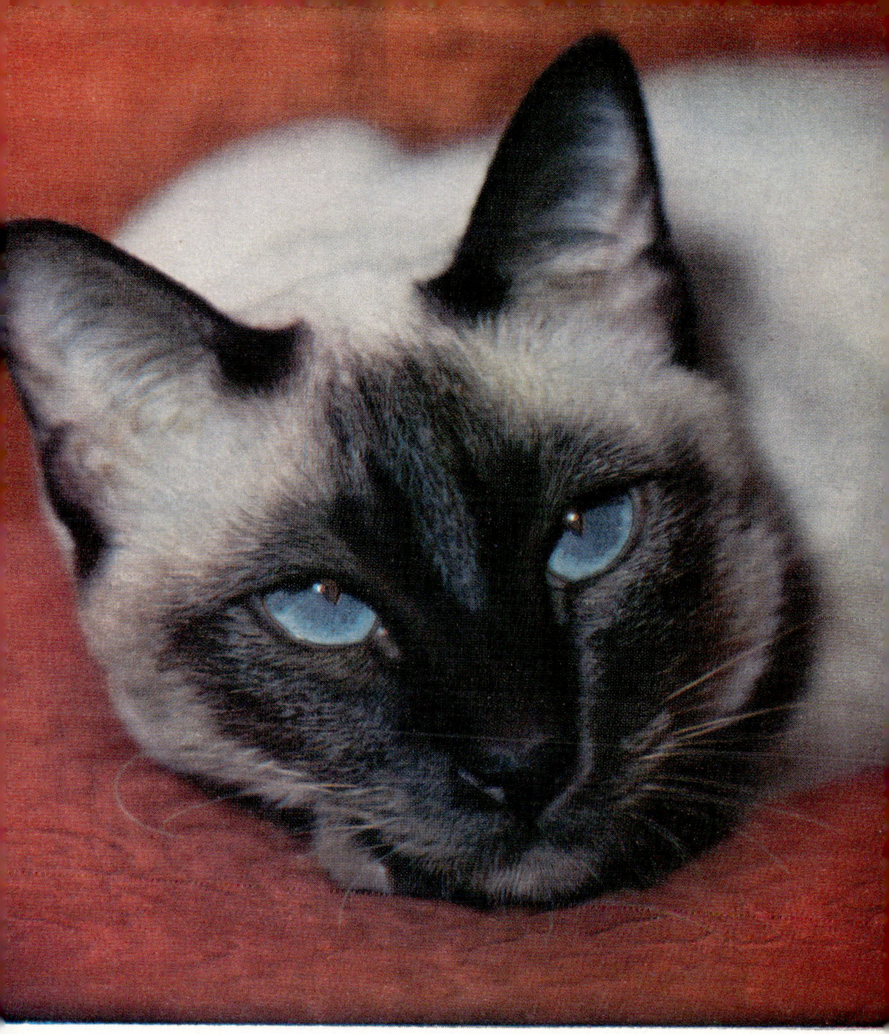

YOU DON'T NEED LOTS OF COLOURS. Use few colours in your first colour picture and watch what happens. The Siamese cat on the red carpet gives a foretaste of it. It proves that a few patches of strong colour can yield a brighter picture than would all the tints of the rainbow crowded into the same shot.—*John Blaxland.*

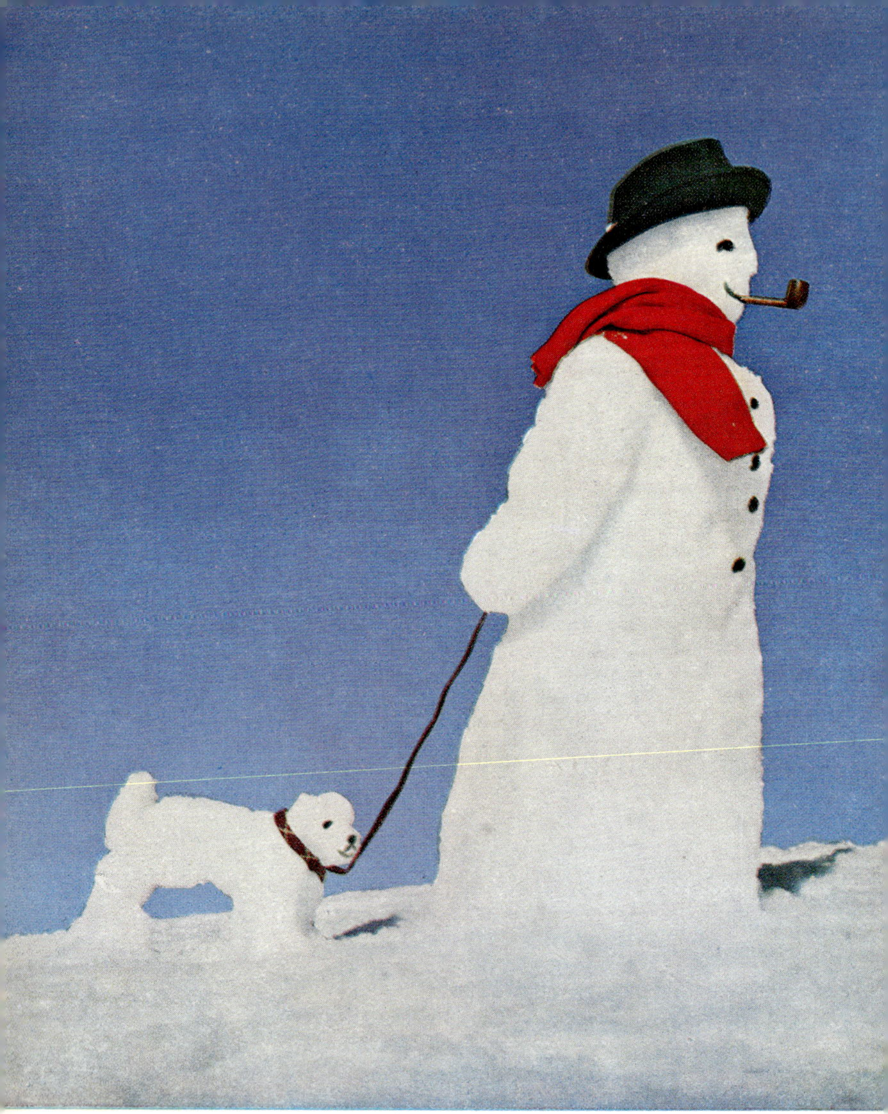

BRILLIANT COLOURS are by no means essential for successful colour shots. The only real spot of colour here is the scarf, which serves to emphasize the brilliance of the snow. Placed against the background of blue sky, the subject stands out in a very striking way.

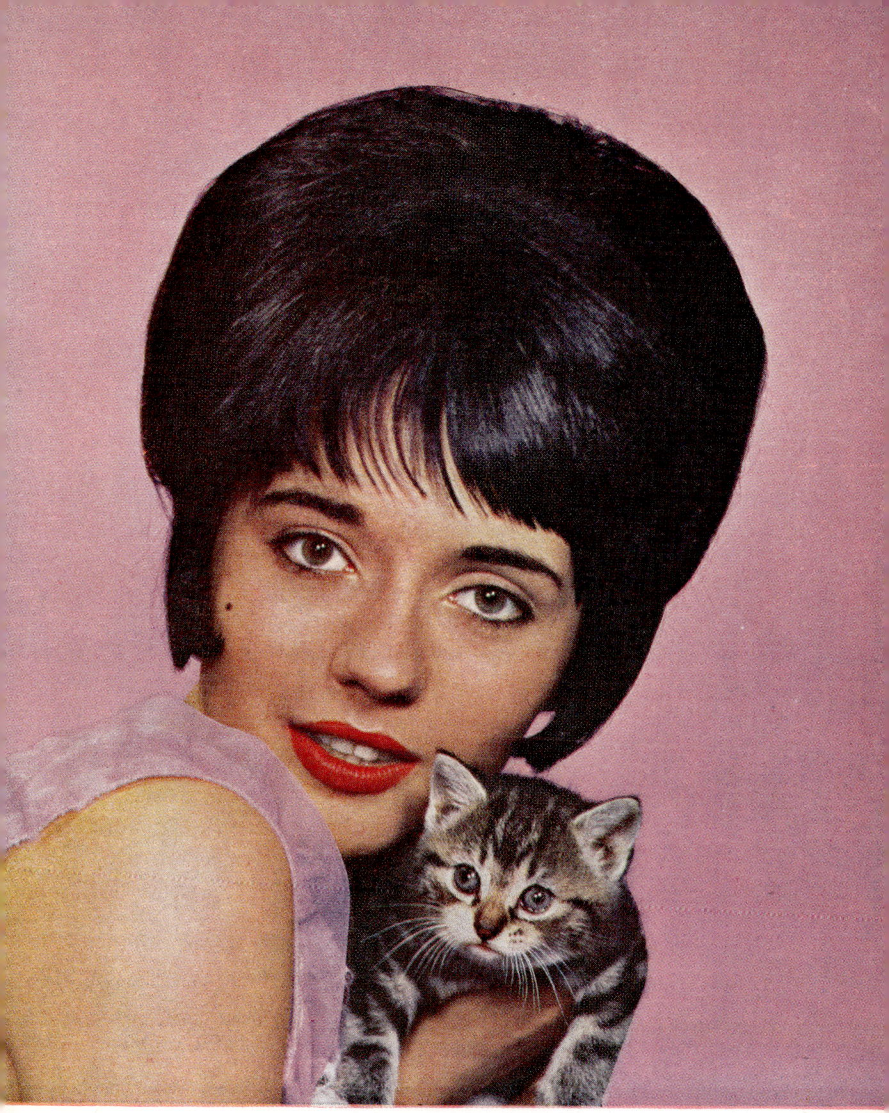

FLESH TONES are always rather tricky in colour. You must be careful to see that there are no strong colours close enough to reflect their hue into the wrong places. The lilac background, for example, must remain behind the head. Otherwise you may find that the girl comes out with a lilac tinged face, or other unnatural colour.

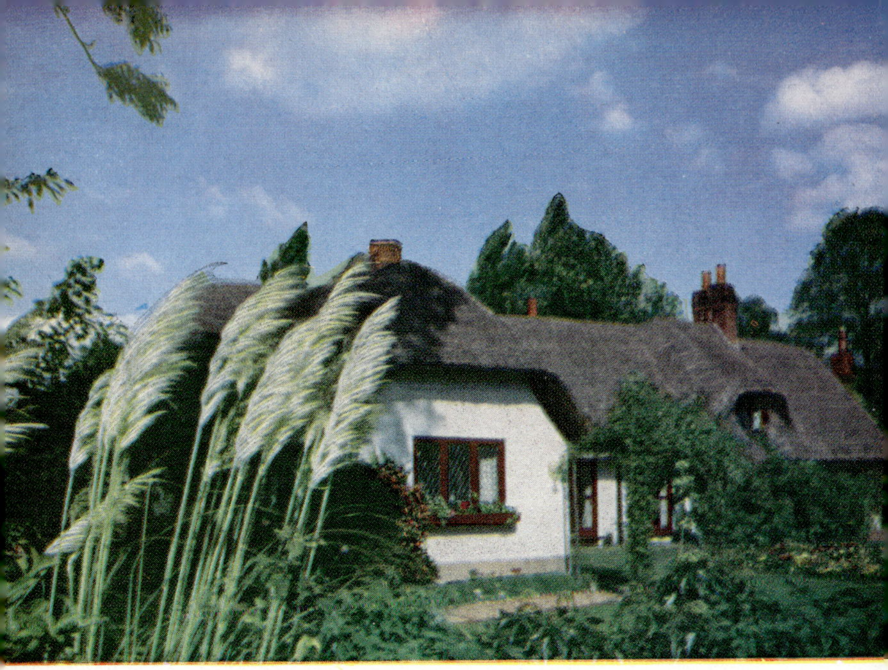

A PEACEFUL SCENE which gains enormously when seen in colour. There is little or no movement so you can safely use a slow shutter speed and a small stop to ensure adequate depth of field. The white walls of the cottage provide a perfect foil for the subtle colouring of the thatch and foliage.—*A. Kavanagh.*

COLOUR CLOSE-UPS (*opposite*) need carefully balanced lighting for best results. One or two blooms seen in close-up will usually look much better than a whole mass of flowers, when the colours tend to look confused.—*C.L.I.*

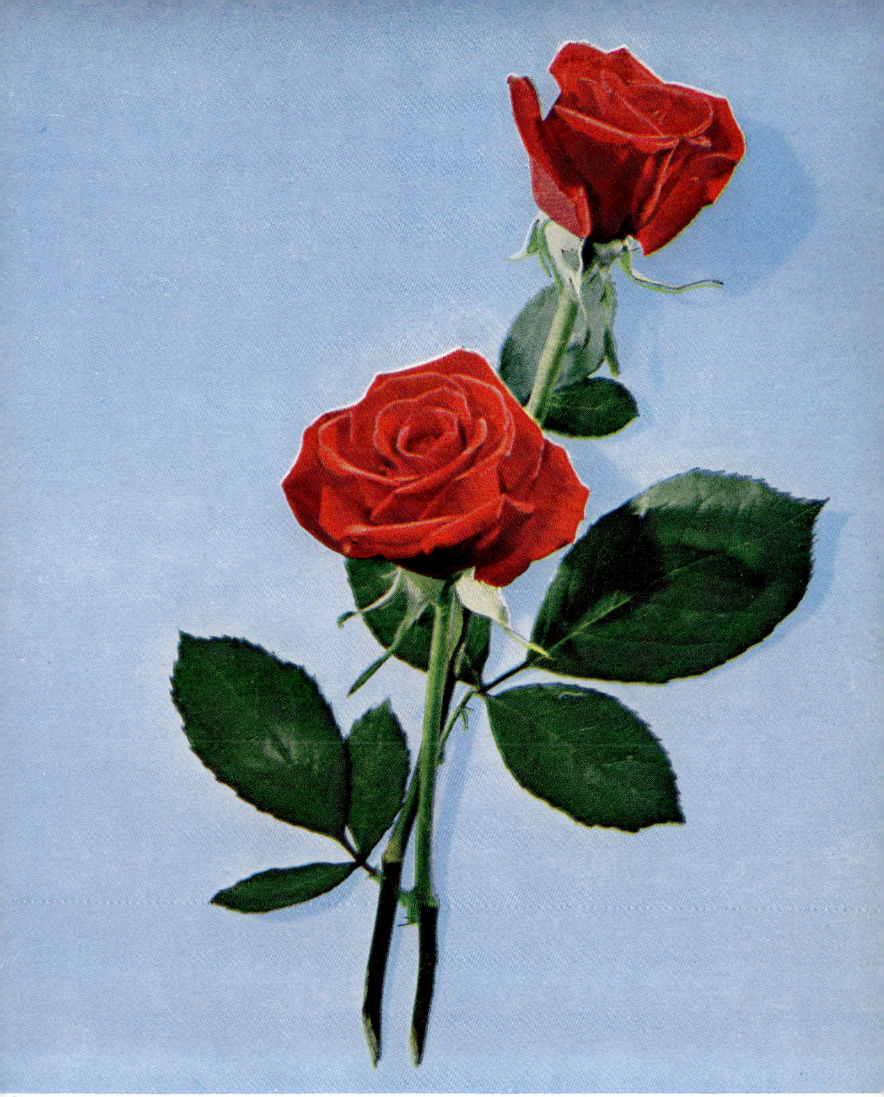

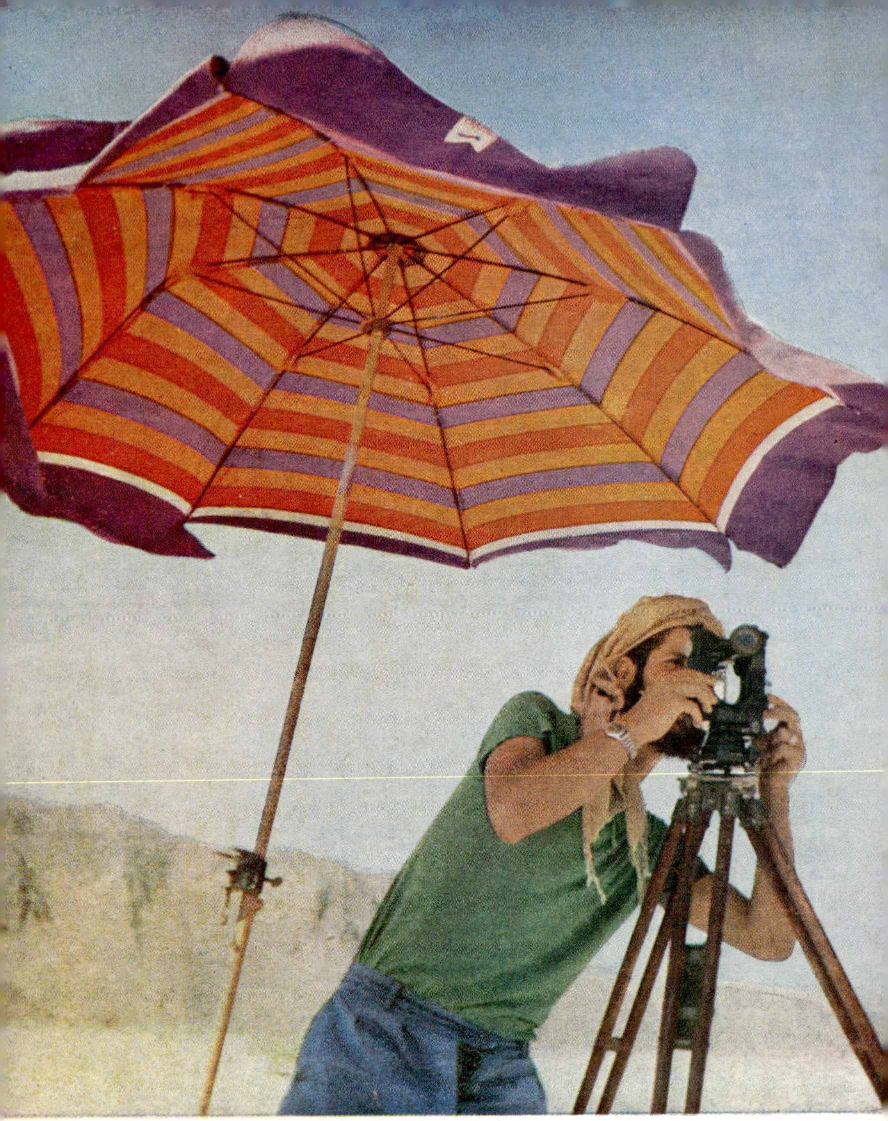

BOLD COLOURS can make a fine picture providing they don't dazzle. Choose your viewpoint carefully; you may be able to contrast one colour against another to good effect.—W. *Herz*.

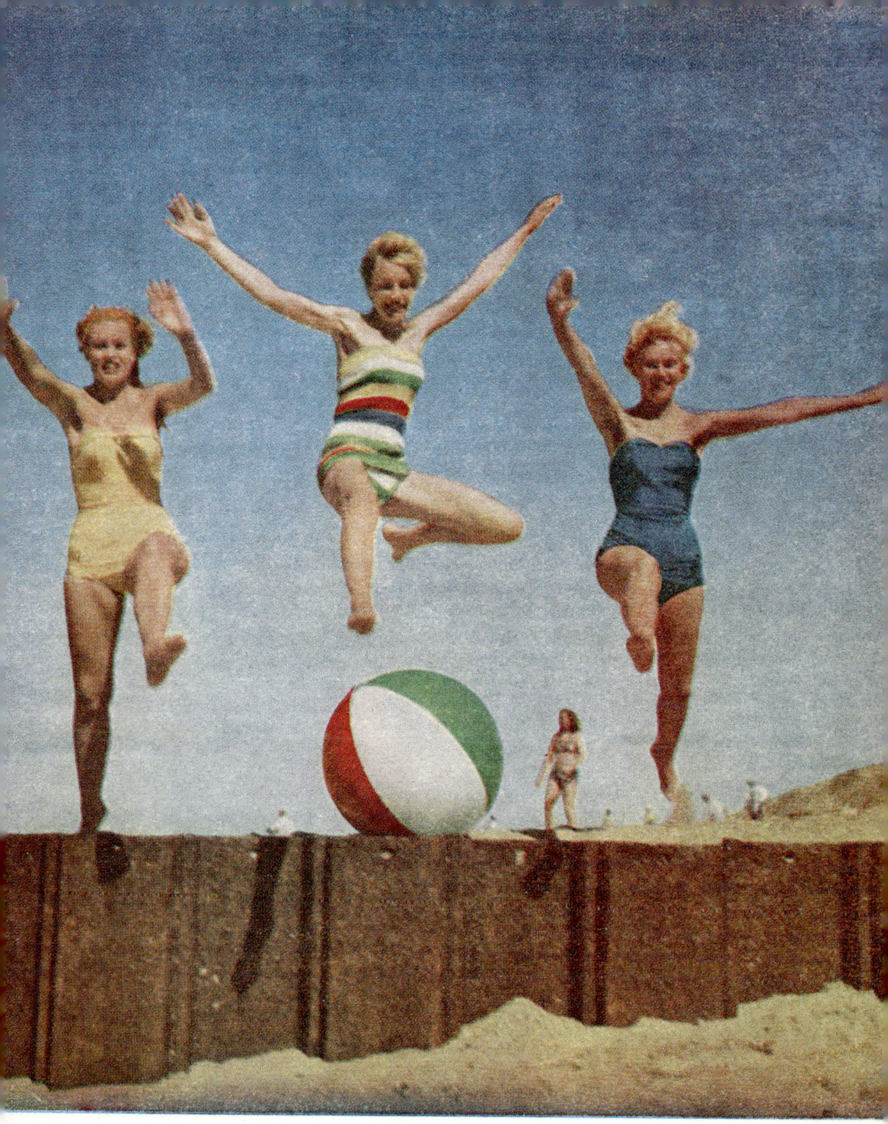

FAST ACTION presents an exposure problem due to the slow speed of most colour film. You need lots of light to catch a shot like this—the sort of light you only find at the seaside.—*W. Boje.*

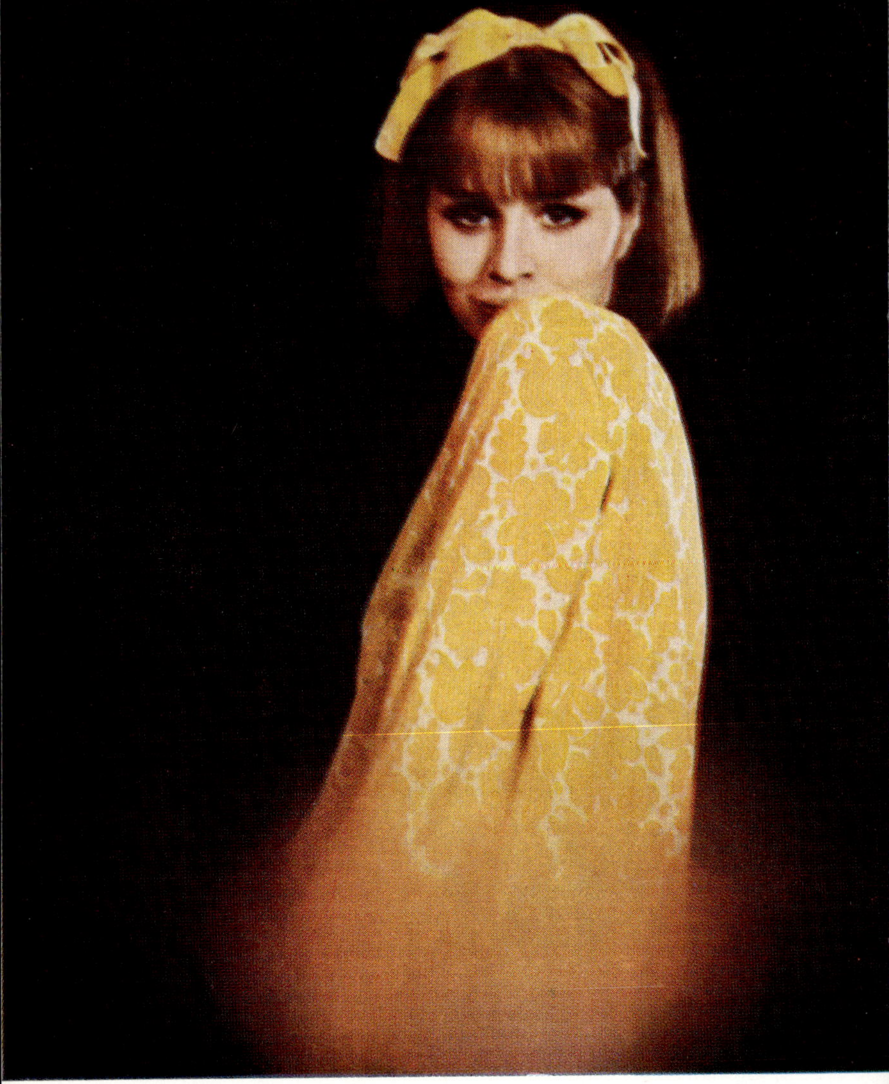

A WHOLE BATCH OF BRIGHT CONTRASTING COLOURS will not easily blend. Two more or less complementary colours are sufficient to create colour contrast. The picture depends on the outline and gradation of tone of each colour.—*Michael Legge.*

COLOUR FILM DATA

Film	*Type*	*Sizes*	*Speed ASA*	*Processing*
Negative (for Prints)				
Agfacolor CNS	Universal	35 mm., roll film	80	U
Ferraniacolor N27	Universal	35 mm., roll film	40	U
Fujicolor FII	Universal	35 mm., roll film	100	U
Kodacolor X	Universal	35 mm., roll film	80	U
ORWO CN17 mask	Universal	35 mm.	40	L
Perucolor	Universal	35 mm.	80	U
Reversal (for Transparencies)				
Agfacolor CT 18	Daylight	35 mm., roll film	50	M
Agfacolor CT 21	Daylight	35 mm.	100	M
Agfacolor CK 20	Artificial light	35 mm., roll film	80	M
Ektachrome X	Daylight	35 mm., roll film	64	U
H.S. Ektachrome	Daylight	35 mm.	160	U
H.S. Ektachrome B	Artificial light	35 mm.	125	U
Ferraniacolor CR50	Daylight	35 mm.	50	LU
Fujicolor R 100	Daylight	35 mm.	100	M
GAF 64	Daylight	35 mm.,	64	M
GAF 100	Daylight	35 mm.	100	M
GAF T100	Artificial light	35 mm.	100	M
GAF 200	Daylight	35 mm.	200	M
GAF 500	Daylight	35 mm.	500	M
Kodachrome 25	Daylight	35 mm.	25	M
Kodachrome 40	Artificial light	35 mm.	40	M
Kodachrome 64	Daylight	35 mm.	64	M
Orwochrom UT18	Daylight	35 mm.	50	M
Perutz Color C18	Daylight	35 mm., roll film	50	M

PROCESSING: M=films can be processed by the maker only. In this case the cost of processing is usually included in the purchase price of the film; L=films can be processed by an approved laboratory through a photographic dealer; U=films can be processed by he user by means of a special processing kit or through a photographic dealer

Colour Balance and Contrast

Colour films can produce brilliant colour transparencies when viewed by projection or looked at against the sky or a lamp. So use soft lighting for colour shots.

One can rely on the maker to provide uniformly good colour balance material. If the transparency is off colour, e.g., too blue or too red, one can generally assume some error in exposure or possibly in processing technique.

The light around us varies considerably from hour to hour and from season to season. It would be impracticable for the manufacturers to make all the films needed to suit the many light variations. As a result they have selected representative light sources to which they balance their reversal films: *daylight* colour film which will give correc colour reproduction in bright daylight; *artificial light* colour film which will give correct rendering in photoflood or similar tungsten light.

Negative films can generally be used in any light. More control over the colour can be exercised after the exposure has taken place, so that the colour balancing is accomplished when making the colour prints.

Filters in Colour Photography

While filters are generally not required in colour photography if the picture is exposed by the light for which the film was balanced, filters are used for special conditions.

UV Filters cut out some of the short-wave ultra-violet radiations which, though invisible, affect photographic emulsions. They are generally required only in very clean air, i.e. near stretches of water or at high altitudes. Such filters may also be slightly tinted yellow or pink to absorb some visible blue light. They are then known as Haze or Skylight filters. The function of these filters is to reduce a tendency to over-blue results.

Conversion Filters enable us to expose reversal colour film when the light source used differs from that for which the film was made. For example, if the exposure is made outdoors with film for artificial light and vice versa.

Polarizing Filters of neutral density are used with colour films to reduce reflections from non-metallic surfaces and render skies darker. They help to produce a more brilliant image by doing so. In colour work the polarizer must be a neutral (colourless) type. In general, from 1½–2 stops increase in exposure is required with a polarizer.

Processing of Colour Films

Once the colour film has been exposed, it is processed either by the manufacturer, through a photo dealer, or by the user, depending on the film and one's own preferences.

The initial price of *Agfacolor*, *Ansco*, *Kodachrome* and *Perutz Color* reversal film, generally but not always includes processing.

Some colour materials are processed by laboratories appointed by the manufacturers. You hand the film to your dealer who sends it to the laboratory.

Some films, where the processing cost is not included in the purchase price, can be processed at home with the aid of special processing kits sold for the purpose. These films are marked "U" in the table on page 137. Many specialized photo dealers will of course also do it for you.

The Basic Rules

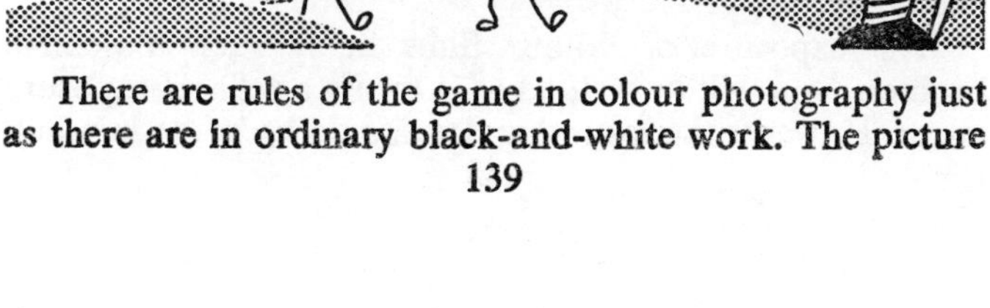

There are rules of the game in colour photography just as there are in ordinary black-and-white work. The picture must, of course, be sharply focused. And even if you have a steady hand, it is unwise to risk a longer exposure than 1/30 second without making use of a tripod or other firm support. A safer rule is to give not more than 1/50 or 1/60 second. Similarly one must avoid getting a blurred image of moving objects (see page 44). And finally, here, as with monochrome photos, a smaller stop will give greater depth of field (see page 47).

Unlike the black-and-white picture, which depends on differences of light and shade, the colour photo consists of a juxtaposition of different colours. Deep shadows look heavy and dead among the lively, gay masses of colour, so avoid them to start with at any rate.

Objects should be taken with *front lighting*, that is, with the sun behind the camera, a lighting arrangement which, on account of the flat, uninteresting light and shade effect it producces, is most unsuitable for black-and-white pictures, but which gives excellent results with colour films.

Watch the Exposure

Colour films have little latitude. This point is all the more important because black-and-white films have spoiled us in this respect. So expose with great accuracy.

If, for example, the correct aperture for any given exposure is *f* 8, the next larger stop (that is 5.6) would tend to over-exposure, whereas *f*11 would be too small and would result in under-exposure of the film.

Wrong exposure of colour films results in distortion of colour values. Over-exposure produces wishy-washy colours, pale faces, a watery sky and greeny-blue shadows. Under-exposure gives hard, deep colours, dark brown faces and a deep blue sky.

The exposure of colour films being such a ticklish business, you will be well advised to use a reliable exposure meter. However the following tips should be borne in mind.

Using an Exposure Meter

The advice already given (page 36) on using the exposure meter holds good for colour. Generally speaking, for close-ups the exposure meter should be held half-way between the camera and the object. This is to prevent the dial reading from being influenced by the surroundings.

For distant views, landscapes, for example, the exposure reading is usually taken at the point from which the photo is to be taken, the meter being pointed downwards somewhat to exclude some of the bright light from the sky.

The reading on the dial of the exposure meter is valid for objects of medium brilliance, in which light and dark colours are to some extent balanced.

For dark objects such as trees in summer and autumn, flower-beds in which green predominates, people in dark clothes, and for dark colours in general—dark green, violet, dark blue, dark red, black—the meter reading cannot be relied upon (see page 42). If your meter reads only the dark tones it will recommend an exposure to reproduce them as middle tones. So you need *less* exposure than the meter indicates for a dark subject.

For light objects such as open landscapes, large squares or wide streets, people in light clothes, for scenes on the beach, in the swimming pool, for snow scenes and for all light colours—white, yellow, light pink, orange, light green, light blue—the meter recommends underexposure, again because it thinks you want the scene to average out to a middle tone, as most scenes do. So you need *more* exposure than the meter recommends for subjects entirely light in tone.

It is preferable in such circumstances to take your reading from a middle tone if you can find one in the same lighting as the subject. Or you can place a grey card or similar medium-toned surface near the subject, facing the camera, and take your reading from that. Ideally, the grey card should reflect 18 per cent of the light falling on it and Kodak produce such a card for photographers. This gives the reading required for a normal subject and should be satisfactory for all subjects in colour. If, however, your subject is excessively dark it might pay you to give half a stop, certainly no more than one stop, *more* exposure than the meter recommends for the grey card.

For such unusual subjects, it is advisable to make more than one exposure of different durations or at different apertures so that you can choose the best one after processing.

People who perforce must do without an exposure meter must rely on the experience they have gained with black-and-white films. Use the exposure tables provided with each film as a guide only.

A further and most important rule for colour snaps is the following: make full use of all the available space on your film. The colours themselves will be more vigorous and more convincing if the snapshot is from close quarters.

Colour Photos by Continuous Artificial Light

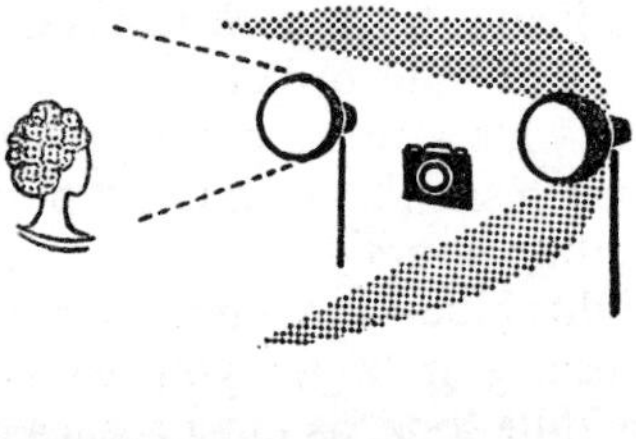

In comparison with daylight, artificial lighting has the advantage of being easier to control. Whereas daylight varies with every hour, every season and every change in the weather, artificial light gives one a constant illumination. It may happen that a colour snap by artificial light shows signs of under-exposure. If so, the picture can be made again under improved conditions. In this way experience will soon be gained to make failures few and far between.

Snaps made on reversal colour film by artificial light require an emulsion specially manufactured to suit the colour components of this kind of lighting. (See page 138.)

Ordinary household bulbs, on account of their relatively low power of illumination, necessitate rather lengthy exposures for colour photography and the resulting pictures have warm, and sometimes even reddish, tones. Photographic lamps are more suitable. Used in conjunction with one of the special emulsions for artificial light, they ensure accurate colour reproduction.

With artificial light, the rules already given for daylight pictures still hold good: use front lighting, give correct exposure and make your picture as large as possible.

When only one source of light is used the flat, shadowless illumination which is essential for good colour effects is best obtained by having the lamp near to the camera. If two lamps are used—and this arrangement is the one that gives the best results—they should be placed on either side of the camera and at equal distances from the object, which is thereby lit as uniformly as possible.

The length of exposure depends in the first place on the brightness of the source of light. Exact indications are con tained in the instructions with each colour film.

Flash Pictures in Colour

It's just as easy to use flash with colour as black-and-white. If you have daylight type film in your camera, you need the standard blue-tinted bulbs or cubes. The blue flashbulbs are right for colour reversal, negative and black-and-white film. Flash should not be used with artificial light film.

With electronic flash use daylight film.

If you find that your particular flash unit gives rather blue results, try fitting a very pale yellow or pink tinted filter such as a haze or skylight filter (see page 138) over the lens.

COLOUR REVERSAL FILM FLASH EXPOSURES

Flash bulb	*Film:*	ASA 25–32	ASA 40–50	ASA 64–80	ASA 100–125	ASA 160–200
Daylight Type Film						
PF IB, G.E.C. IBS, MFIB, AGIB		65	85	105	130	170
PF6B (focal plane)		62	80	100	124	160
PFC4 (cube)		50	65	80	100	130

Find the guide number in the table above for the flash bulb and film speed in use. Then divide it by the distance between the flashgun and subject. The answer will give you the correct aperture to use (e.g., with a PF IB bulb and 25 ASA film the guide number is 65, Divide this by the distance from the subject, say 10 ft., 65÷10=6.5. Therefore the correct aperture to use is 6.5 about mid-way between *f*5.6 and *f*8).

Displaying the Picture

With reversal colour film you will get only one copy of each picture—or rather, you get the original. Moreover, this is a transparency, a coloured lantern slide. Paper prints can be made from this transparency (see page 127) but it is primarily intended to be viewed by transmitted light.

On the other hand, colour transparencies can be produced from colour negatives for viewing or projection.

There is a whole series of "gadgets" for viewing colour slides in comfort. The 1 × 1½ inch (24 — 36 mm.) or smaller pictures made by a miniature camera are altogether too small to be seen comfortably without enlargement.

A simple and inexpensive piece of apparatus for viewing colour slides by daylight consists of a magnifying glass set in a frame into which the pictures can be inserted. If the holder is then held up against a light background the picture appears large and well lit. There is a ground-glass or opal screen to diffuse the light and ensure uniform illumination.

Even handier is the viewer designed for use with artificial light. Here the screen is lit by an electric lamp. This type of illumination, being soft and yet powerful, and employing a suitable combination of light rays, provides excellent colour reproduction.

The colour quality of the light by which you view your transparencies and prints has a marked effect on the appearance of your photographs. It is therefore important that, to make fair comparisons, both the transparencies and the prints are viewed in the same light. The colours in the prints won't look quite as vivid as those in the transparencies.

Undoubtedly the finest method of viewing colour slides is by using a projector which throws on to the screen a really large picture in which every detail can be admired by several people at the same time.

Colour prints can also be projected by using an Episcope.

HINTS AND TIPS

Some Good Advice on Taking Colour Snaps

Keep to one make of film long enough to become familiar with its peculiarities and with its special requirements with regard to exposure. In this way you will get the best out of whatever material you may use.

Colour snaps should, of course, be coloured, but they need not look like a patch-work quilt. There is no necessity to include all the colours of the rainbow in your picture. You will get a much better effect with a few large patches of well assorted colours—yellow and blue, for example, or green and red. Close-ups serve almost automatically to limit the picture to one or two large surfaces, each of one colour only.

In choosing suitable subjects for colour photographs, an important psychological fact should be taken into consideration. This is that most people are apt to notice many more colours in a picture than they do when looking at their surroundings. In everyday life nearly all of us—with the exception of painters—content ourselves with a superficial perception of local colours, whereas when looking at a colour picture we notice secondary shades, coloured reflections, coloured shadows and so on, and in consequence even a picture which faithfully reproduces natural colours is likely to be considered too variegated. Although it is probable that we shall eventually become familiar with the richness of natural colours as rendered in the photographs, it is advisable to avoid subjects which are over-full of strongly coloured shades and reflections.

A deep blue summer sky needs careful handling. The real thing, of course, is enchanting. Even so, without clouds it is apt to look a bit gaudy. If there are dark-coloured objects in the foreground, the danger is already less, because the exposure is taken from these. This means that the sky will be somewhat over-exposed and will appear a little paler, which is all to the good.

Green is an awkward colour. If it comes out too dark it looks like spinach. Slight over-exposure immediately produces a violent hue. The eye is much more critical of distortion in green than in the other colours, red and orange, for example.

In the case of reflections the photographer should remember that a green shadow on a face will give an extremely strange effect when the tree which causes it is not shown in the picture. This is also true for red reflections, such as may be caused by a fire or a red coat, whether or not the object throwing the reflection is included in the picture.

Snow scenes in colour sometimes show definitely blue shadows. This may at first offend one's vision. But a little experience with snow in the same conditions, that is, beneath a blue sky, will prove that the colour film was right. The shadows, thanks to the reflection of the sky, are blue.

Portraits are a very interesting but rather tricky task for the colour photographer. Deep shadows under chin and nose and in the eye-sockets should be avoided by a carefully levelled lighting, which in the case of artificial light should rely on not less than three photolamps and some reflectors. But if the photograph consists only of head and shoulders, two photolamps, or even one, may be sufficient. Be sure the reflectors are colourless and don't place anything coloured over the lamps to achieve soft lighting effects unless you want special colour effects, too.

Although front lighting, i.e., with light behind the camera, is the rule, a lens-hood will be found useful for excluding unwanted light from the sides, reflections from white walls, water, and so on. It likewise protects the lens from disturbing light from a cloudless blue sky above and from the bright reflections from the road surface below. The result is a clearer reproduction of colours.

The rules for taking colour photos of firework displays and thunderstorms are the same as for black-and-white pictures. Shutter release on B, shutter open, stop 2 or 2.8, focus at infinity. The shutter is closed when the photographer considers that the film has accumulated a sufficient store of light impressions.

For photographs by night of advertisement signs, etc., an artificial light film should be used but many prefer the warmer colours obtained on daylight film.

The old trick of using a household or photographic lamp for lightening the shadows of an object near the window will not work with colour film in the camera if daylight material is used. The side of the object which is lit by the electric bulb appears reddish on the picture. If, on the other hand, you use an artificial light colour film the colours on the daylight side of the picture are not true to life.

Once they have been exposed, colour films should not be left undeveloped too long. Otherwise the colour reproduction may suffer. So once a film has been started, finish it off quickly, and when the whole film is exposed, do not leave it lying about for longer than you need.

In all cases where colour films are not sent back from the photographic firm already cut and mounted, it cannot be too strongly emphasized that they must be divided into individual pictures immediately on receipt. Each individual film should be framed between two cover-glasses and surrounded by a mask. Only then are they in a fit state to be handled and admired. This is the only way to prevent damage from dust and dirt, finger marks, scratches, etc.

Colour films and prints should not be exposed for long to bright sunshine, or the colours may fade.

Black-and-White Prints from Colour Films

It is possible to get black-and-white prints and enlargements from reversal colour films. All you have to do is to make a contact print on panchromatic film. This print appears as a black-and-white negative, which can be printed like any other negative.

From colour negative film you can get black-and-white prints even more simply by printing or enlarging in the same way as from black-and-white negatives, preferably on a panchromatic enlarging paper.

Although technically every colour photograph can be transformed into black and white, it must be borne in mind that a good colour picture will not necessarily result in an equally good black and white one. In fact, while the beauty and the expressiveness of a colour photograph depended on colour combinations and harmonies, the black-and-white picture relies only on the relations between black, white and the different shades of grey.

Two points should be remembered. The black-and-white negative from a colour film is inclined to be hard. One uses, therefore, soft material and makes the development as soft as possible. (*See formula on page 228.*) *In the second place, since colour film is reversed, the negative is a mirror image of the real object. In order to correct this do not as some cunning fellows might, place the emulsion layer of the pan film against the celluloid side of the colour film. This would only produce a blurred image, since it has been printed through the thickness of the celluloid. You can, on the other hand, put the reversed negative into the enlarger with the emulsion side turned towards the lamp and so produce an enlargement the right way round.*

PHOTO-SUBJECTS A—Z

How your photography should be adapted to whatever you want to photograph

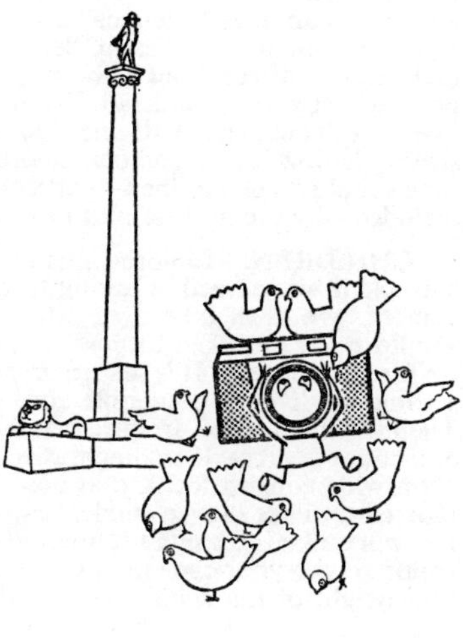

ANIMALS.—*Our Pets.*—We only need to watch them at play or in repose to get not one, but a whole series of pictures. The camera is best pre-set for zone focusing (page 46). A low viewpoint is essential, otherwise we shall dwarf our subject. To get close-up heads, it is best to pre-set the camera at a fixed distance, attract the attention of the animal and expose just as the head comes into range. *In the Zoo* animals behind bars and coarse mesh netting can be photographed by putting the lens right into the space between the bars or netting to avoid their appearance in the picture. With fine meshed netting we may also push the lens against the netting, which will then be so far out of focus that it fades out of the photograph. The chief problem will be the usually distracting and ugly background. By choosing side lighting we can eliminate background detail. At the same time the animal will receive satisfactory modelling and will "stand out" boldly. One should make sure of generous exposure to secure good rendering of fur, skin or feathers. Subjects with a very wide range of colours are better taken on panchromatic film and with a medium yellow filter.

ARCHITECTURE.—The typical "picture-postcard" view can be bought but not the small architectural discovery. So concentrate on detail. Any normal camera will cope with such tasks. The camera has to be held straight, otherwise everything will appear distorted and toppling over. (Still, *intentionally* distorted views may be effective. For these you must go quite close to the building and take it at a sharp angle from a low viewpoint. You will have to stop well down to about *f* 16 to make sure of adequate depth of field.) If you must get a lot into the picture it is essential to stand well back from the building, otherwise a special "wide-angle lens" has to be used to cover a wide field at a short distance. A "tele-lens" also has its uses for architectural work, enabling you to get distant details large in your picture. With all architecture direct front light is bound to give a flat, uninteresting photograph with little detail. Front-side lighting is almost essential to liven up the subject. Extreme side lighting may produce disturbingly strong shadows casting across important lines and shapes. The exposure time should be determined—particularly if large patches of shadow are included—by the darkest part in which details are clearly visible.

CHILDREN.—Children are the most rewarding of all photographic subjects if we succeed in taking them as they are—unconscious of the camera. We must take them when they do what they like and they should never be asked to pose, to look into the camera or be dressed up for the occasion. It is best to prepare the camera without being seen, setting the lens at a suitable zone-focus combination (see page 46). Then watch until you are sure that the camera does not attract attention and shoot quickly. If a comparatively long shutter-speed is required to get a wide zone in focus, that need not worry you unduly, as slightly blurred outlines due to sudden movement will not show unpleasantly but will make the picture if anything more alive. Never look down on children with your camera but keep to a normal angle with the camera at a height of the child's head or, better still, take them from a low angle, say the height of your knees; the impression will be more natural and pleasing. As far as lighting, film, filter and general technique are concerned, what is said on pages 187–9 applies here too.

Books on all aspects of portraiture are "Camera Portraiture", by H. Williams, and "The Photoguide to Portraits", by Günter Spitzing.

FIREWORKS.—The camera is supported by a tripod, the lens directed in such a way as to avoid moving sources of light (like motor-cars), the shutter set to "B" and preferably worked with the cable release. Set the aperture to *f*8 and then all you have to do is to press the release while a rocket, for instance, goes up, and to close the shutter again. Open the shutter once more when the next firework goes up, and so on. In this way half a dozen or more single units can be collected on one negative to produce an impressive picture.

Books on this subject and similar tricks are "All the Photo Tricks", by Edwin Smith, "Effects and Experiments in Photography", by Paul Petzold and "The Photoguide to Effects and Tricks", by Günter Spitzing.

FLOWERS, PLANTS.—For close-up studies, the simple camera will have to be equipped with a close-up lens (full particulars on page 55). A tripod or tabletop stand with a ball and socket head is indispensable. Medium-speed film, colour or black-and-white, is the most suitable material. In black-and-white there are few flower subjects whose delicate tone rendering cannot be improved by the use of a light or medium yellow filter. Flowers and plants should be photographed where they grow, but they need to be isolated from the surroundings. This can be done by choosing a suitable viewpoint for the camera and by clearing the ground near the subject. Both fore- and background should be watched, for if blurred parts of other plantsare included in the picture they will spoil the effect, especially in colour A sheet of not too white paper fixed to two sticks may be used to form a neutral, restful background; set in a slight curve around the flower it will serve, at the same time, to shield the plant from the wind. The hard midday sun will be found unsuitable, and diffused, hazy sunlight as a rule most effective. A hand mirror, reflecting light to the shadows, may sometimes be useful. The exposure time should be kept as short as possible to avoid blurring from the movement of the plant in wind.

"Camera Close Up", by O. R. Croy, deals with all aspects of usıng the camera at close range.

GROUPS.—While the technicalities of photographing groups are not different from those involved in taking portraits (see pages 187–9), the pictorial side is a problem which needs study if the group is not to look like the all-too-famous "football eleven". Some sort of occupation serves to join a number of people together in the garden, around the tea table, at sports. If nothing of the kind can be arranged, then group them roughly together, let them talk to each other, but do not let them look into the camera—deceive them as to the moment of exposure, even pretend that you have taken the picture and actually expose when they feel free again. To avoid over-cutting when taking a large number of people you should use a higher viewpoint, a chair, a table or a first-floor window, for example; but do not make it too high, otherwise you will dwarf the figures too much.

Portraiture in general is well covered in "Camera Portraiture", by H. Williams, "The Photographic Portrait", by O. R. Croy and "Light on People", by Paul Petzold.

INTERIORS.—With the ordinary camera you will have to content yourself with small sections. However, if your camera is one in which the lens is interchangeable, you can obtain the widest possible angle of view by fitting a lens with the shortest focal length available. The first essential for indoor work is a solid tripod, as the exposure time is bound to be long—as a rule a few seconds. If a mere "record" of the building is all that is required, the camera should be placed centrally near one wall; for a pictorial effect it should be in or near a corner. In public buildings, churches, etc., where artificial light cannot be arranged one will sometimes get striking pictorial patterns by making use of sunshine streaming through windows, though there is a danger here of producing a "patchy" effect. A safer medium, however, is soft, diffused, outdoor light, which will bring out details more clearly without too many heavy shadows. The strong midday light should be avoided. It is essential to stop well down—*f* 16 or smaller to obtain sharp reproduction of the largest possible area. Where the light can be arranged, as for example at home, one can combine daylight with artificial light except with colour film, using the artificial light to lighten deep shadows, or work in artificial light only. (See also pages 105 and 108). A simple way to get an even, shadowless illumination with one lamp only is to hold the lamp in the hand and swing it slowly in large circles on either side of the camera towards the part of the room to be photographed.

LANDSCAPES.—Distant landscapes rich in small details will usually be disappointing in black-and-white, as will those consisting mainly of "green" values, e.g. meadows with woods in the background. By including a subject of known size, such as a tree, in the foreground, we get a measure of distance in the picture and create an impression of depth. By choosing a high viewpoint we may be able to disentangle an otherwise confused view; low viewpoint, on the other hand, will increase the importance of things near the camera. The skyline, too, may be raised and lowered according to whether a low or high position is chosen for the camera. Even tilting up or downwards is permissible so long as you keep the camera otherwise level and there are no buildings included in the view to give you away. Tilting upwards will emphasize foreground and diminish background, a downward tilt will give you more of a bird's-eye view. The mood, or atmosphere, of a landscape depends to a great extent on two factors—sky and distance. In colour, there is the further factor of brilliance or otherwise of the colours. In sunshine, they are full and clear. In more sombre conditions, colours are degraded and sometimes totally obscured. In black-and-white, clouds can be made to stand out better against a *blue* sky if you use a light yellow filter. A deeper coloured filter will give a dramatic emphasis to clouds,

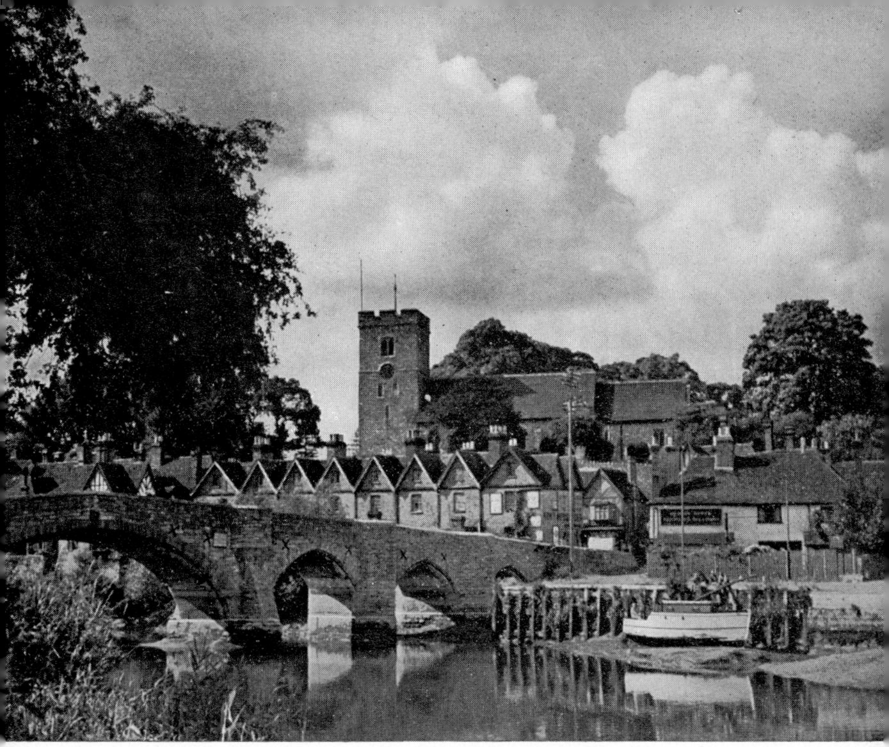

ARCHITECTURE AND SCULPTURE are best taken with angled lighting to show form and shape. Level the camera carefully to avoid tumbling verticals. Small stops are needed to yield good definition in depth. Foliage, sky and water will provide pleasant contrast for livening up the picture—but they call for a filter if we want them recorded in good tones. Introduction of "human element" is seldom too successful.—Photographs by *L. and M. Gayton* (page 153), *W. Knoll* (page 154), *H. van Wadenoyen* (page 155).

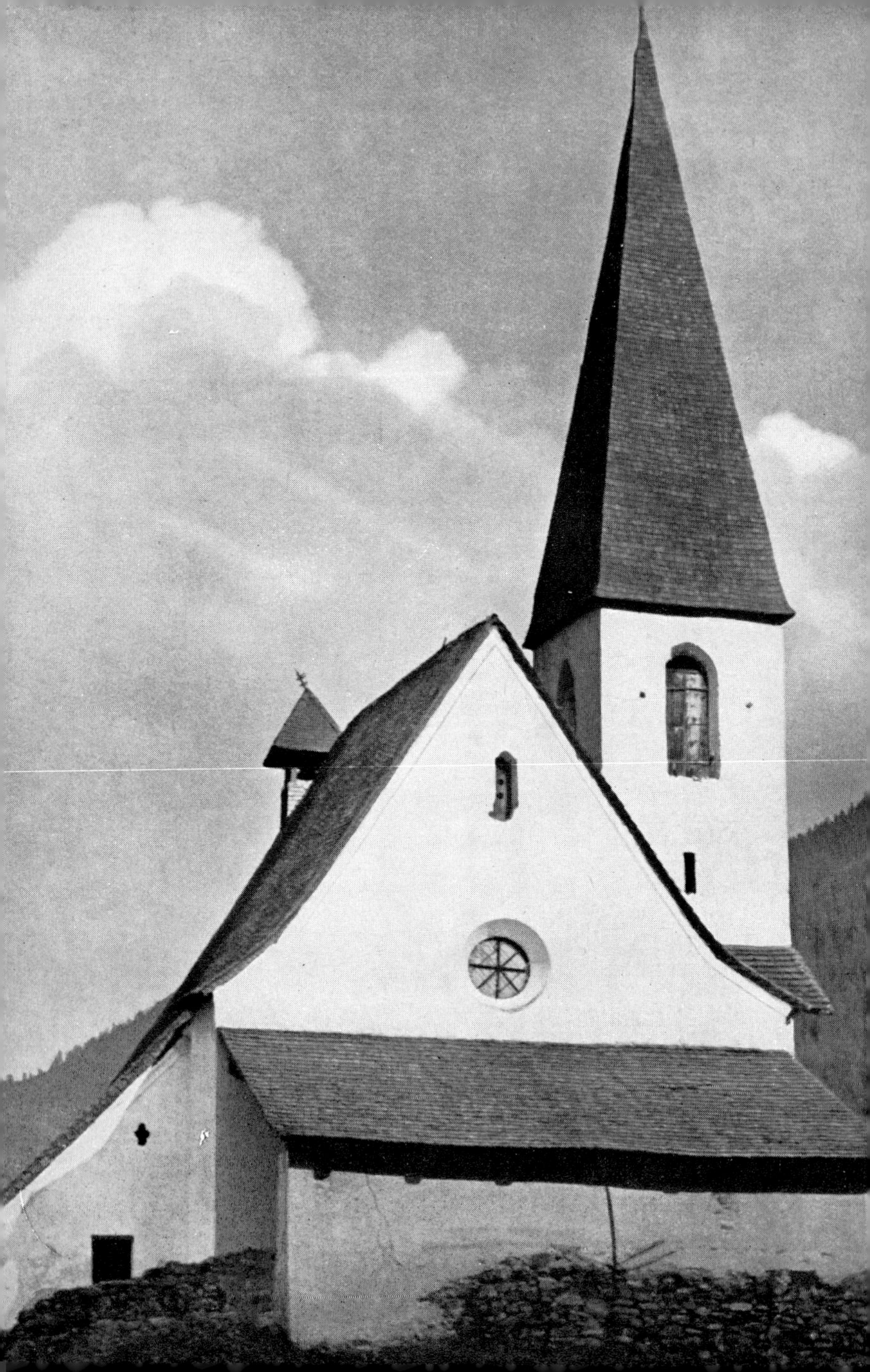

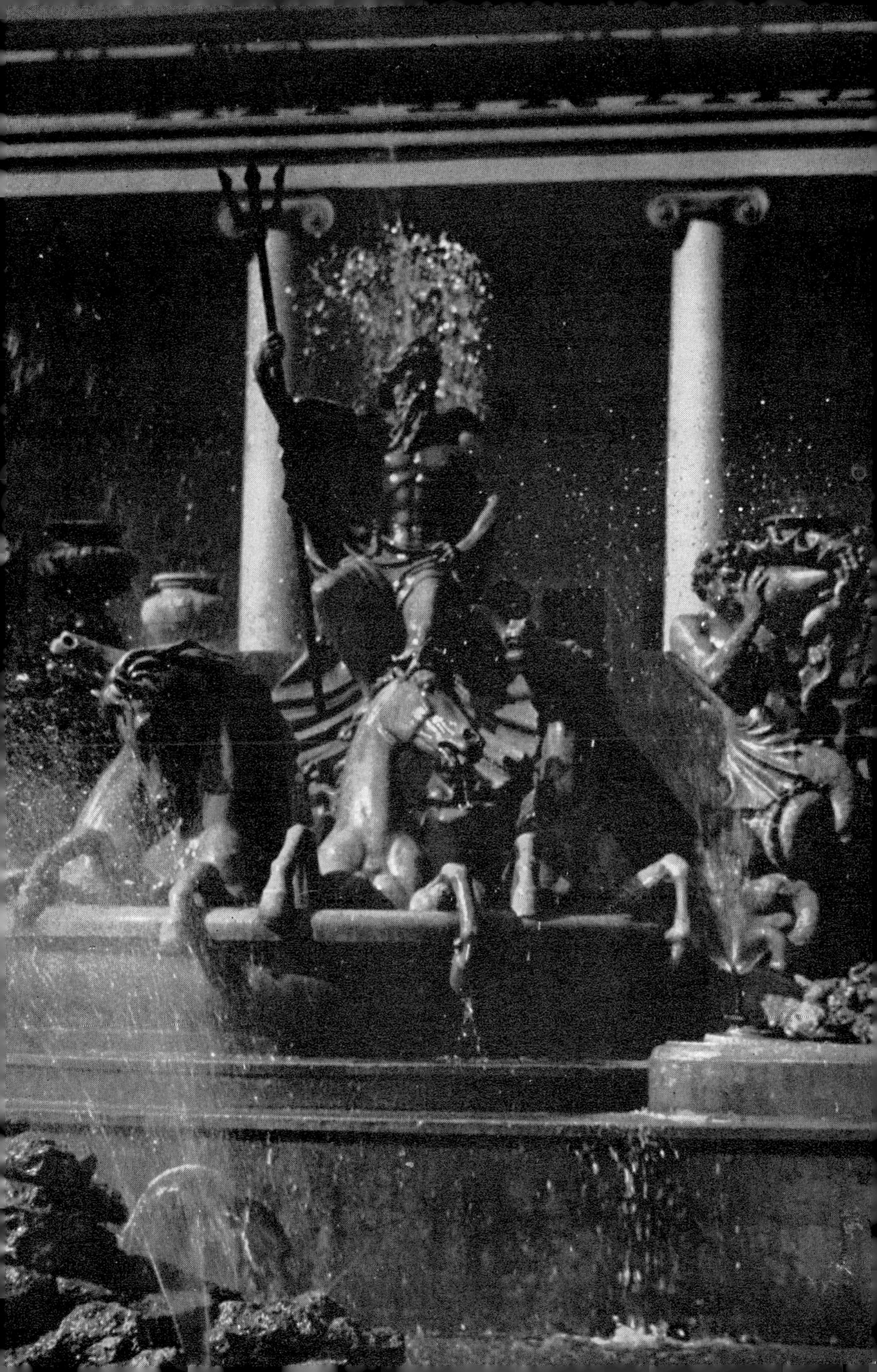

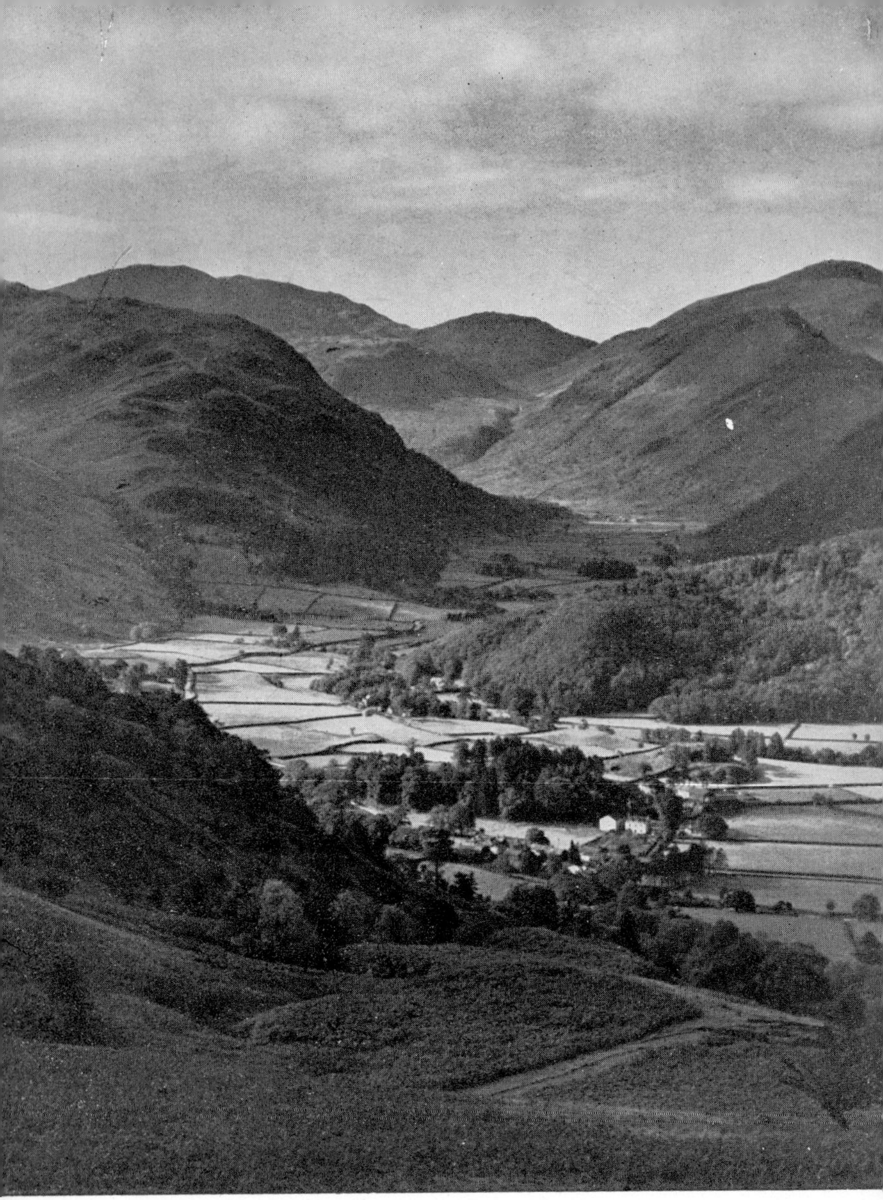

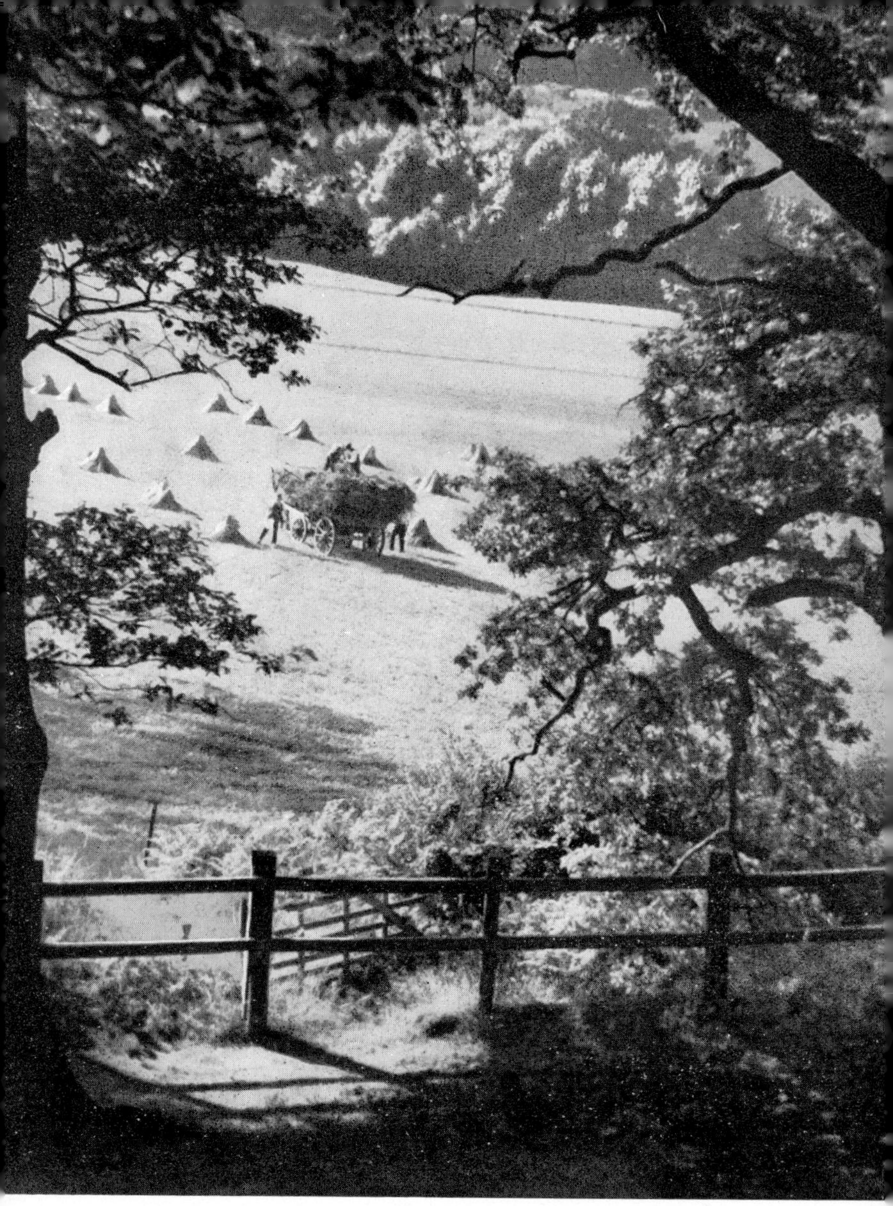

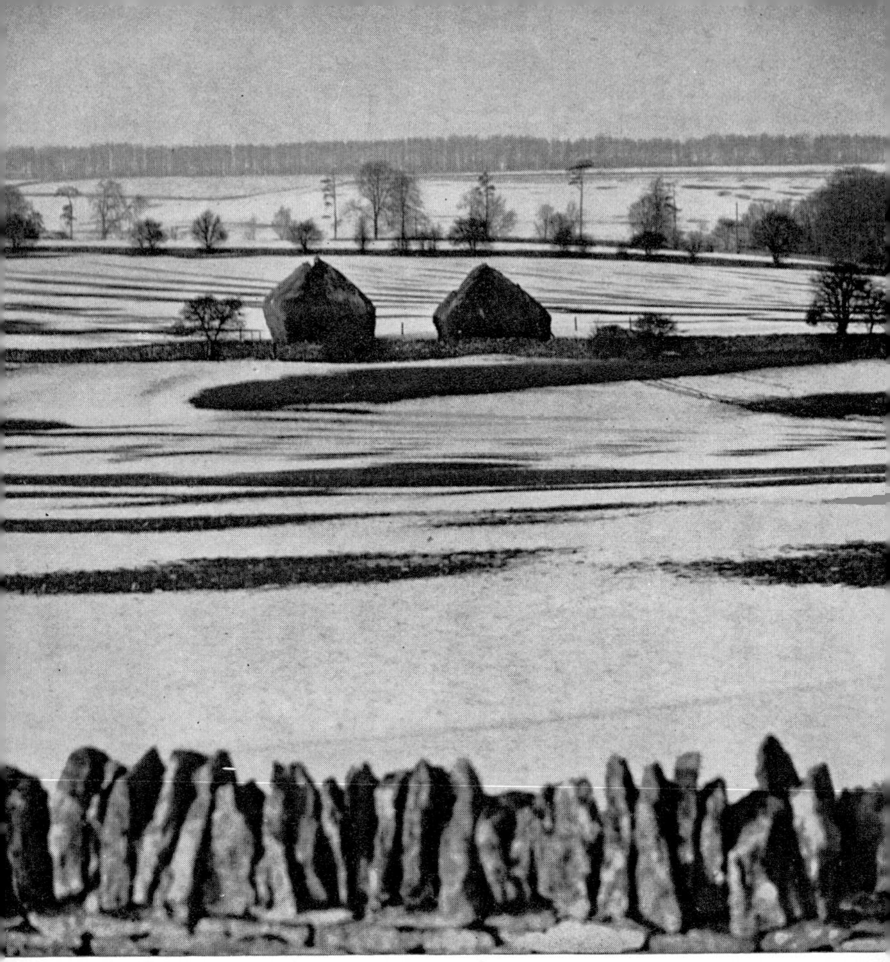

LANDSCAPE PHOTOGRAPHY has as many varieties as there are varieties of landscapes. High viewpoints will yield broad vistas, low viewpoints are best to bring out some detail. The wider you cast your view the more you will need something in the foreground to give an impression of depth. The distance seldom need be sharp but stop down sufficiently to ensure sharpness for foreground and centre. The main point of

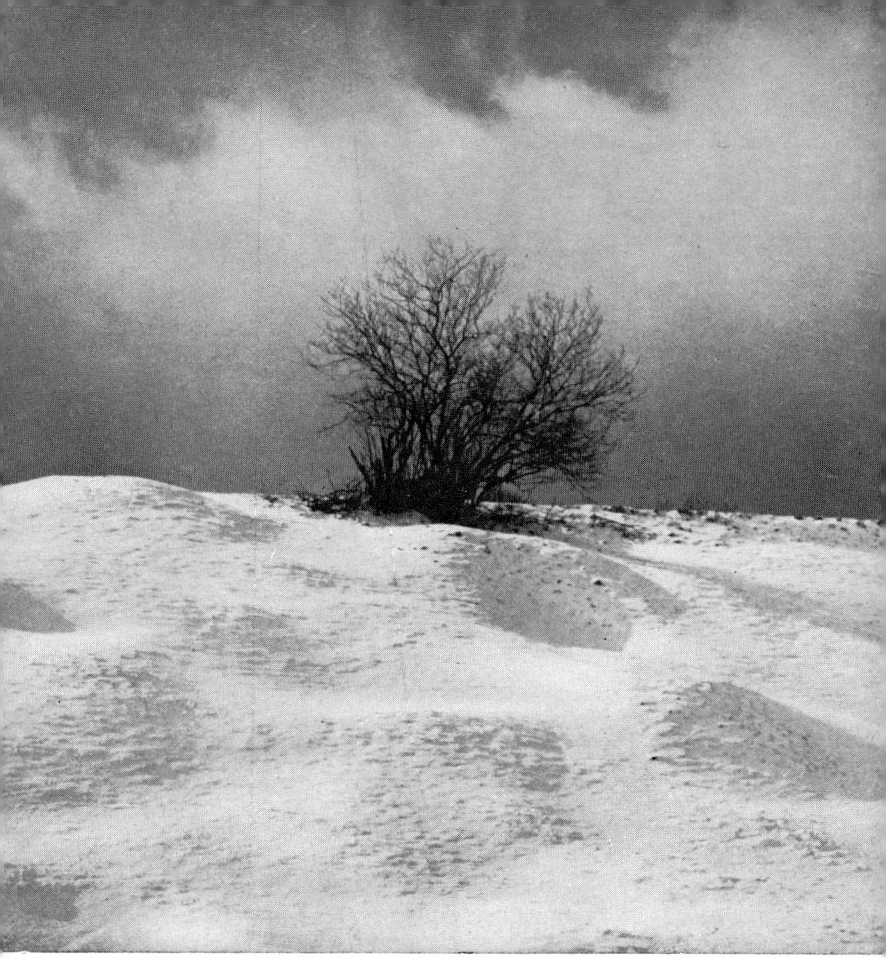

interest should be well lit; cloud shadows on the rest will make the most important subject stand out better. Side-light will bring out modelling. For tone and clouds in the sky you need a filter.—Photographs by *L. and M. Gayton* (page 156), *John Erith* (page 157), *H. van Wadenoyen* (page 158), *H. Gorny* (page 159).

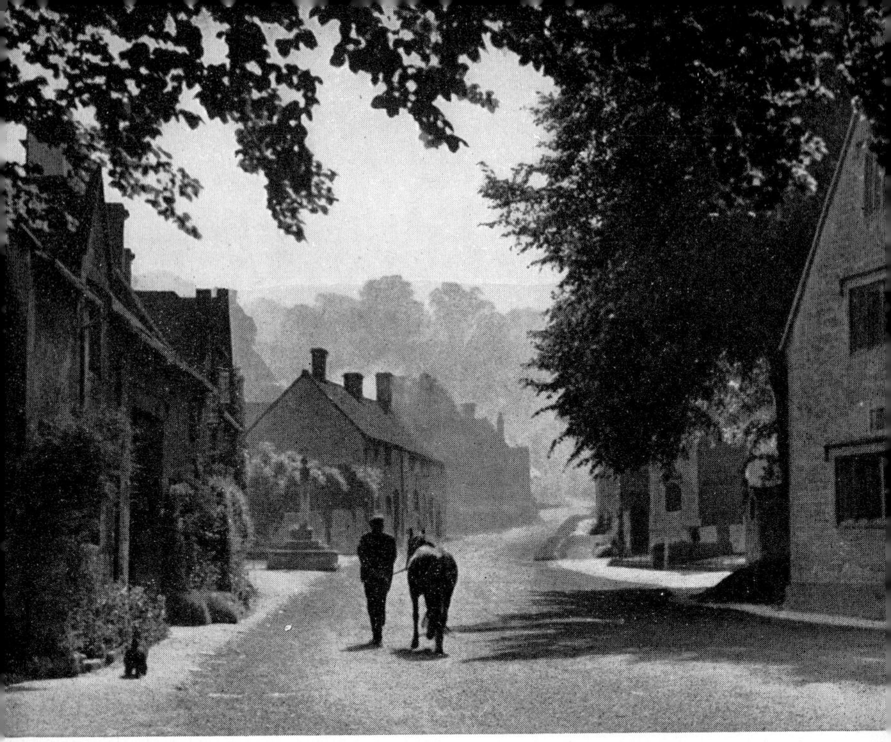

STREET SCENES need careful preparation and quick action at the right moment to produce good living pictures. Focus, stop and shutter must be pre-set and you should carry a lenshood on the lens to be able to turn in any direction without fear of unwanted light on the lens. Have

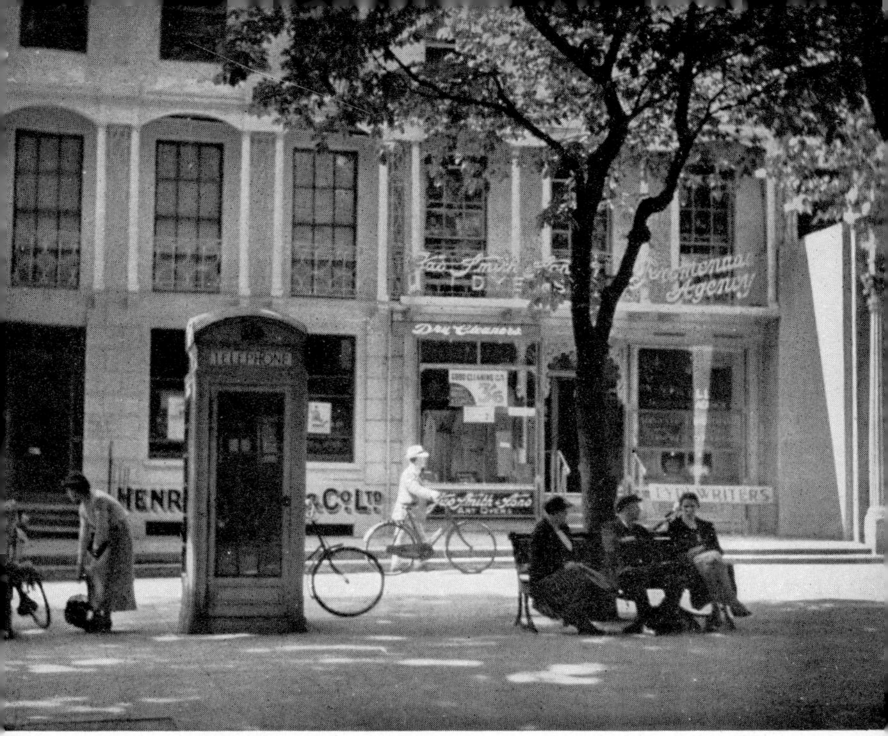

the picture ready assembled in your eye before pointing the camera; if you search for it through the finder—you will have attracted attention and lost an opportunity.—Photographs by *B. Alfieri* (page 160), and *Hugo van Wadenoyen* (page 161).

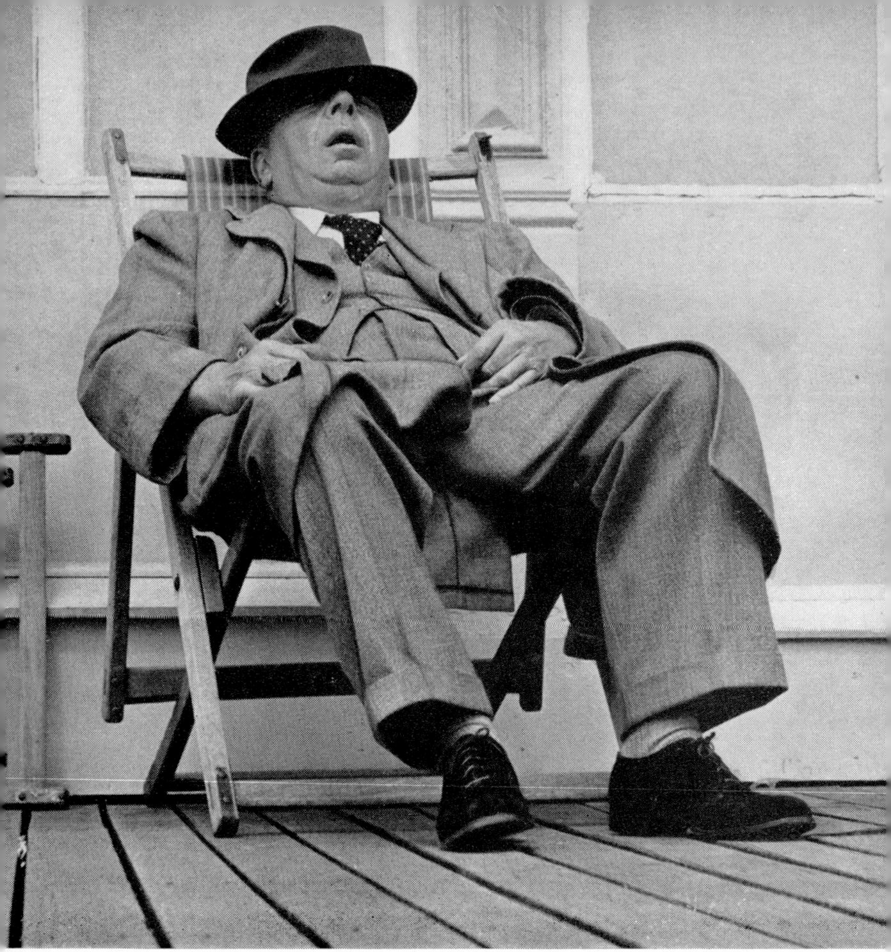

HOLIDAY SNAPSHOTS will catch more of the holiday spirit in human faces and posture than in all the backdrop of mountains, lakes and cathedrals. Plenty of people have tried to get their whole holiday party plus Buckingham Palace on one negative but nobody ever made a decent

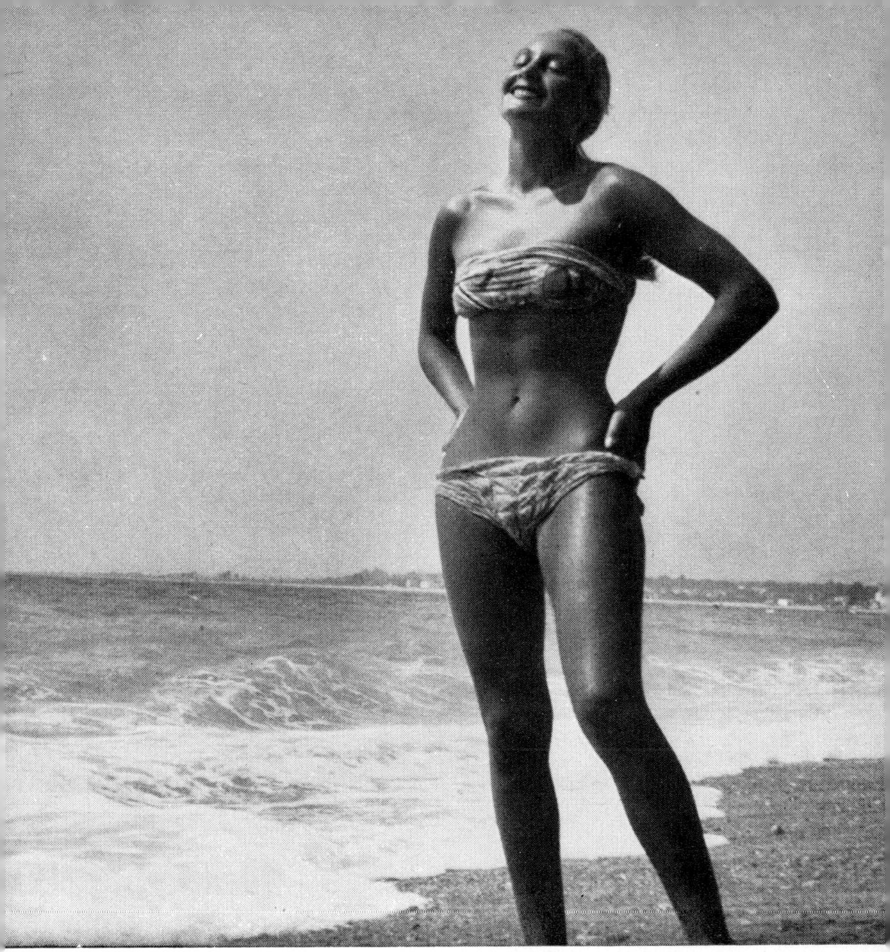

picture that way. Do one thing at a time. If it is to be a snapshot of your friends you had better have only just a fringe of the scene around them. Get as close as you can with the least possible fuss and take them unawares. —Photographs by *Clifford Robinson* (page 162) and *E. Morton* (page 163).

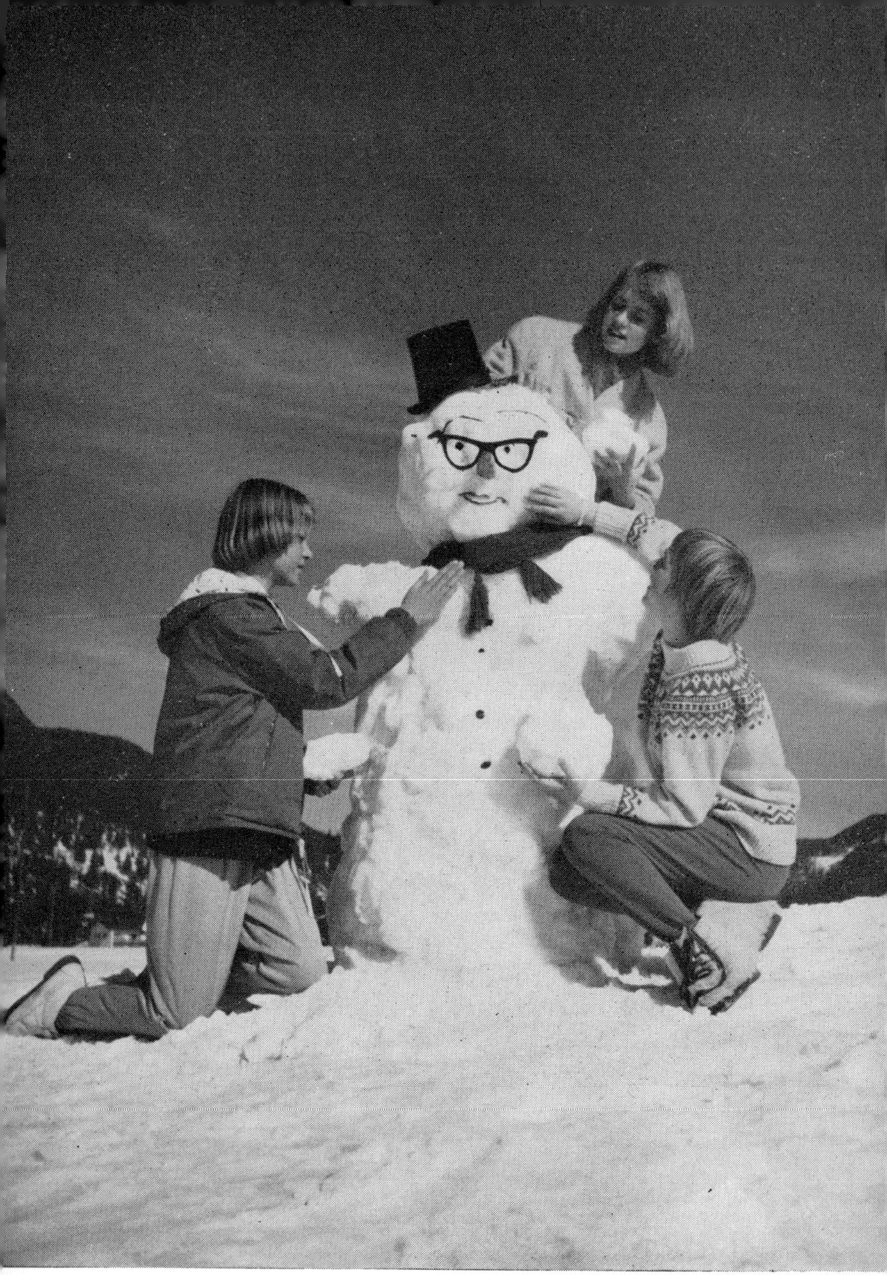

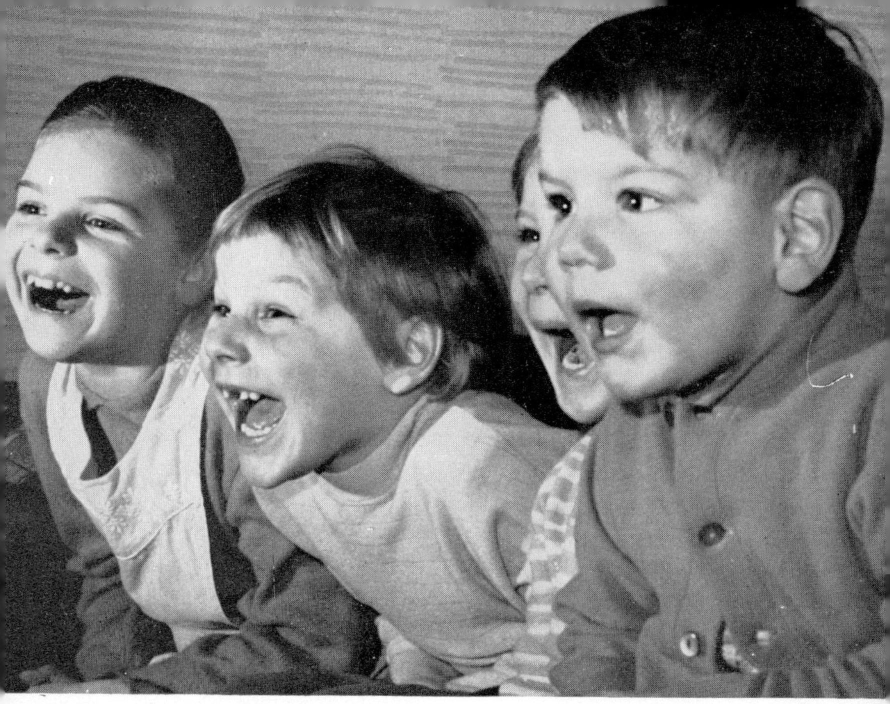

GROUPS are always somewhat of a problem. If you take them as you find them figures and faces are likely to cut across each other, but that is preferable to a stylised arrangement giving an orderly assembly of lifeless dummies. More than anything you need time for the job. Wait until the people sort themselves out and relax. Just to ease the tension make a "fake" exposure or two and try the final picture when they have almost forgotten about it all. Should light conditions compel you to ask them to "hold it" do so only if the positions can be held without an effort.—Phot. by *Ullman* (page 164) and *Gerhard Jacob* (page 165).

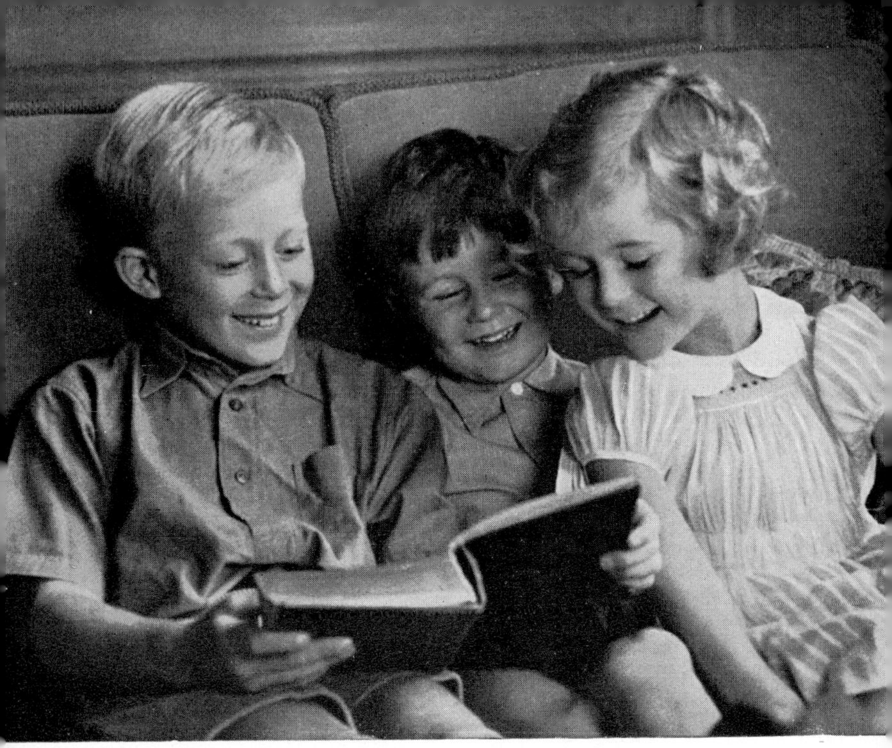

CHILDREN are easy to photograph. Should you and your camera be strangers to them first get acquainted. Give them something to play with: a book, paper and pencil, some toy. You want an assistant who is good at tricks or telling stories if big eyes and startled expressions make the sort of pictures you are after. Keep the camera at the children's own level to avoid giant heads on dwarfed bodies. Stop and focus are better pre-set if you do not want to miss the best shots especially if you want to capture children in action. Indoors, fast lenses are preferable to fumbling with lamps or scaring the kids with flash. Such large apertures give little depth of focus—but a sharp background is hardly ever needed.—Photographs by *H. van Wadenoyen* (above and opposite), *A. Tritschler* (page 168) and *F. W. Lang* (page 169).

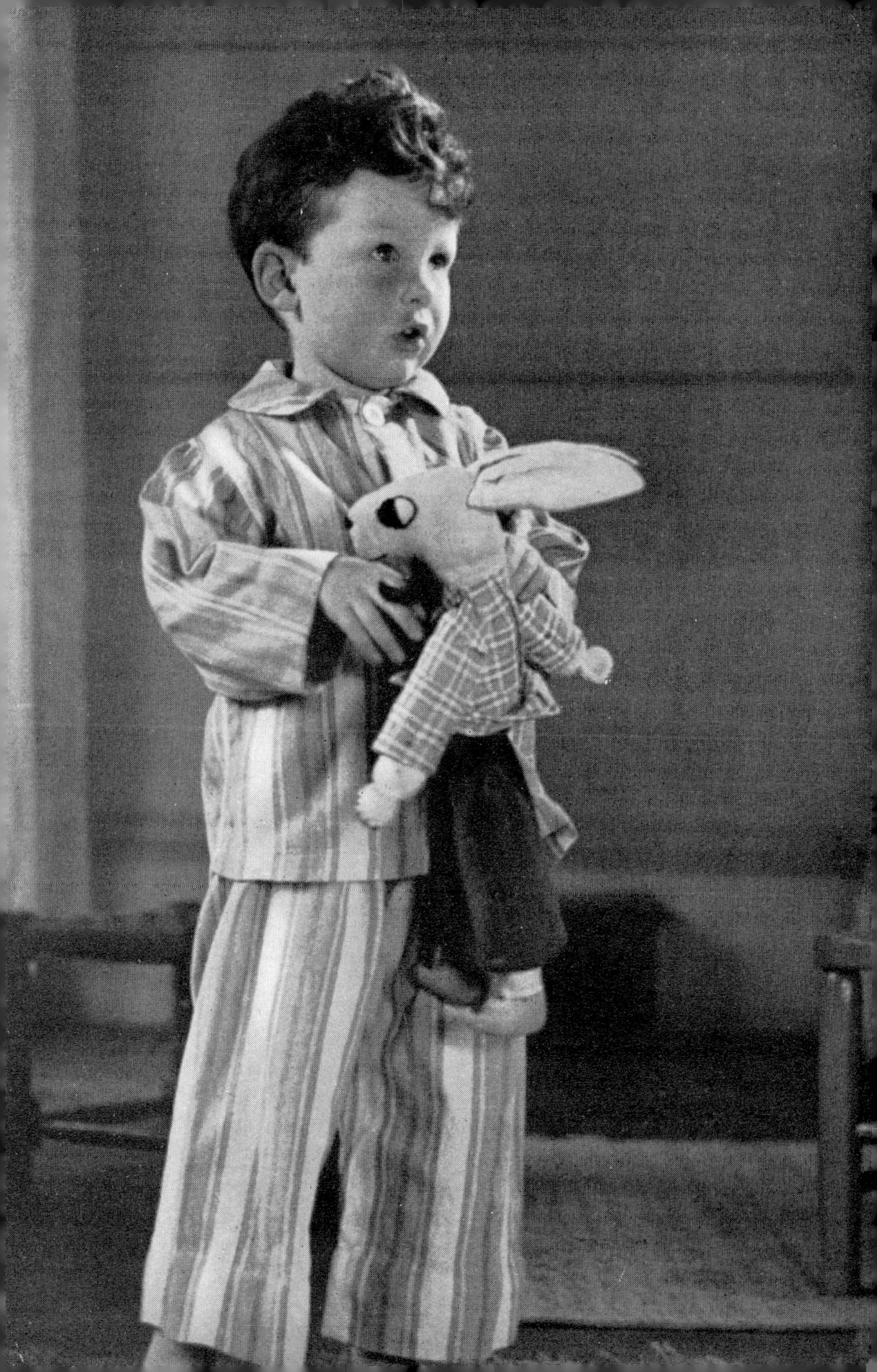

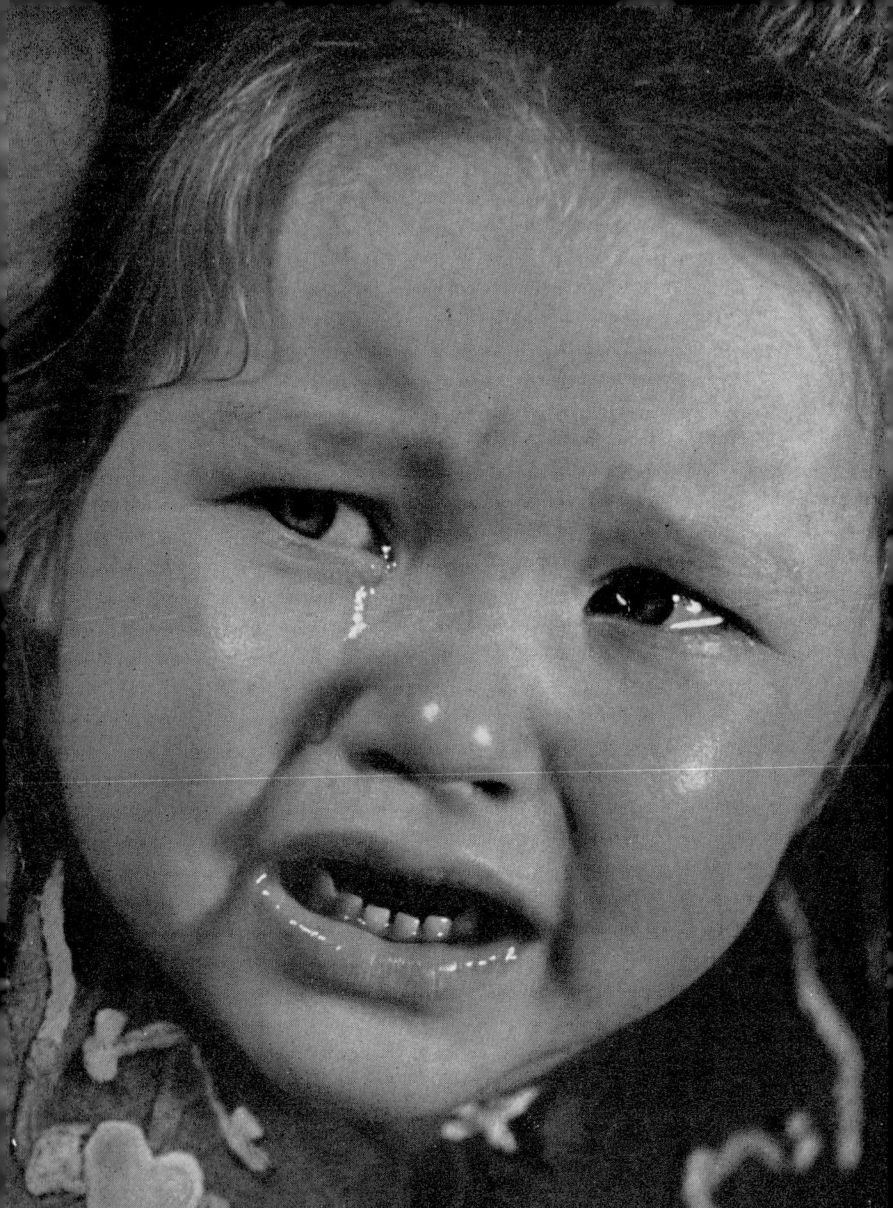

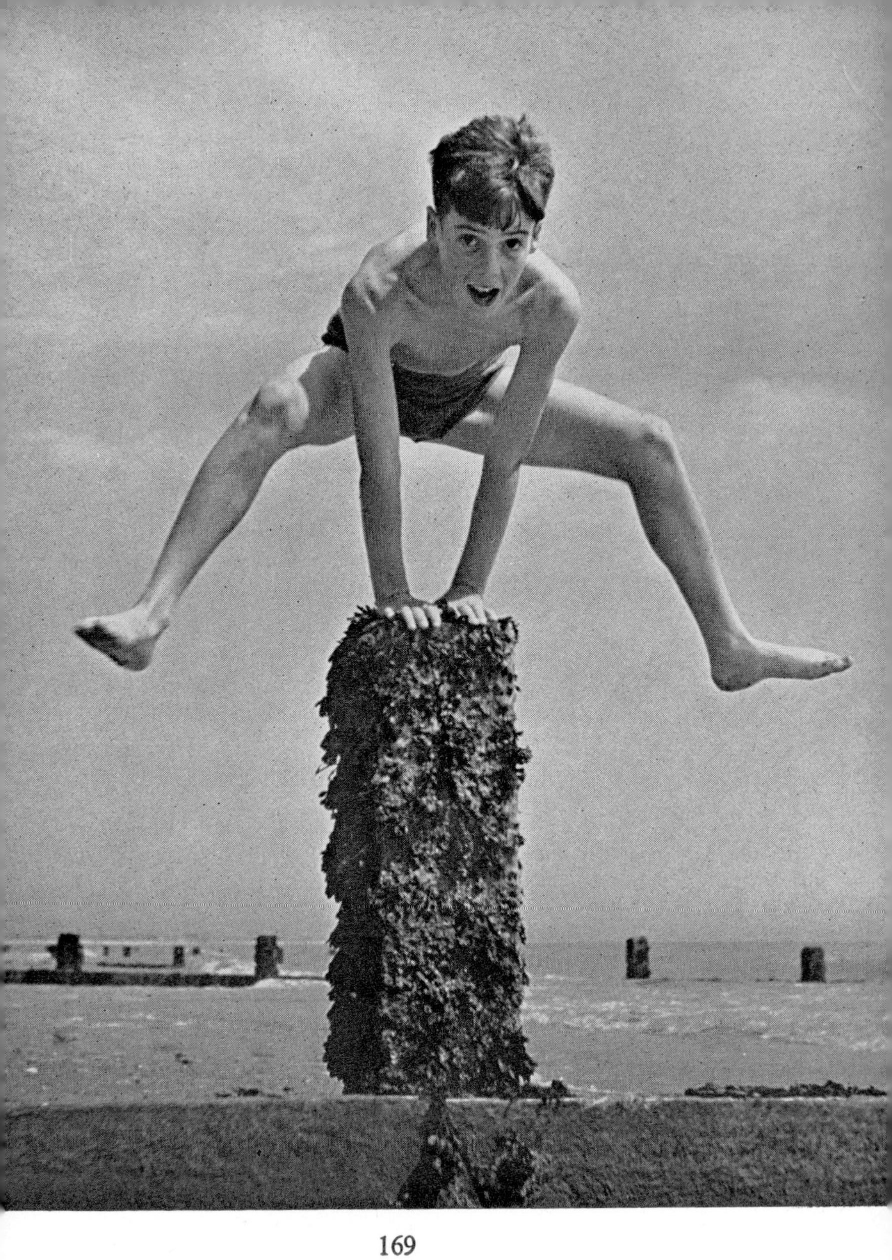

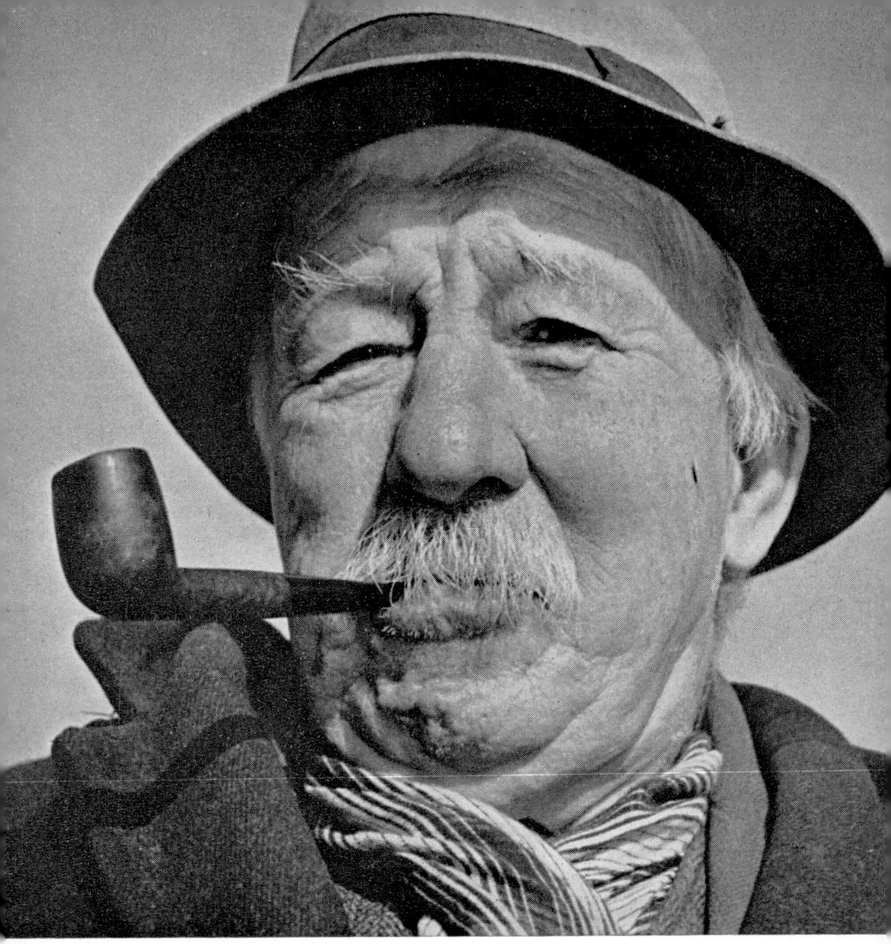

CLOSE-UP PORTRAITS are not quite as simple to take as they look. With the cheaper type of camera and its average lens it is better to keep some distance away from the model and get an enlargement from a portion of the negative. At close range you almost inevitably picture over-life-size noses and hands. Genuine close-up portraits are better

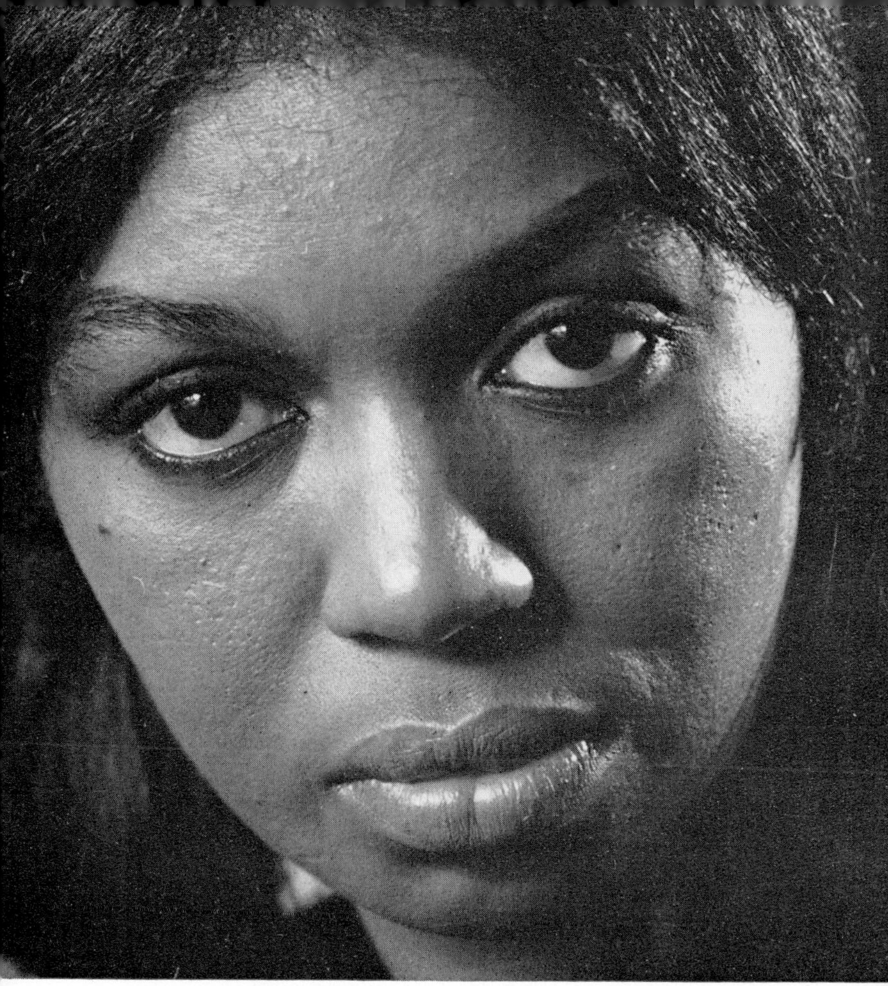

made with portrait lenses of longish focal length. The plainer the background the better. If you cannot have it plain, leave it out of focus. For "character" use side-light, for "smoothness" the light should be more from the front.—Photographs by *Douglas Glass* (page 170), *H. Kröbl* (page 171).

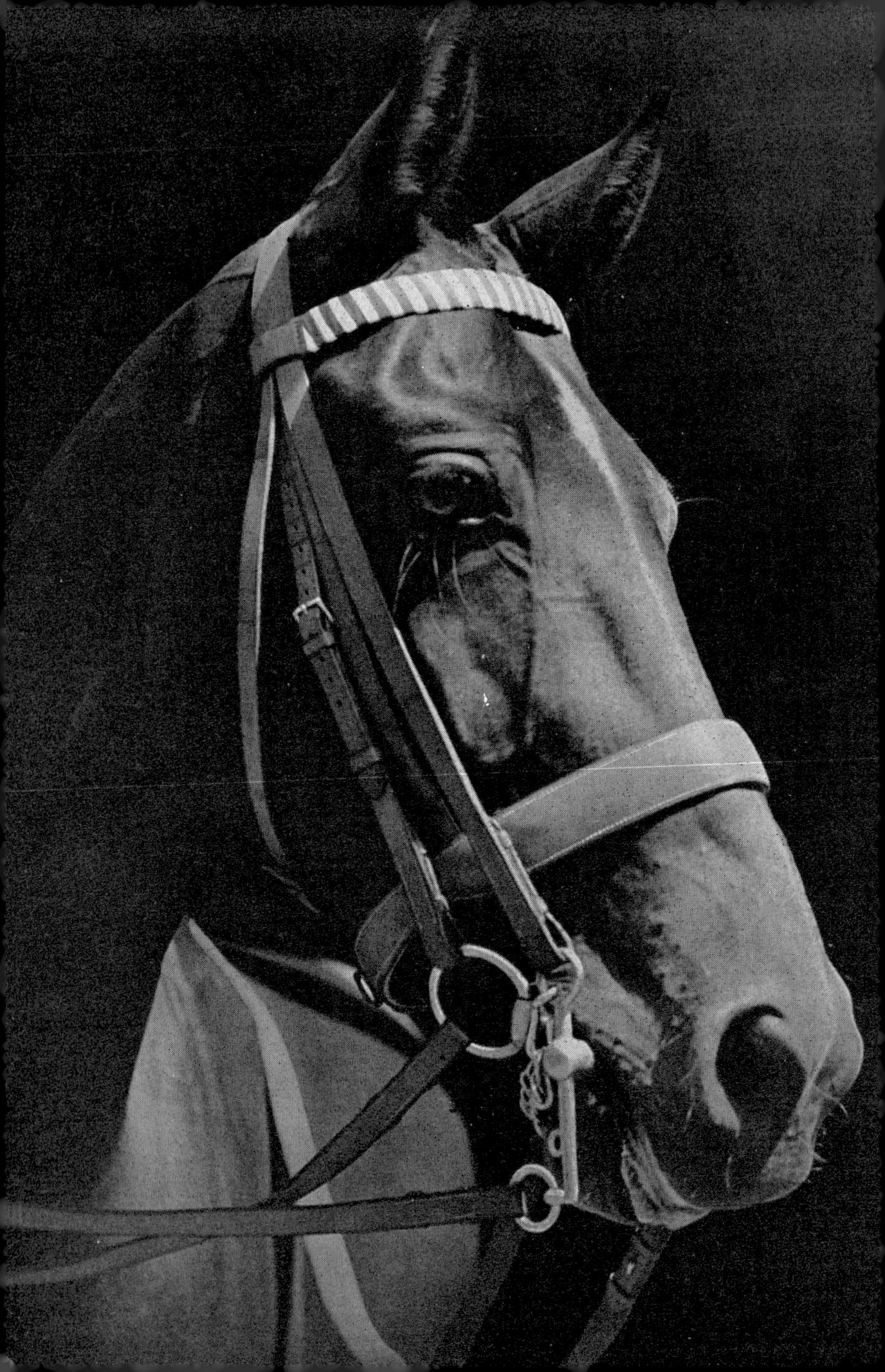

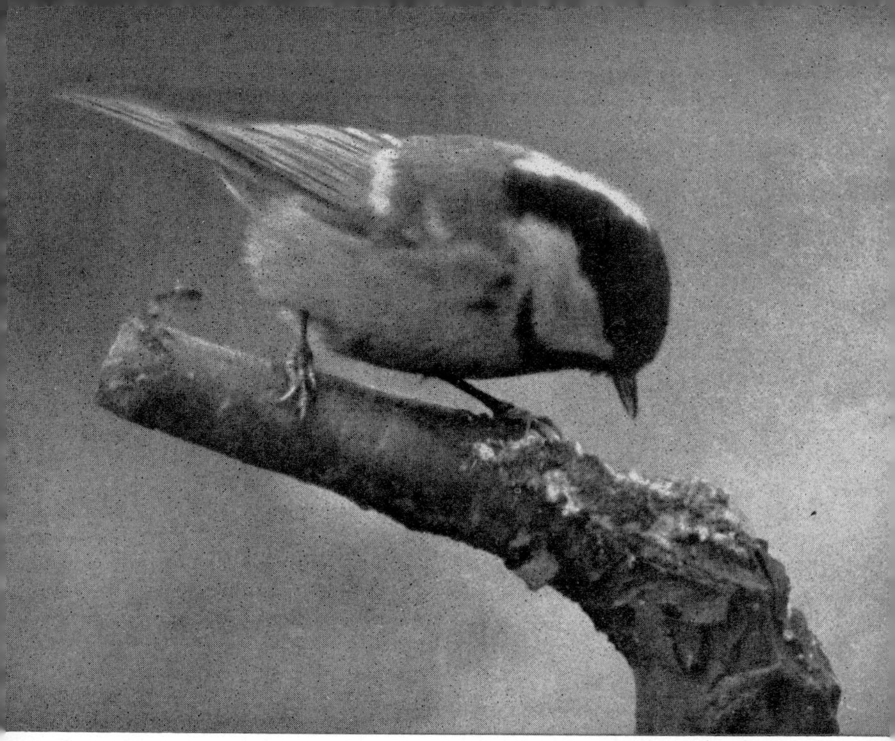

ANIMALS require patient approach. You cannot stage Nature; if you do, it will cease to be natural. Nobody can hope to become a successful animal photographer without some knowledge of animal habits and haunts. Search for the best point of view; if possible for one that ensures plain background and side-light to draw modelling. Sort out

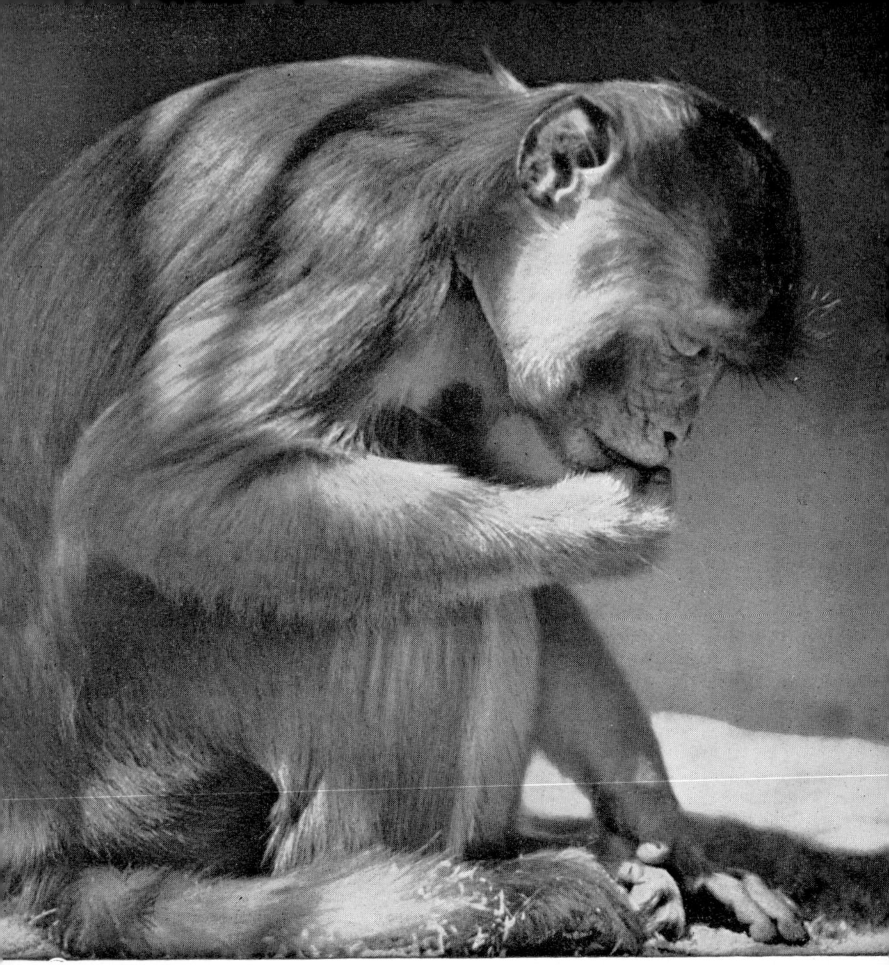

your technique (focus, stop and shutter speed) well in advance. Unless you take domestic animals or work in a Zoo (where you must get right up to the nets and bars to avoid showing them) lenses of longish focal length are needed to get large pictures at some distance. Wherever

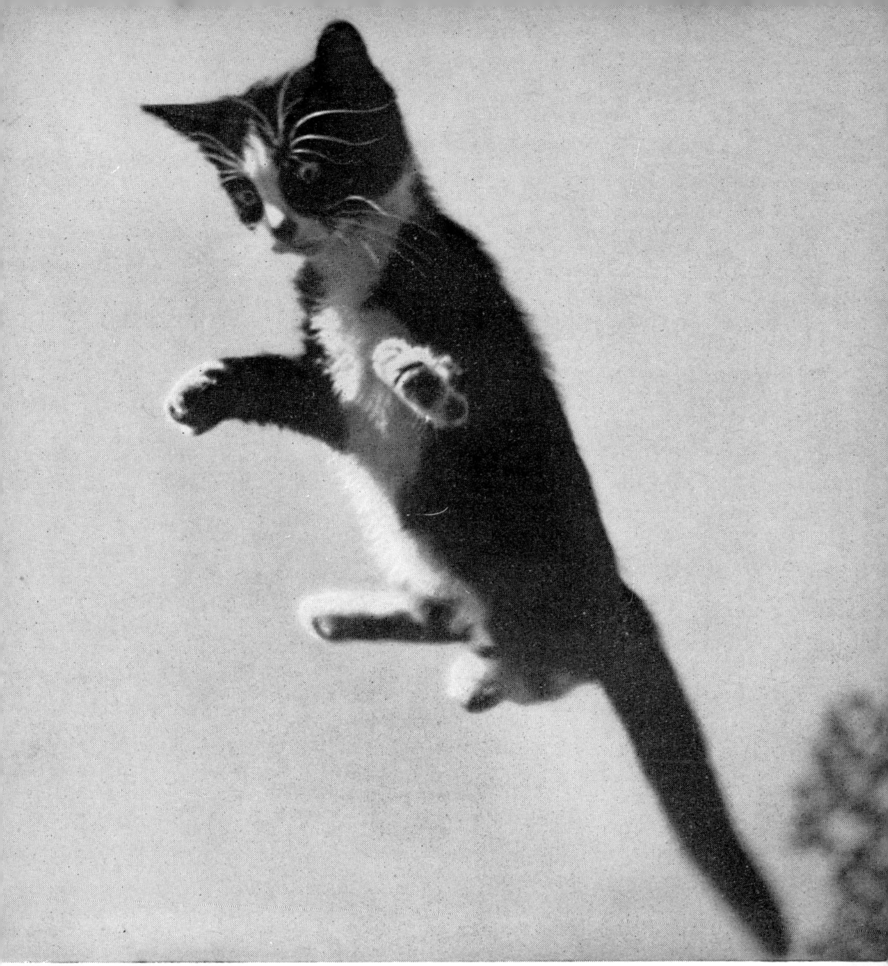

you stand, keep quiet and wait for your chance. Motion is least blurred when photographed coming towards the camera. Photographs by *H. Gorny* (page 172), *Oliver G. Pike* (page 173), *H. Gorny* (page 174), *Ylla* (page 175) and *Unknown Photographer* (page 176).

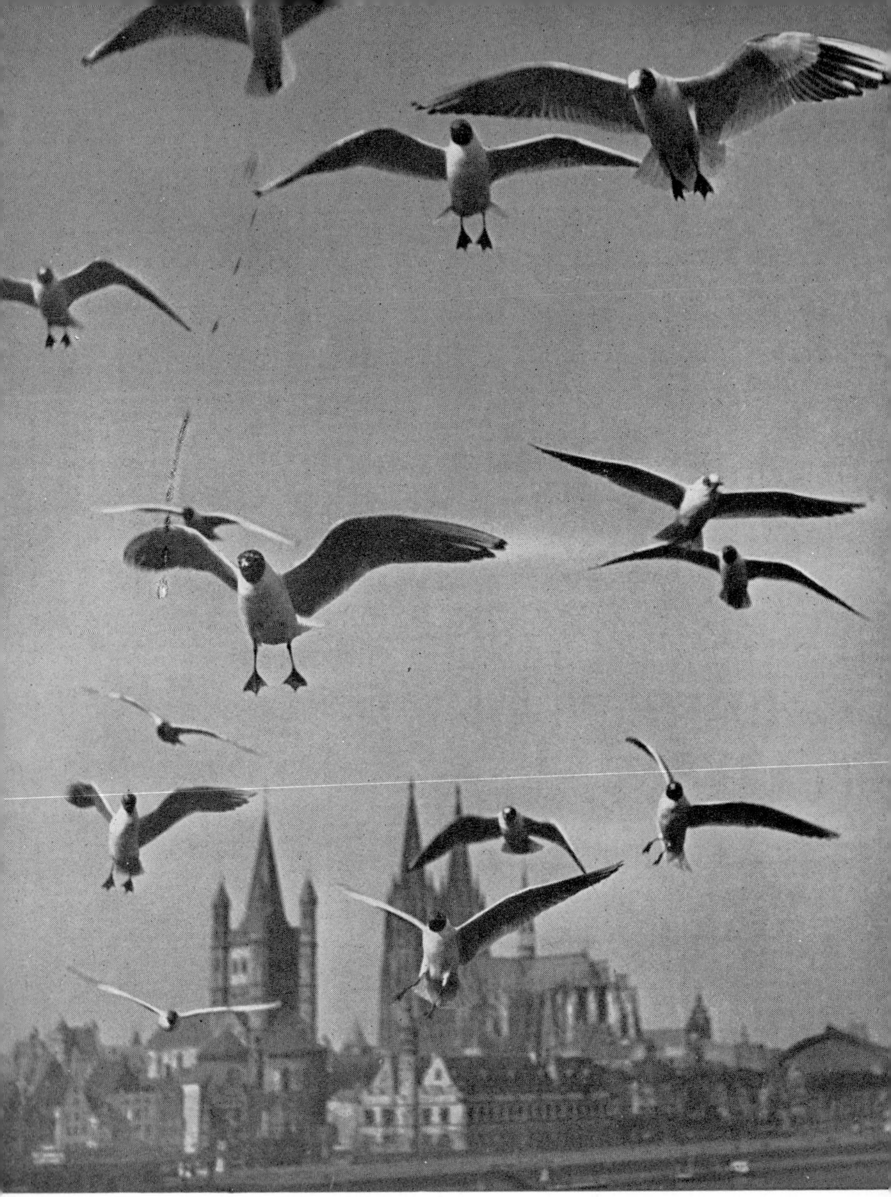

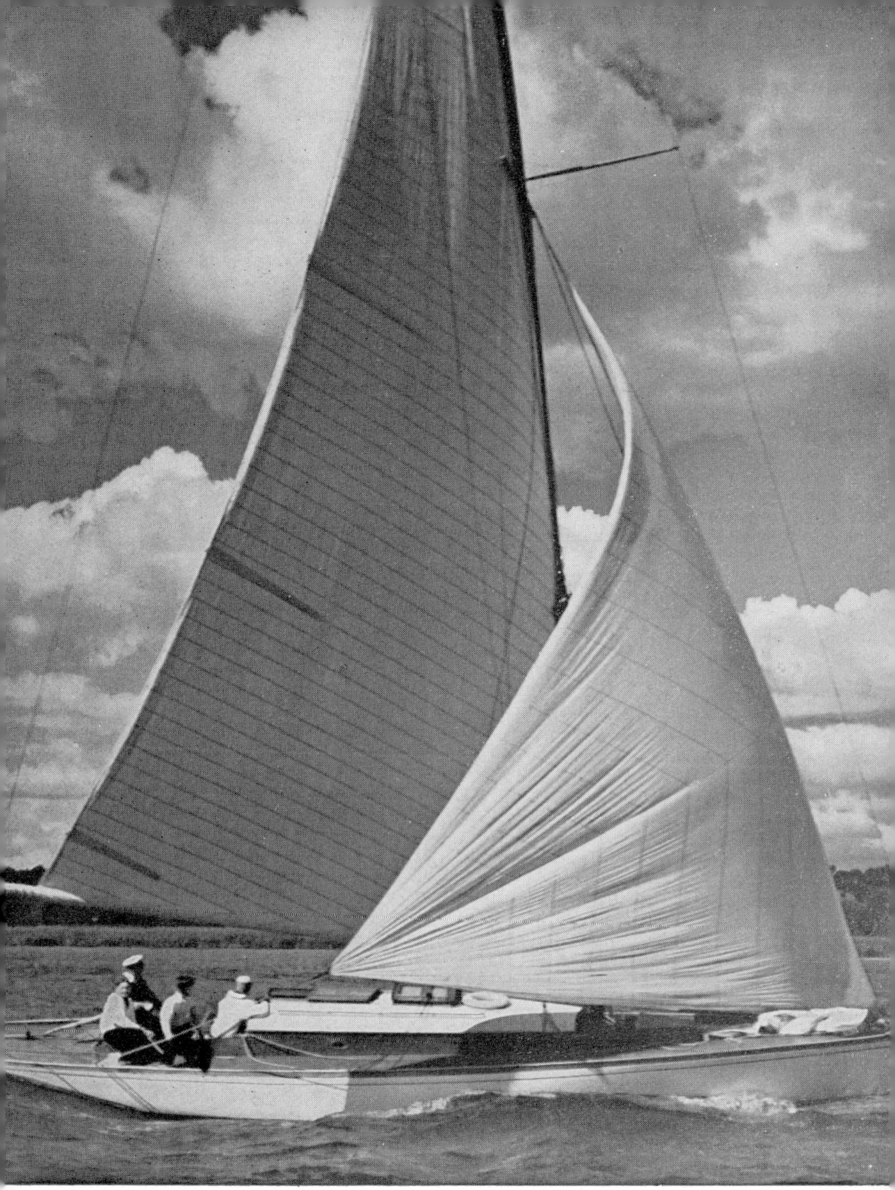

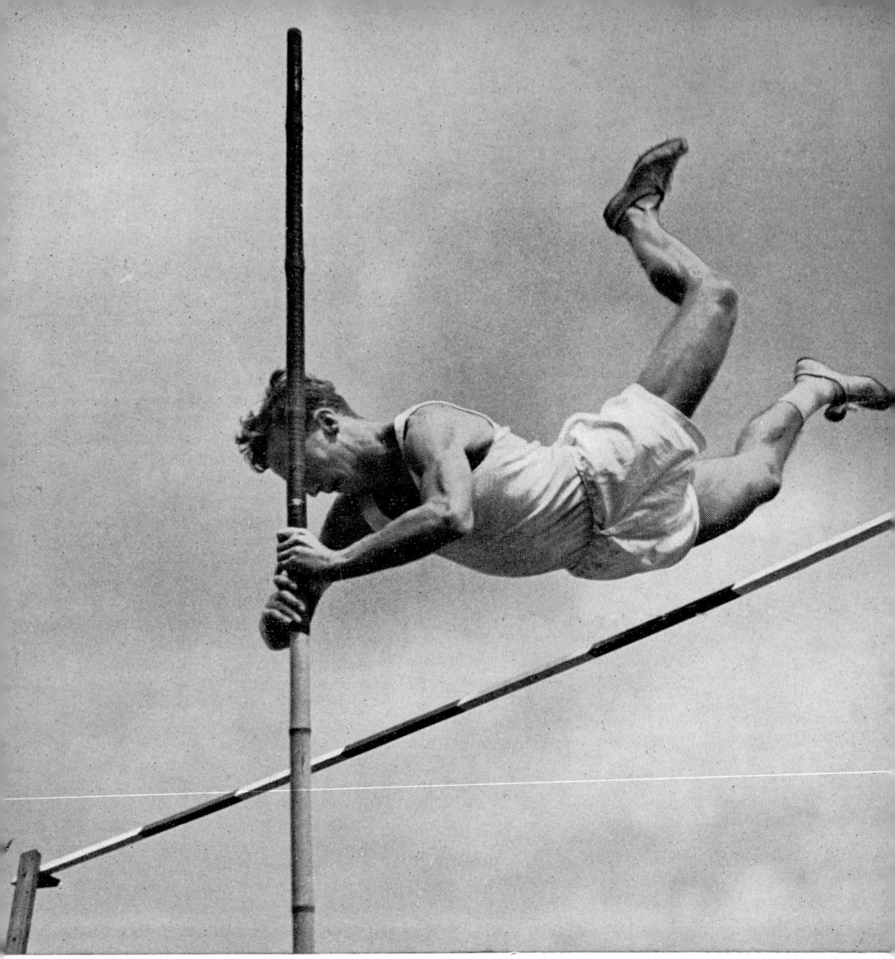

SPORTS photography cannot succeed without some experience of the kind of sport photographed. You must know what to expect, where to expect it and when. Pre-focus at the critical distance and stop the lens down to ensure a safety zone of sharp definition. Pre-set the shutter so as to freeze the speed at the rate expected. If either your equipment or

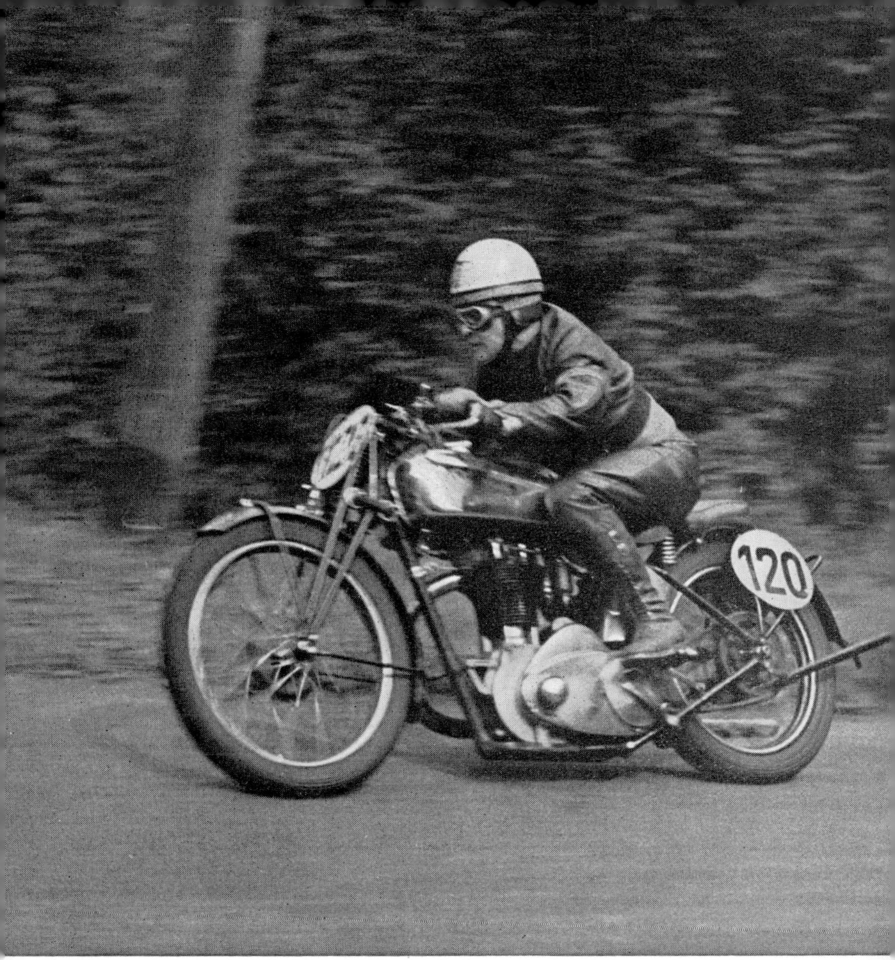

light conditions confine you to slower exposure times than the rate of speed would demand, take an oblique viewing angle to the direction of the moving subject or wait for the movement to slow down for changing its direction or swing the camera in step with the moving subject while you expose.—Photographs by *Unknown Photographers*.

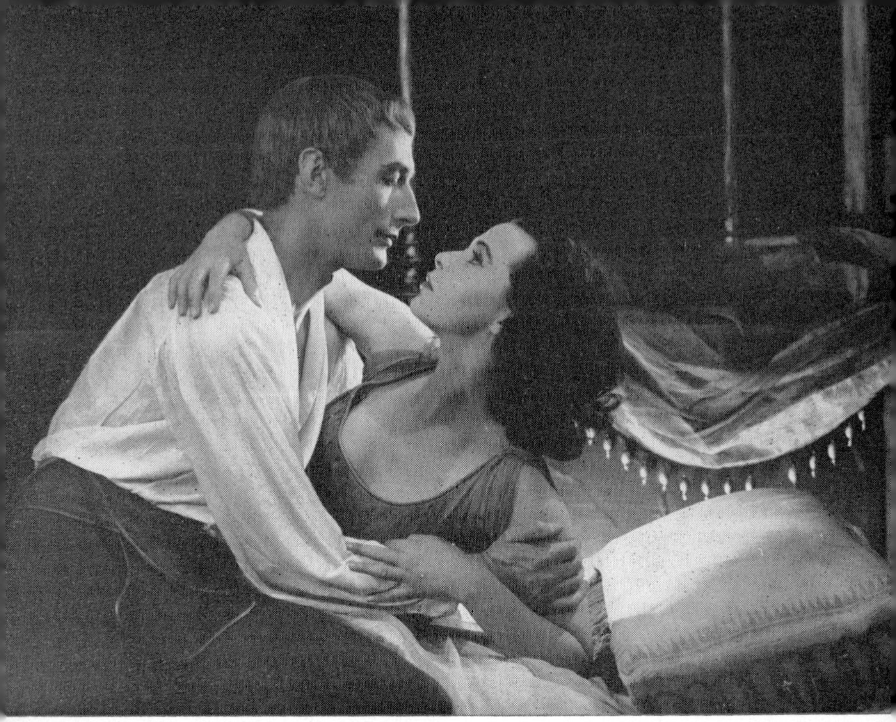

THEATRE and show photography demands good seats, fast lenses, and that you too have seen the show before. Theatrical lighting is difficult to judge and often calculated to be uneven, and so you are not likely to hit the correct exposure without trying to do it in more than one way. As every bit of the speed of the lens will be needed you cannot stop down much and so will have to pre-focus carefully.—Photographs by *Angus McBean* (page 180) and *Oreste Bianolli* (page 181).

FLOWERS must be carefully illuminated to retain some of their colourful charm in black-and-white photographs. Both outdoors and indoors reflecting screens are needed to throw light wherever there is too much shadow. Again screens are called for to provide even backgrounds and to protect the plant from the wind when working in the open. (All the screens can simply be made from pieces of flexible cardboard fastened to a couple of sticks.)—Photographs by *Van de Poll* (page 182) and *C. W. Teager* (page 183).

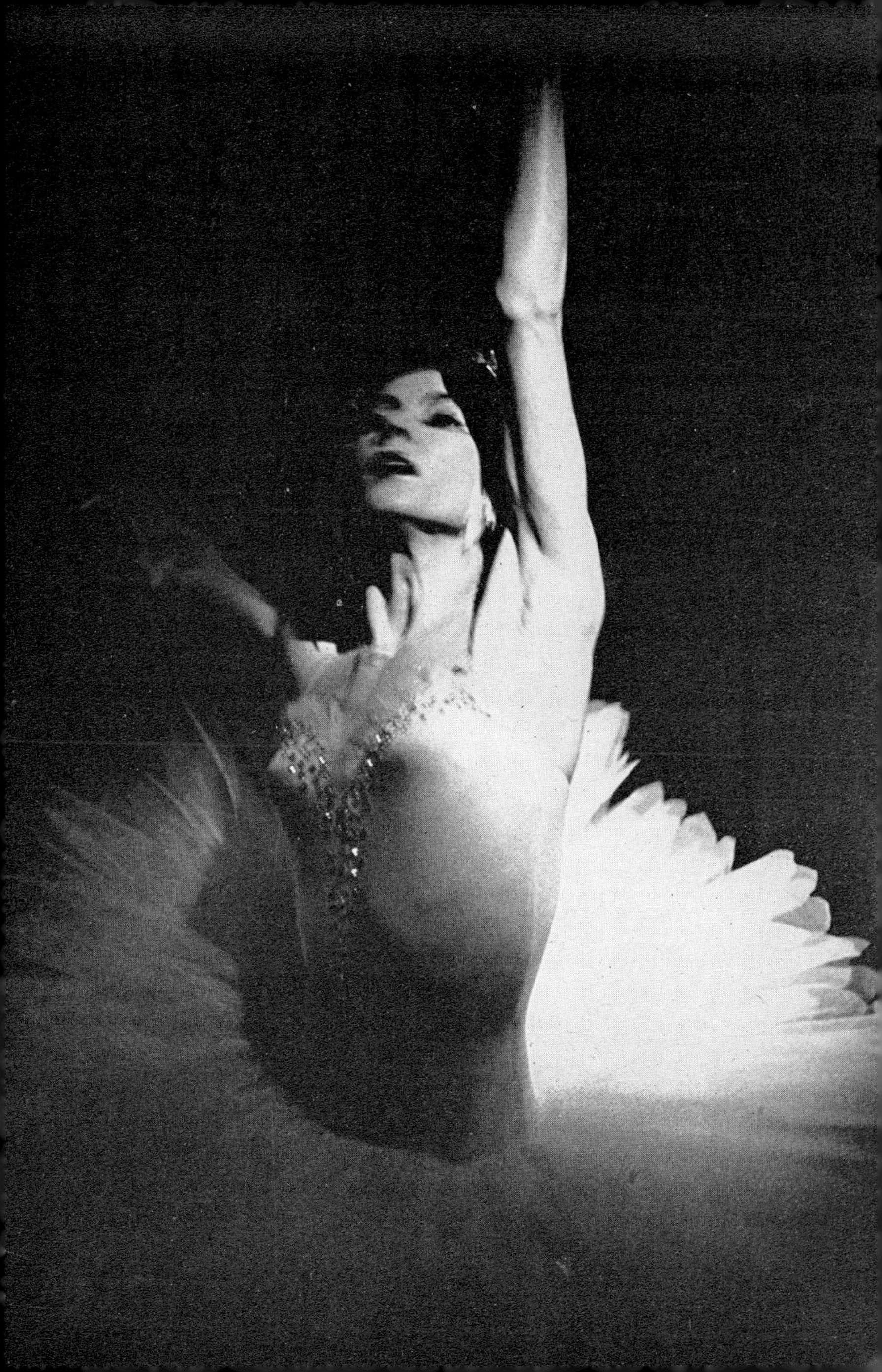

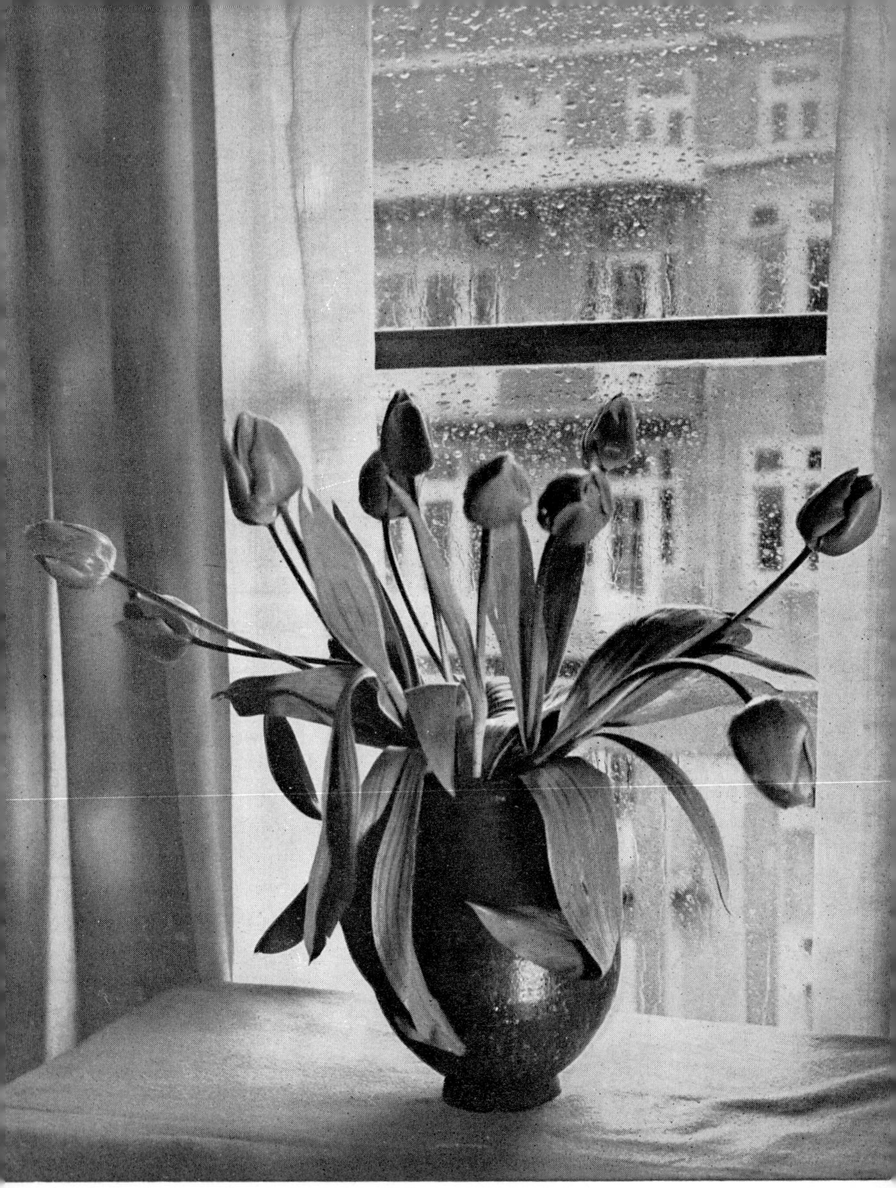

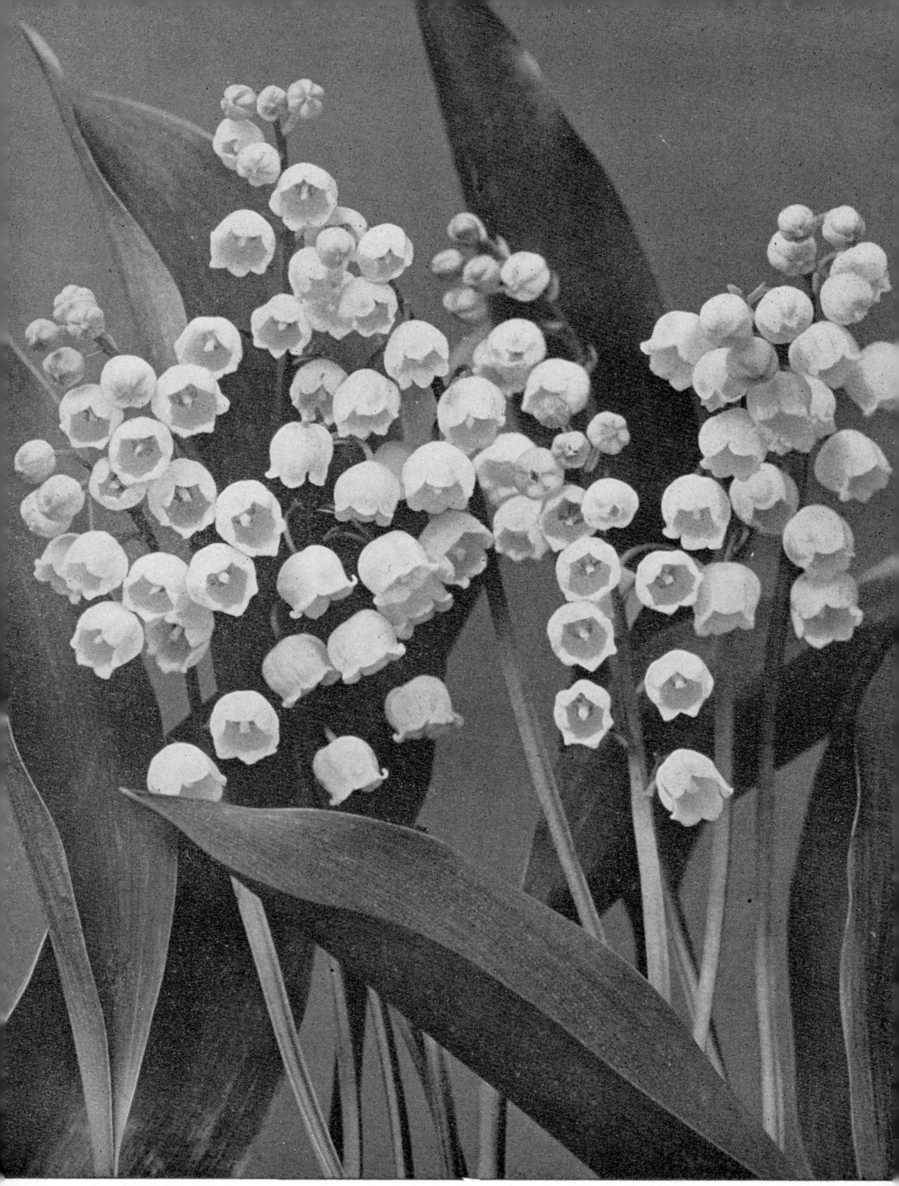

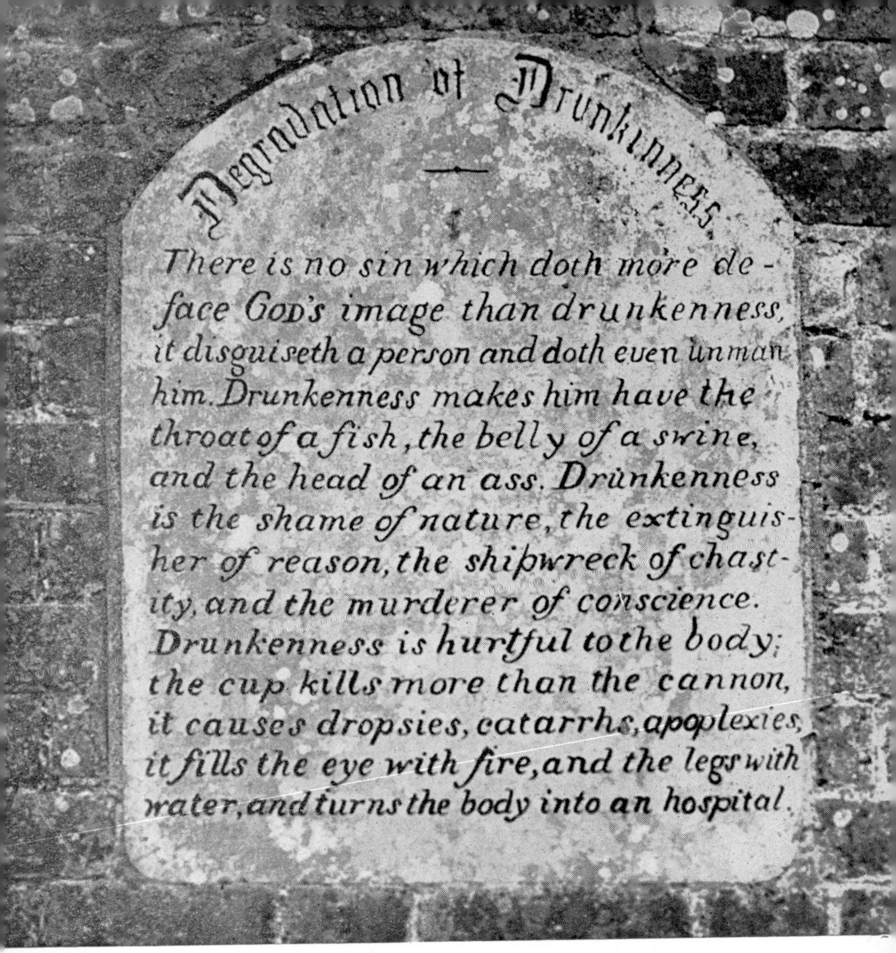

COPYING. Approach as close as possible to fill the finder frame. If necessary use auxiliary close-up lenses. Diffused light is best. The camera should be carefully centred and levelled in line with the subject. Strong filters are often necessary to get not very legible writing in strong contrast to its background.—Photograph by *H. S. Newcombe*, F.R.P.S.

possibly with some loss of atmospheric perspective. To differentiate between the various shades of green in a landscape, a green filter is preferable to a yellow one. A red filter will give an even more striking effect of dark sky with brilliantly lit clouds; green will be darkened and sunlight strongly emphasized. Front lighting, which is bound to give a flat, lifeless impression, is to be avoided for black-and-white but is preferable for colour. The interplay of light and shade resulting from side-lighting will give the picture body and life. Back-lighting, that is, with the camera directed against the light, may produce striking effects, emphasizing outlines and suppressing details, but it requires the use of the lens-hood to prevent direct sunlight from falling on the lens and the exposure time will have to be generous.

MOONLIGHT.—Pictures by moonlight may be taken just as in daylight, but as the available light is weak the exposure time has to be considerably lengthened. In fact, to get well-exposed moonlight pictures one must give one hundred thousand times the exposure one would give to the same picture in direct sunlight. This means that a landscape in bright moonlight without deep foreground would probably have to be exposed for 10 minutes at *f* 5.6 to get the real moonlight effect. Avoid including the moon itself in the picture, as its movement would be reproduced in the shape of distortion. ***Faked moonlight pictures*** can be taken in sunlight by giving a very short exposure time; the negative will then have to be printed so dark that only the highlights appear while the rest will be black. To get convincing effects the hour of sunset should be chosen and a sky with clouds; the sun itself may be included in the picture to appear as "moon". Moonlight pictures on colour film, whether genuine or faked show very little colour, unless fully exposed. Then, in theory at least, the colours should look reasonably natural but the moonlight effect is lost.

Good books on such tricks are "All the Photo Tricks", by Edwin Smith and "Effects and Experiments in Photography", by Paul Petzold.

MOUNTAINS.—With the normal lens, impressive distant peaks will appear miserably small; taking the same subject with a tele-lens magnifying two to three times, foreground and background will stand out in something like their true proportions. On the other hand, when moving among or upon the mountains, the comparatively wide angle of the normal lens will come in useful to produce a survey, particularly when care is taken to include sufficient foreground to create the impression of depth, it is always possible subsequently to enlarge part of the negative only in order to get a more concentrated effect. A yellow filter can be used with black-and-white film or a haze filter with colour at heights up to about 6,000 feet, 2000 m. Above this level the ultra-violet filter is used to eliminate the ultra-violet rays, which otherwise would "clog-up" the distance and make it appear very hazy and over-blue. Medium and dark filters should not be used at these heights as otherwise the distant prospect becomes too hard and the impression of "space" gets lost. In particular, in photographs of glaciers the sky becomes too dark. The values given by your meter remain correct if you use a U.V. filter, for which no allowance is necessary. To eliminate haze and to bring out the background clearly a red filter can be used. This gives an unnatural but often highly pictorial effect. With colour film, a similar darkening of the sky can sometimes be obtained with a polarizing filter. Ordinary coloured filters cannot be used with colour films.

Filter effects are described in "The Photoguide to Filters" by Clyde Reynolds.

NATURE PHOTOGRAPHY.—*To photograph birds* the best place and time is at the nest and early in the morning or before 3 o'clock in the afternoon. To illustrate the technique with an example, we will assume that we are after a song bird whose nest we have found in a bush. First, the camera position for the best lighting has to be determined, taking into account the change of light during the time you are hiding. Tie back branches which would obstruct your view, fix up your tripod with the camera, and then focus, making sure that the nest is in the lower part of the picture. The distance of the camera from the nest is determined by the focal length of the lens. If you work with a normal focal length lens you may have to go as close as 5 feet. It is, of course, better to work with a long-focus lens which will enable you to keep farther away from the nest and still get a close-up view. Now both camera and you yourself will have to disappear from the bird's keen eyes behind an efficient and camouflaged screen. Finally, you will have to show your patience by waiting to get your photographs until the bird arrives. Some birds, such as buzzards, kites, crows, may be attracted by bait. Good sites are small pools in woods where birds bathe, and the sea shore and mud flats at low tide. Most of the successful work is done from hides, which have to vary according to the surroundings. When no hide can be used, a remote control release or a piece of string attached to the shutter release, may prove helpful. *To get birds in flight* is largely a matter of luck and persistence. The larger birds with slow wing beat are easier to get than small ones. As the movement even then is relatively fast and the working distance mostly a short one, the shortest possible exposure time should be employed. 1/300 to 1/500 second will suffice if one is not too close and the camera is directed along the line of flight. A good hunting ground is the sea shore where sea birds can be attracted by bait. Fastest negative material and bright weather are required for good results. The eye-level frame finders or sport finders are the only ones with which one can successfully keep track of the motion. *Mammals*, such as otter, badger, fox, polecat, stoat, weasel, squirrel, mouse, water vole, hare, rabbit, deer, etc. have a strong sense of smell and are shy. Their habits should be studied to find out the best position for the camera. As many mammals rest during the day, the early morning and evening hours are the most likely times to catch them. All photography should be done up-wind. If bait is used, any kind of flesh will attract the fox, honey the badger and fresh fish the otter. The use of tele-photo lenses is a great help in getting a sufficiently close view, as the working distance will not often be less than 15 feet. The exposure time for mammals in normal movement (if not chased) varies between 1/60 to 1/500 second at a distance of 15 feet with movement across the lens. Fast films are, therefore, essential, particularly as most exposures will have to be taken in the early or late hours of the day.

A good book on this subject is, "The Technique of Bird Photography" by John Warham.

NIGHT PHOTOGRAPHY.—The average camera must be mounted on a tripod, a small aperture (*f*16) used. In such conditions a medium speed 125 ASA film will require an exposure time of 3 to 7 minutes according to the illumination available. The small aperture with its relatively long exposure time will not record an occasional passer-by at all. Should, however, the strong light of a car or bus approach the field of view, the lens must be covered until it has passed. The total exposure time may thus be made up of a number of partial exposures. The use of a lens hood is essential to ward off stray light from the lens. Floodlit buildings, lighted shop windows, illuminated advertisements, brilliantly lit shopping centres, can be taken with relatively short exposure times of about 1/2 second on the fastest film, even with modest lens apertures of *f*4.5 and *f*5.6. The man with the fast lens *f*2 to *f*2.8 will be able, without the use of a tripod, to get action shots at night of people looking in windows, of slow traffic in main streets and similar subjects with fastest pan film and exposure times of 1/8 to 1/60 second.

A general book with much information on this subject is "Photography with the Eye-level Reflex", by H. S. Newcombe.

PANORAMAS.—A panorama view can be obtained by taking a number of photographs which slightly overlap each other. These photographs are joined together to form one picture after the overlap has been cut off. The camera should be used on a tripod with a panoramic head. The panoramic head allows the camera to be turned smoothly, a degree-scale indicating the angle through which the camera has been turned. Normal cameras require, when used horizontally, about 10 pictures for a full 360° Panorama, or in a vertical position about 13 pictures. It is essential that the camera should stand strictly level otherwise the horizon line cannot be linked up.

"The Rollei Way", by L. A. Mannheim, has a chapter on this subject.

PORTRAITS.—First and foremost, get away from the fear of approaching close to your subject. The photograph which is half landscape with a figure placed half-heartedly somewhere in it is not a portrait. With the average camera, about 4 feet is the most useful portrait distance which will avoid distortion and still produce a large portrait. If your camera allows for a change of lenses and you can use a long-focus lens with twice this working distance, it is even better. Next, keep in mind that most viewfinders, even those of reflex cameras, show a little more than you will get on your film, therefore keep every portion which must be included away from the very margin of the finder. The background deserves special consideration. The less prominent it is the better; it should be kept strictly neutral, a self-coloured wall or a sky being excellent. The most important point in producing the "lifelike" portrait is the approach to the subject. You will not get a good portrait by asking for a smile, you will only make the sitter self-conscious and that is the one thing to avoid. Prevent your model from thinking about being photographed by giving him something to do—let him read, smoke, play or work—and then watch for your opportunity to snap. *Outdoors:* the perfect light for outdoor portraits is hazy sunlight, strong enough to give good modelling to the face and soft enough to avoid hard shadows. Failing this, the shadow of a building, etc., will give good results but, in colour be careful of reflected colour from the wall. In strong midday sun it is just as well to give your camera a rest. Morning and late afternoon sunlight will be helpful, particularly when the sun shines from the side, and slightly in front of your subject. The possibilities of a reflector in the form of a large sheet of white cardboard to lighten deeper shadows, are worth keeping in mind. Wide apertures should be employed to get *little* depth of field, to render the background less prominent. *Indoors:* with fast films it is possible to take pictures indoors with any normal camera as long as one works in reasonably good light and not far from the window. While practically all that was said about outdoor portraits is also applicable to indoor conditions, one should take into account the fact that if the light is coming from one window only it will cast heavy shadows. These heavy shadows have to be lightened to produce a reasonably balanced negative. This can best be effected by a reflector consisting of a large sheet of white paper, or any other white material, for example, a bed-sheet, a pillow case and so on. There are two ways in which, even with a slow lens, you can keep the exposure time reasonably short. The sitter may either be placed to one side of the window, with a reflector to lighten the shadows, while the camera is pointed towards him from the other side of the window, or he may sit facing the window, in which case no reflector is needed. The camera may then be placed either in front or to one side of the window. If two windows are available in one wall, the sitter should be placed between them so that both front and back lighting is given; a reflector should be used to lighten the shadow side and the camera can be used either parallel with the windows or pointing slightly away from them into the room. If the windows are at an angle to each other the sitter should be placed in the corner between them and looking into the room. The reflector is placed facing the corner, while the camera can be put between a window and a reflector. *Artificial Light:* a good background is supplied by a self-coloured wall, a piece of light or dark cloth stretched taut or simply the frame of an open door leading into an unlighted room. The sitter should be about 3 feet away from the background. Even with a slow lens the exposure time will be fairly short, particularly when two lamps are used. With a fast film, 5.6, the lamps about 5 feet from the subject, 1/30 second will suffice. One can straddle a chair, supporting the camera on the chair back and so dispense with a tripod. If one lamp only is available, a reflector must be used to lighten the shadows. The position will be the same as for daylight indoors, the lamp being substituted for the window. When two lamps are employed, one should be used as a main light source while the other one, farther away, should lighten the shadows. Different lamp positions can give different effects. Do not be afraid, therefore, of moving your lights, or the subject or the camera. The film to be used for indoor portraits should be reasonably fast to allow of short exposure times. Where ample light or wide aperture lenses are available, slower films, including colour can be used.

Good books on this subject are "Lighting for Portraiture", by Walter Nurnberg, "Camera Portraiture", by Herbert Williams, "The Photographic Portrait", by O. R. Croy, "Light on People", by Paul Petzold, and "The Photoguide to Portraits" by Günter Spitzing.

REPRODUCTION (COPYING).—With the fixed-lens camera which does not focus at less than about 3 feet we have to employ a close-up lens. (See pages 55.) It is important to know the field that is covered when using the close-up lens, as the viewfinder will no longer be correct at these short distances. While the exact field varies with focal length and negative size, the average for the normal camera is:

focusing to 3 feet without supplementary lens, the field covered is 18 × 24 inches.

focusing to 1.7 feet with supplementary lens plus 1, the field covered is about 9 × 12 inches.

focusing to 1.1 feet with supplementary lens plus 2, the field covered is about 5½ × 8 inches.

The original to be copied is best placed on the floor, the camera fixed on the tripod with a ball and socket head turned downwards and carefully adjusted so that the negative-plane is parallel with the original. The correct distance between camera, with supplementary lens, and original is set by suitably extending and straddling the tripod legs. To prevent the tripod and camera from toppling over a heavy weight may be suspended by a string from the tripod head. It is important to have an even illumination of the original without light being directly reflected into the camera lens. In daylight the centre of a bay-window would be ideal, while if artificial light is used, there should be two lamps in reflectors, one on either side of the camera, shining down on the subject. The use of a filter will often be found necessary to darken certain colours, that of blue ink, for example. The filter is best chosen in accordance with the table given on pages 70–71. Interchangeable lens cameras are more versatile for close-range work because extension tubes can be placed between lens and camera to allow closer focusing. Reflex cameras can use extendible bellows for the same purpose because focusing is carried out through the camera lens.

A detailed treatment of the more advanced aspects of copying is contained in "Camera Copying and Reproduction", by O. R. Croy. General works such as "Commonsense Photography", by Leonard Gaunt and "Photography with the Eye Level Reflex", by H. S. Newcombe also contain useful information on this subject.

SEASIDE.—By using a low viewpoint for the camera you will get impressive waves or a pleasing still life of sea-grass against a background of water and sky; from a high viewpoint—the top of a cliff—you will show the stretch of a coastline photographed against the light, the water glittering and shining. You may tilt the camera downwards to get a lively impression of the pattern produced by the backflowing water in the sand. But do not bother about the steamer which comes up over the horizon; it would appear as a mere pin-point on your film. Snapshots of anything alive with 1/125 second and *f* 11 with 125 ASA film should in sunshine give well-exposed negatives. For close-ups make use of zone focusing (see page 46). A light yellow filter will help to get good colour rendering, an orange filter will give you dramatic cloud effects and clear distances. A lens hood is absolutely essential; it will protect your lens from glare and reflections whether you work with or against the light and so your picture will be more brilliant and have better shadow detail. Protect the camera well from sand, which has a habit of creeping into shutters, bellows and all other essential parts. The film should be changed away from sand and in the darkest spot available. A UV filter may be necessary with colour film to avoid over blue results. Be careful, too, that the meter is not misled by the general lightness of tone (See page 42.)

The use of filters is fully covered in "The Photoguide to Filters" by Clyde Reynolds.

SHOWS.—Hundreds of photographic possibilities exist here for the man with a fast lens of not less than *f* 2.8. The technique varies with the type of show, the lighting conditions available and the camera position. Fast film is generally advisable. Coloured lighting has to be treated with care as often our eye finds it difficult to estimate its lighting value for our film. While a front row position will give large figures, one has to put up with a low viewpoint which leads to distortion. Seats on the side are as a rule to be preferred, as a centre view usually produces flat lighting. The distance is best pre-set to the spot on the stage where action is likely to take place; then wait for the dramatic movement which at the same time coincides with the dead-point of motion, so as to make longer exposure times possible without fear of image movement. While the exposure time will vary according to the light prevailing, an average setting for fast film at *f* 2.8 is 1/30th second. Colour film is not easy to use, owing to the low lighting level. Shots can be obtained, however, on fast artificial light film.

SNOW AND ICE.—Snow and ice, which might seem to be colourless, are not so to photographic material. The shadows in snow—which give it shape and feel—contain much blue. Black-and-white film being very sensitive to blue will register this particularly strongly, thus reproducing the shadows and sunny patches on the negative with equal strength, with the result that, instead of powdery snow and glittering ice, we get a wide even field of white, devoid of just those fine details which may have made us want to take the photograph. For ice and snow, therefore, use a yellow filter. Colour film should not need a filter unless the sky is excessively blue ,when a pale-tinted haze filter may give a more acceptable, though less accurate result. Wide open snow-scapes are usually disappointing in the picture (see *Landscapes*, page 152). Near distance and close-up shots are more satisfying. The cold glittering brilliancy of snow and ice, particularly in close-up work, is best brought out in strong side-light or better still, back-light. Use your exposure meter with care. A direct reading of snow will recommend underexposed because the meter thinks you want the scene to average out to a mid-tone. You need about one stop more exposure than the meter recommends, perhaps more in bright sunshine. This is particularly important with colour films.

Photography in exceptionally cold conditions is one of the subjects of "Photography on Expeditions", by D. H. O. John.

SPORTS.—Any camera may be used but, where interchangeable lenses are available, a long-focus lens is often helpful. This allows you to get close-up shots without approaching the object too closely, which would not be possible in many instances. As actions worth recording happen, as a rule, without warning, it is essential to be ready for them. It is here that the knowledge of the game will help. The first question will be to find a suitable zone focusing which covers the most likely field of action without having to stop down more than is absolutely essential (see page 46), as a small stop would necessitate a relatively long exposure time, while on the other hand, short shutter speeds are needed to arrest movement. It goes without saying that fast film is the best safeguard against under-exposure if the weather is not particularly bright; on the other hand if a fast lens or good lighting conditions are available, the medium speed film, on account of its finer grain, will give a better chance of getting sectional enlargements (see page 57). In athletics, conditions are as a rule simplified because the position of the athlete is fixed, or at least can easily be pre-determined; in athletics, too, there is sometimes a dead-point of movement which usually coincides with the moment of greatest interest. Therefore, the distance may be set beforehand and the exposure time will not have to be too fast, speeds of 1/125 to 1/250 second being adequate for reasonably close-up pictures. Where movements are taken it has to be borne in mind that arms and legs move with at least twice the speed of the athlete's body as a whole. The direction of the movement plays an important part in all sports pictures. For fast movements, or where one's shutter only allows of comparatively slow speeds, it is essential to avoid snapping at right angles to the moving subject, but to take the movement towards (or away from) the camera.

TECHNICAL SUBJECTS.—Technical subjects, such as machinery with its component parts, the technical and industrial processes, etc.—require first and foremost a clear, sharp and detailed rendering. To get this, accurate focusing on to the main part is essential; adequate stopping down to cover sufficient depth of field will almost always necessitate the use of a tripod and the camera should be exactly level in order to show true perspective. The exposure time should be determined with the greatest possible care for the *shadow* parts, which should still show all details. The illumination has to be arranged so that no deep shadows occur: these might be helpful in producing a pictorial effect but are definitely not useful in a technical record. Where artificial illumination can be arranged, a shadowless picture can be produced by swinging the lamp from behind the camera in a large semi-circle (with the camera position as centre). For small technical subjects one should refer to what is said under "Reproduction" on page 189. For large technical subjects, outdoors and indoors, much of the advice given for "Architecture" (see page 150) may be applied, always taking into consideration the essential rules given above.

More on this subject can be found in "Lighting for Photography", by Walter Nurnberg.

TRAVELLING WITH THE CAMERA.—Decide beforehand what you are really likely to need and travel as light as possible. If you should have a whole battery of lenses, don't carry them all with you. Two lenses are generally enough for all purposes and a good choice would be a moderate wide angle and a slightly long-focus. If you have a good tele-extender, just that with the standard lens should suffice. Unless you know for certain that your usual film is easily obtainable, take a good supply with you. Other films may be just as good but you will not be familiar with their characteristics. Carry your camera where it is reasonably free from vibration or heat. The glove compartment or rear window ledge in the car is not a good place. Check your insurance, if you have any, to see that it covers your travels. Keep your exposed films well away from the unexposed ones. Either wind the leader (of 35mm film) completely in or tear it off to positively identify exposed film. Take plenty of pictures, looking out for local features or peculiarities, even if they are not exceptionally pictorial. You will find them intriguing in future years when the journey is almost forgotten.

There is a great deal more on this subject in "*35mm Photo Technique*" *and* "*Photography with the Eye-level Reflex*", *by H. S. Newcombe.*

TROPICAL PHOTOGRAPHY.—It is a mistake to assume that no exposure can be too short under a tropical sun. Both reason and experience show that one can rely on the photo-electric meter as well as on exposure charts in so far as they apply to the latitudes in question. The light in tropical countries is deceiving as far as street scenes and architecture are concerned. Although the intense brightness of the sunny parts might induce us to give very short exposures, this would be wrong, for here, as everywhere else, we have to adhere to the principle: expose with due regard to the shadows. In sunny countries these shadows are relatively all the darker. The best rule is to take the middle exposure between the number indicated for the shadows and the one for the sunny parts. There is no great difficulty about material. Films should not be kept longer than six months in their original airtight tins (tropical packing) at continual temperatures of 90°F (32°C). At continual 100°F (38°C), the life of most films is limited to a month or two. Keep films for as short as possible a time in the camera. Films should be processed as soon as possible after exposure—within a week or two or, in very hot humid climates, within a few days. Keep the film in an airtight container with desiccant (to absorb moisture). If possible, keep in a refrigerator, but only if you can dry out the exposed film and the container is sealed. If one wants to develop one's films, no difficulties need arise provided that baths, developer, fixer and washing water can be cooled to the same temperature. But it is better to work with the prevailing high temperature than to have appreciable change of temperature from bath to bath. A "tropical" developer should be used and *Kodak D.K.*15 in powder form should be found most useful. After developing, a short rinse in water should be given and the negative immersed in a tropical hardener (*Kodak S.B.*4) for 3 minutes. After hardening, fix for at least 10 minutes in a hardening fixing bath (*Kodak F.*5) and then wash in running water for 10 to 15 minutes (or in three changes of water of 5 minutes each). To dry, wipe both sides of the negative with a swab of wet cotton-wool, then dry in a current of air or the draught from a fan—if necessary, keeping insects away with mosquito netting.

High and widely varying temperatures with low humidity, as occur in desert regions and dry seasons, and very high humidity in rainy seasons, call for special precautions to protect the lift and continued good performance of the camera. These conditions also cause the growth of moulds on organic matter. Sand, dust and insects may present problems. The camera should be kept dry and clean. Leather parts should be wax polished, metal parts lightly greased. Never leave the camera unnecessarily exposed to heat. Always keep it in its case. The lens should be covered with the lens cap when not in use. Outer lens surfaces have to be kept clean, dirt and grit removed with an air-blower and by tapping. Wipe the lens surface with cotton wool or open mesh fabric (butter muslin) when required. Store photographic equipment in an airtight metal box or a tin which should be sealed with adhesive (e.g. medical) tape. In a humid atmosphere, add some desiccating agent, e.g. silica gel. Condensation on the lens may occur when the camera is moved from a cool place into humid heat; this has to be removed before use and the whole camera carefully wiped before re-storing.

A useful book on this subject is "Camera in the Tropics", by G. C. Dodwell. Advanced information is supplied in "Photography on Expeditions" by D. H. O. John.

WOODS.—As in landscape photography, it will be best to concentrate on detail, to select, for instance, a small group of trees standing out against a background of cloudy sky, which will suggest more than a whole wood. More worth while but technically more difficult to tackle will be scenes in woods: a few tall tree trunks between which the rays of the sun cast interesting light patches on the undergrowth, the morning mist slowly clearing, and so on. A light or medium filter may help to disentangle the various shades of brown and green on black-and-white film. Careful use of the light falling through the trees is the most important factor. While pictures with the light are usually uninteresting, side light or photographs taken against-the-light will show up the rays of the sun against a dark background and the irritating details will be smoothed out. The exposure time should be carefully determined for the darkest parts, which should show detail. One has to take into account that woods and particularly undergrowth are very dark even on a bright day and the predominating brown and green colours swallow most of the incoming light.

For more detailed information on any kind of photo-subject, you will find complete articles written by specialists in the "Focal Encyclopedia of Photography". All of the above subjects are separately and fully covered together with many others—ranging from archaeology to zoo photography.

Most subjects are also covered in general books such as "Photography with the Eye-level Reflex", by H. S. Newcombe. The technical aspects of exposure, exposure meter usage, close-ups, processing, etc., are dealt with in "Commonsense Photography", by Leonard Gaunt. The use of particular cameras is the specialist subject of the Camera Way books, Camera Guides, and the new Camera Book series such as "Rollei Way", "Leica and Leicaflex Way", "Pentax Way", "Praktica Way", "Canonet Guide", "Yashica Guide", "Nikon Guide", "Praktica Book", "Pentax Book", "Minolta Book", etc. The guide series also includes the "Lens Guide" and "Electronic Flash Guide", dealing with the choice and use of extra lenses and flash equipment.

DARK-ROOM

A few simple tips for those who like to develop and print their own black-and-white films. In order to follow these instructions you need no dark-room, very little apparatus and very few chemicals. (Colour film developing, printing and enlarging is for the advanced photographer and expert only).

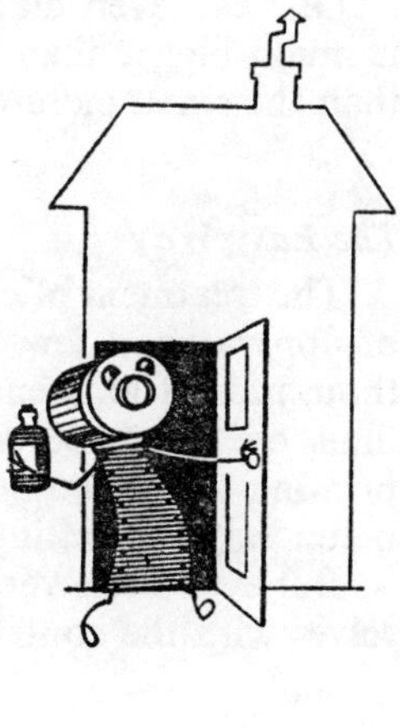

TWO METHODS

From the "Negative" to the "Positive"

When the film has been exposed you cannot tell from examining the emulsion that anything has happened. Yet there has been a change; the fleeting image thrown by the lens has left its mark on the film. Not that anything can be seen of this impression, even under the most powerful magnifying glass. It must be treated chemically before it appears. And then the details appear gradually, one by one, until the picture is complete.

But it is a funny kind of picture. All the things which in real life were white appear black on the film, and the dark parts of the real object look light. People we know very well look like negroes, while Blackie the cat looks like Snowball next door.

This topsy-turvy state of affairs, however, need cause no worry, for a second process produces from this "negative" as many "positives" as you require, with the blacks and whites where they should be.

One can even make enlargements, in which the picture is much bigger than the negative and much more striking than the small picture.

The Easy Way

The treatment of exposed films requires a certain amount of apparatus, a few chemicals and a little knowledge. Yet thousands of amateurs solve the difficulty by handing their films over to experts who take charge of the developing, printing and enlarging. And for busy people there is no better way for getting good results.

But even these very people could usefully acquaint themselves with the contents of the following pages. The knowledge which they may acquire in this way will be helpful in putting their orders in a more precise form than they did before.

More Fun This Way

But other people get a great deal of satisfaction out of the hours they spend developing, printing and enlarging their own films. The enjoyment they get from their labours more than compensates them for any failures. What do a few fuzzy negatives, a few "flat" prints matter if they can be said to be "all my own work"? The method may be more laborious, but it's much more fun.

The Usual Method

In most handbooks on photography for beginners the procedure adopted is always the same. First, the amateur is shown how to obtain a negative from the exposed film or plate and then how to make paper prints and enlargements from the negative. Now this is a nice logical procedure, because one must, of course, have a negative before one can get a positive from it. But even so, it is questionable whether this is the best way of going about things for the beginner.

For if there is anything difficult about photography it is undoubtedly the development of negatives. The emulsion coating on films or plates is not nearly so resistant as that of printing paper. And if in the course of development there is a little too much here and not quite enough there, the negative is already damaged, if not entirely spoiled. And a lost negative means that everything else is lost, too.

A spoiled print, on the other hand, is by no means the end of everything, for another one can easily be obtained from the negative, this time without making any mistakes. With prints, in fact, it is a case of: "If at first you don't succeed. . . ."

A New Suggestion

From the above considerations comes the rather unusual suggestion which follows. Give your films to a photographic dealer to be developed and begin your own part of the business with printing, developing and fixing the paper copies. When you are an old hand at this, you can go on to enlargements, and last of all—when all the other manipulations come naturally to you—undertake the development of your films.

This method, which is the exact opposite of the one usually recommended, is undoubtedly the safest. It leads you step by step from the easier to the more difficult and arranges things so that the mistakes and failures which inevitably occur at the beginning do not affect the negative, which is often irreplaceable, but only the copy.

Variations

For owners of miniature cameras the order of procedure is somewhat different. They are not very interested in prints made direct from the negative, for there is not much to be seen on a picture 24 × 36 mm. (1 × 1½ inches). So they usually leave prints alone and go straight on to enlargements. On the other hand, there are amateurs who are satisfied with prints because their camera gives them pictures of 6 × 6 cm. (2¼ × 2¼ inches), 6 × 9 cm. (3½ × 2¼ inches), or even bigger. And therefore—more's the pity—they are not interested in enlargements, and can proceed direct from printing to developing their own films.

Unnecessary Expense

Learned men, familiar with every aspect of every branch of photography, occasionally produce treatises in which they describe all the gear which they consider necessary for home developing and printing. In the first place they prescribe a dark-room, equipped, if possible, with heating installation and running water. Then comes a respectably long list of apparatus and a fearfully long catalogue of chemicals.

Now all this is very disheartening for the beginner. He becomes anxious, for, having a tremendous respect for anything he sees in print, he imagines that all these highly-desirable luxuries are necessities. So he sits down with pencil and paper and begins to reckon the cost. The total is staggering!

Dark-room not Indispensable

Fortunately it is easy to demonstrate how a dark-room—(what flat-dweller can find the space for a dark-room?)—and all sorts of *comfort moderne* can be dispensed with, and how apparatus and chemicals can be reduced to a minimum.

If you use a film suitable for contact prints (the usual term for prints the same size as the negative) you need very little room or equipment at all. These are the films giving negatives of 2¼ × 2¼ in. (6 × 6cm.) or larger.

The other things which will be wanted later on for enlarging, and for developing and fixing films and plates, can be acquired gradually. Then all the luxuries will come along bit by bit, for although they are not indispensable, they do add to the ease and accuracy of one's work.

FIRST OF ALL—CONTACT PRINTS

Things You Need

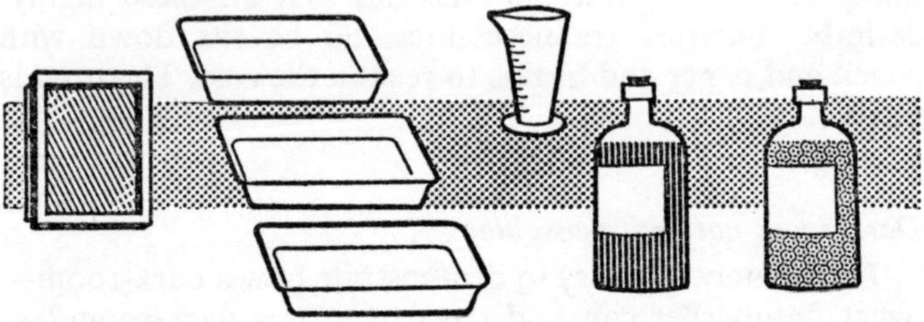

You will need a printing frame in which you put your negative and the sensitive printing paper, three dishes (trays) and a measuring glass containing 300 cc. (about 8 fluid ounces). And that completes all the essential apparatus.

The printing frame must, of course, be the right size to take the film, but it is better to make the trays too big, so that they can be used later on for enlargements if required. They should be big enough to take postcard size ($5\frac{1}{2} \times 3\frac{1}{2}$ inches) (9×14 cm.) paper comfortably, or, still better, large enough for the $\frac{1}{2}$-plate ($6\frac{1}{2} \times 4\frac{3}{4}$ inches 13×18 cm.) size, since prices do not rise proportionately to the size of tray.

As chemicals you will require a paper developer, in powder or liquid form, with directions for making-up, and a box of acid-hypo fixing salt. And that is all.

For developing prints a dark-room is easily dispensed with. For one thing most people have their living to earn during the day, so that they have to do their photography at night, when it is dark. You choose a corner of the room as dark as possible, but as this type of paper is not highly sensitive, a glimmer of light does not matter very much.

It is advisable to have two pieces of cardboard in readiness to cover the developing and fixing trays, and to work in your own shadow. In this way you will not need any special yellow light to work by. If you procure a yellow dark-room bulb, you will be able to have considerably more light on the dishes.

All Ready

First cover the table on which you are working with newspaper to protect it from stains which might result from spilled developer or hypo. Then place your three dishes next to each other.

In the first dish you have 100 cc. (3½ fluid ounces) of developing solution made up according to the instructions on the bottle.

The second one is filled fairly full with clean water.

The third contains the fixing solution, again not too shallow.

And now you can start. It goes without saying that you don't wear your best suit for the work. Some of the chemicals leave nasty stains.

Printing

Under the protection of your own shadow you open a box or packet of contact printing paper, take out one sheet, and put the remainder, carefully wrapped, back into the box where it is safe from stray light. Make sure it is *contact* paper. The paper used for enlargements is much more sensitive to light and cannot be used in even very dim room lighting.

You have already put your film, dull side up, into the printing frame. You now place the paper on the emulsion side (the dull side) of the negative. As only glossy contact paper is now available there is very little danger of putting it in the frame wrong-side up. The glossy surface, of course, must be next to the emulsion of the film.

Having assured yourself that the film and printing paper have been correctly placed, you close the frame, cover it with one of your pieces of cardboard and take it to, say, about 12–18 inches from a 60-watt lamp. Having removed the cardboard you expose the loaded frame to the light for 10 seconds, timing yourself by your watch. Keep the frame the same distance from the light each time.

If you choose to count your seconds, "seventy-one, seventy-two, seventy-three," etc., you need not be afraid of being a second or so out. It will make little difference.

Developing

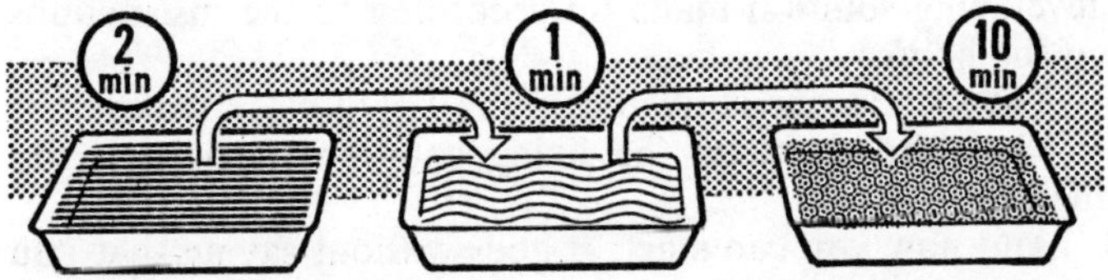

After the printing, cover up the frame again and take it back to your dishes. Remove the paper from the frame and *submerge* it in the developer, glossy side up, taking care to see that no air-bubbles are allowed to remain on the surface.

Keep the liquid constantly moving by gently rocking the tray. The tray can remain uncovered, provided it is in the shadow of your body. Make sure that the paper remains totally immersed.

At first the paper remains as white as when it came out of the box. But soon the positive picture begins to appear, faintly at first, and then stronger every second. It is really exciting to see the details emerging out of nothing.

You cannot expect to get perfect results with your first print. It may, for example, be much too dark, or even entirely black. This means that the exposure was too long. The fault can be remedied by leaving the second piece of printing paper under the light for less time.

If, on the other hand, the picture appears too slowly, and

has not reached its full strength after *two minutes'* development, it shows that the exposure to the light was too short. So next time you hold your printing frame at the same distance from the light, but for a longer time.

You will soon learn by experience how long must be given to the only variable factor, that is the exposure to the light, in order to get good pictures.

The Next Steps

If all has gone well with the developing—(remember: minimum time allowed—2 minutes)—the print is well swilled in clean water in the covered dish.

When the traces of developer have been removed in this way, the paper is put into the fixing-bath, still covered, as it is still sensitive to light. And there it remains for 10 minutes.

The fixed print, which cannot now be affected by light, is washed in clean water. As you cannot use too much water, take a large kitchen dish for the purpose and change the water six times in the course of an hour. A quicker and more thorough method is to wash the prints in running water. (See page 214.)

Lastly the prints are removed from their bath, the free water on the surface is carefully absorbed by white blotting-paper, or filter-paper, and the prints are laid on clean blotting-paper to dry. This is rather a lengthy process, but as you do your printing in the evenings the prints will have all night to dry.

In the morning you will find them dry, but curled up. To straighten them out you first bend them very carefully, picture side up, over the edge of a table, taking care that no cracks appear. Finally they are pressed between the leaves of a thick book.

If you must have dry, flat prints within a few minutes, you will have to invest in an electric dryer and press.

The Printing Paper

As contact printing is now rarely practised, the paper is not always easily obtainable and is only supplied with a glossy surface. This gives the best and clearest reproduction of detail in small pictures.

Hard or Soft?

Certain faults in the negative can be corrected to some degree by using the right kind of printing paper. The paper is supplied in different degrees of "hardness" (gradation).

For a film that has been *correctly exposed* and developed, which has the normal gradations from light to dark, a *normal paper* is used.

A *hard negative*, on the other hand, that is, one with great contrast in light and shade (page 221) requires a *soft paper* which tones down these extremes.

Conversely, a *flat negative* (page 222), on account of its lack of light contrasts, needs a *hard* or an *extra-hard paper*.

Both *dense* and *thin negatives* (page 222) are printed on *normal*, or, at the most, on *hard paper*, and the time is regulated according to the density of the film. If it is over-exposed, that is, densely covered, the time allowed for printing must be long, whereas the thinly-covered negative will print quickly.

ENLARGEMENTS—STILL BETTER

Prints are Too Small

Most amateurs have cameras using film of the 35 mm. size or smaller. Contact prints are of little use to them because they are too small to show any real detail.

The result is that many amateurs are amazed by an enlargement of a section from one of their own negatives. They can hardly believe that they took the picture themselves. The result is so vastly superior to the print, that the author of it does not recognize his own child. And once the man who hitherto has always found contact prints quite good enough for him is bitten by the enthusiasm for enlarging, his printing frame grows rusty from lack of use. He hardly condescends to look at small prints. For him it is enlargements or nothing, and he is quite right, too. For the joy of photography begins all over again for the amateur who once discovers the possibilities of enlarging.

Additional Apparatus

The extra material does not amount to much. Many of the things required for enlarging are the same as those which have already served for contact printing.

The trays, for example, were chosen at the very beginning to take the half-plate size of paper ($6\frac{1}{2} \times 4\frac{3}{4}$ inches or 13 $\times$ 18 cm. continental size) with ease. You can use, too, your same measuring glass and the same chemicals, developer and fixing solution.

The new apparatus consists of the enlarger which, although not precisely inexpensive, is not nearly so costly as many people imagine.

Then you will need a special means of lighting your work-table, as enlargement paper is rather highly sensitive.

Whereas it was quite sufficient, working with contact printing paper to protect the emulsion by your own shadow, you will now need filtered light, either orange or yellow-green. The latter is preferable as it gives a much brighter light to work in and makes the task of estimating the density of the enlargement much easier. The cheapest system is provided by the coloured dark-room bulbs with which the usual bulb is replaced.

Just Like Printing!

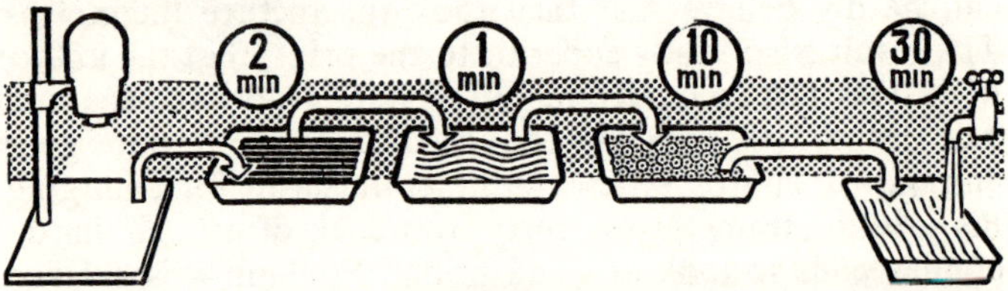

The procedure for enlargements is just the same as that for making contact prints: first expose, then develop, rinse, fix, wash. Even the times are the same. The paper is exposed long enough for the image to appear after developing for a maximum of two minutes. then rinsed for one minute and left for 10 minutes in the fixing bath. You can get high speed fixers where the fixing time is reduced to 30 seconds. Finally the enlargement must be very thoroughly washed and dried. The final washing must, of course, be even more thorough than it was in the case of small prints, and the volume of water used correspondingly greater.

Focus Sharply

A great deal of the knowledge gained in making contact prints is useful for enlarging. But the actual printing, that is, the exposure of the paper to the light, requires special care.

There is nothing very difficult about it, however. You put your film in the enlarger and switch on the light. An enlarged image of your negative now appears on the baseboard of the apparatus. To get the details as clear as possible, you lay a sheet of white paper where you will subsequently put your sensitive paper. Some enlargers have an automatic self-focusing device, but with others the focusing must be adjusted by hand and eye.

The greater the distance between negative and paper, the larger the image. But the beginner should be satisfied with moderate magnification. If, for example, he has hitherto contented himself with prints of V.P. size (2¼ × 1⅝ inches or 4 × 6½ cm. continental size), he will probably find some satisfaction in an enlargement of ¼-plate (4¼ × 3¼ inches = 8.2 × 10.8 cm.). This represents an almost four-fold magnification of the 24 × 36 mm. (1 × 1½ inch) picture given by the miniature camera.

But it is not necessary to drag in every detail of the original negative. It is much better to enlarge one section only. Not only is the enlarged section more satisfactory in itself, but it may be possible at the same time to leave any blemishes on the film out of the picture.

Once the image on the white sheet of paper is sharp, and the section to be enlarged has been decided on, the enlarger lamp is switched off, and, by the red or green light of your special bulb, the sensitive enlarging paper is substituted for the sheet of ordinary paper. When the paper is firmly fixed in position on the board, either with drawing pins, but, better still, with the special masking frame sold for the purpose, the light is switched on.

Time of Exposure

The length of time required to produce a well-defined print must depend on several factors; the density of the negative, the size of enlargement desired, the strength of the lamp in the enlarger, the lens aperture, and even the sensitivity of the paper. But for practical purposes the only variable factors are the negative, the size of the enlargement and the lens aperture.

As in the case of contact prints, the time must be fixed by experiment. A 20 second exposure is given first and this figure is subsequently reduced or increased according to the behaviour of the print in the developer. If the image appears with a rush, and if even the parts which should remain white, appear grey, the time of exposure must be shortened. If the image appears very slowly, exposure was insufficient.

When examining the developed strip, the highest lights should be watched, as they are an indication of the exposure.

1. Where the highlights are white and chalky, and the shadows are a medium grey without any full black, exposure was too short.

2. Where the highlights are just white, and show full details, while the very densest shadows of the image are just full black and also show details, the exposure was correct.

3. Where the highlights are veiled over, and appear grey, and the shadow details are too dark to be seen, the exposure was too long.

When you have made enlargements from fifty or so different negatives, you will have had enough experience of various densities and the various exposures required, to proceed to make bigger enlargements for your films.

The extent to which you can enlarge the image is limited only by practical considerations of obtaining sufficient separation between lens and baseboard, while still being able to focus accurately. Naturally, the quality of the enlargement depends on the quality of the negative. Unless the image on the film is really sharp, you cannot make a very satisfactory enlargement. And if the film is a fast, relatively coarse-grained type or has been overexposed or overdeveloped, the grain may be too obtrusive for extensive enlargement.

The Right Paper

When a negative is enlarged its image is spread over a wide area. On its way to the enlarging paper it has to pass a wide cone of air, filled with more or less dust, which correspondingly weakens the enlargement.

So even *normal* negatives may need a *hard* paper for enlarging purposes, whereas a *hard* negative will enlarge well on *normal* paper, which will do the necessary softening. For *flat* negatives a hard paper is not enough; the *extra-hard* variety must be used.

The reader will see that this is rather different from what happens with contact prints.

As far as the density of the negative is concerned, however, the same rules apply as for ordinary printing: the denser the negative the longer the exposure of the paper to the light. If a negative is exceptionally dense, it is preferable to reduce it first (see page 222) rather than to increase the time of exposure. The prolonged stay beneath the lamp might result in over-heating the emulsion, causing actual damage and making it useless.

Hard enlarging paper such as can be recommended for normal negatives, unfortunately emphasizes not only the desired light and shade contrasts, but the grain of the emulsion. For this reason it is better, if very big enlargements are required, to use "normal" paper.

Matt or Glossy?

For clear reproduction on all sizes up to full-plate ($8\frac{1}{2} \times 6\frac{1}{2}$ inches) or 10×8 inches (18×24 cm. continental size) use a paper with a glossy surface, just as you would do in the case of contact prints. A high gloss can be imparted by drying pressed against a glazing plate.

For larger sizes, and in cases where something more than a strictly practical clearness is sought, enlargements are best made on matt or semi-matt paper, which can be white or cream according to the subject of the picture. The coarser-grained papers are not suitable for the smaller sizes. The rough surface serves to some extent to conceal the grain from the film and gives interest to large uniform surfaces in the picture.

Toning Rarely Used

Enlargements can be toned in a variety of hues, either by using a toning-developer or, more often, by a process involving first bleaching and then toning. It is a treatment to be applied very sparingly, as the result may so easily be in contradiction to the canons of good taste. No picture can be saved by toning, but a good enlargement may be ruined if toned unwisely. The formula of a reliable Brown developer is given on page 216.

Retouching Even Rarer

The amateur need not bother his head about retouching in the bad old sense, which involved an interference with the whole character of the picture.

The best way to avoid the necessity for retouching is to handle the film so carefully that any scratches, which would later show up on the enlargement, are avoided. The great enemy is dust, which settles on the emulsion of the negative and produces white spots on the dark parts of the picture.

But as it is well-nigh impossible to abolish specks of dust altogether, one should be prepared to make white marks invisible by what is known as "spotting". Matt papers will take marks from a very soft pencil quite well. Or else the spot can be obliterated by putting a number of tiny dots of paint on the offending part by means of a fine sable brush.

Glossy paper can also be treated with the brush, but care must be taken to see that the paint used is one that dries glossy.

If black marks, due to some damage to the emulsion, appear on the enlargement, they must be carefully scraped with a razor-blade and then coloured to the correct tone with water-colour. Retouching sets can be bought for a few shillings.

The Finishing Touch

The saying about spoiling the ship for a ha'porth of tar applies to photography as well. Having lavished a great deal of care on exposing, developing and producing your enlargements, it would be a pity not to find a way of keeping the pictures clean and easily available.

You can either invest in one of the many handsome albums or, better still, mount each enlargement on separate cardboard sheets which you can keep together in a suitable file or folder. This loose-leaf system allows for rearrangements and additions *ad lib.*

The enlargements can be stuck on to the mount with an adhesive made for photographic purposes (free from acids which in time would spoil the picture) or with transparent "corners" unless the clean working "Dry mounting tissue" is preferred.

HINTS AND TIPS

Enlarger and Enlarging

A red filter can be useful in your enlarger. It allows you to focus the picture on to the sensitive paper itself without affecting the emulsion. An orange filter can be used for the same purpose.

An over-exposed film, the denser the better, is useful for enlargers which are not fitted with automatic focusing. Two diagonal cuts are made in the emulsion with a pen-knife, and the test negative is ready for use.

An old trick for settling the question of exposure in printing or enlarging is to cover the printing frame or the enlarged image, as the case may be, with a piece of cardboard, leaving one strip free, and then second by second to expose an ever wider strip. The whole sheet is developed and the correct time can be seen by comparing the various strips.

If miniature films (24 × 36 *mm.:* 1 × 1½ *inches) are put into an enlarger made for films of a bigger size, the empty space in the negative holder must be blocked by a paper mask. Otherwise the enlargement will be spoiled by stray beams of light.*

"Hard" or "soft" papers can do no more than improve the tone-gradation of black and white pictures, whether prints or enlargements. That is, a picture from a hard negative can be softened somewhat, and vice versa. But thick or thin negatives, that is, those with too much, or too little, density, demand a longer or shorter printing on normal or, possibly, hard paper.

An enlargement from a hard negative will naturally show heavy masses of black in the shadows and large white blanks in the highlights. The missing details in the light parts may appear if the exposure is prolonged. But this will make the shadows even more solid.

So many photographers prolong the exposure and cover the dark parts of the enlargement with their hand. Better still, since the hand is not likely to fit the required shape, a number of paper masks, cut to all kinds of fantastic outlines, are prepared beforehand, so that an area of almost any shape can be shaded. To prevent hard dividing lines between the shaded and unshaded parts of the picture, the mask is moved slightly from side to side.

Coarse grain can be reduced during enlarging by placing a ground-glass plate, smooth side up, on the enlarging paper.

For enlargers with condensers an opal disc on the upper condenser lens gives softer reproduction.

Normal photographs can be softened during enlargement by placing a soft-focus screen in front of the enlarger lens. Another method consists in stretching a piece of thin net or silk in front of the lens. But none of these post-development processes is quite satisfactory. If soft outlines are sought it is better to fit the soft-focus apparatus at the time of taking the photograph. (See page 81.)

Although a small stop cannot help to correct a negative which is out of focus, it can increase the depth of focus of the lens in the enlarger. This means that any slight error in focusing on to the baseboard is of no account.

The small stop, with the correspondingly deeper band of sharp definition, is essential when "vanishing lines" on buildings, due to the tilting of the camera, are to be suppressed. Here the baseboard is purposely set at an angle to the negative, but it is essential for every part of the paper to be in focus.

It is quite easy to make a gentle ski-ing slope into a breakneck descent by taking an oblique section of the picture. But be careful that there are no perpendicular objects, such as houses or towers, to give the trick away. As a matter of fact, the practised eye is rarely taken in by these artificially steep slopes. Gravity has a knack of giving objects a certain poise which indicates at once how the plumb-line falls in reality.

You can use your enlarger for making photographs of pictures in books. You first place any normal negative in the enlarger and focus it on to the page in question. The dimensions of the negative show how much of the page will be reproduced in the subsequent photograph. If the area is too small it can be enlarged by raising the lens.

The negative is then replaced, in total darkness, by a photographic plate or a section of film, emulsion side towards the lens. Then the page of the book (uncovered, of course) is illuminated by an ordinary electric bulb. The exposure time must be fixed by experiment. When the film is developed you will see whether the exposure was correct.

During this procedure, the lamps used to illuminate the page must not be allowed to spill light on to the enlarger head, where it may reach the film. It is advisable to cover all gaps around the negative carrier with black cloth or hinged pieces of card.

If the experiment described above entails an exposure which is too short to be manageable, the time can be lengthened by *using a thick yellow filter, or even a red one, as a "brake". This system can also be used in the preparation of lantern slides.*

Washing, Drying, Finishing the Print

It is of the utmost importance that paper prints and enlargements are thoroughly well washed so that no trace of the fixing bath remains in the fibre of the paper. To do this without wasting water, place your vessel under a slowly running tap and put in it a rubber tube with one end near the bottom of the bowl and the other end hanging over the side and reaching below the level of the end in the water. Begin the outflow by sucking the water to the free end of the tube. This now acts as a siphon and draws off the soiled water from the bottom of the bowl while clean water is constantly supplied from the tap.

The prints, which should float about in the bowl, are anchored to cork clips.

In one litre (20 *ounces*) *of fixing bath* 300 ¼*-plate prints may be safely fixed.*

If prints and enlargements are immersed for two or three minutes after fixing in a solution of 1 *litre of water and* 10 *grams* (154.3 *grains*) *of anhydrous sodium carbonate* (*or* 27 *grams—about* 1 *ounce—of crystals*), *the paper will take the subsequent washing water better and be more thoroughly cleansed from traces of fixing salts.*

A pleasing glossy surface can be obtained by pressing the wet prints, face downwards, with a rubber squeegee, on to a sheet of glass where they are left until they spring off by themselves. The glass must be scrupulously clean, of course.

Wet paper prints, left to themselves, take quite a long time to dry and even then they are rolled up in a tube. It is quite a business to straighten them out and press them until they lie flat. A great deal of time and trouble can be saved by investing in an electric drying and glazing press.

If the prints emerge from the press rolled instead of flat, it means that the press was overheated. So switch off the current at the end of two minutes and allow another few minutes to complete the drying slowly.

COMMON PAPER SIZES

British Standard Sizes	*Metric Equivalents*	*Nearest Continental standards*
3½ × 2½ in.	8.25 × 5.7 cm.	6 × 9 cm.
4¼ × 3¼ in. = (¼-plate)	10.8 × 8.25 cm.	9 × 12 cm.
5½ × 3½ in. = (Postcard)	13.9 × 8.75 cm.	9 × 14 cm.
6½ × 4¾ in. = (½-plate)	16.5 × 12 cm.	13 × 18 cm.
8½ × 6½ in. = (1/1-plate)	21.5 × 16.5 cm.	18 × 24 cm.
10 × 8 in.	25.4 × 20.3 cm.	—
12 × 10 in.	30.4 × 25.4 cm.	24 × 30 cm.
15 × 12 in.	38.1 × 30.4 cm.	30 × 40 cm.

PRACTICAL FORMULÆ

Metol-Hydroquinone for Papers

Metol	9 *gr.*	1 *grm.*
Sodium sulphite (anhydrous)	220 *gr.*	25 *grm.*
Hydroquinone	40 *gr.*	4.5 *grm.*
Sodium carbonate (anhydrous)	150 *gr.*	17 *grm.*
Potassium bromide	9 *gr.*	1 *grm.*
Water: to	20 *fluid oz.*	1,000 *ccm.*

The above developer is used undiluted and gives pleasant neutral black tones on bromide and chlorobromide papers. It may also be used with ordinary contact printing chloride papers, but in this case the quantity of potassium bromide should be doubled in order to stop any tendency to fog.

In the fresh developer, bromide papers will develop in approximately 2½ minutes. Chlorobromide papers will require a rather shorter time, while developing out chloride papers of medium sensitivity will require about 90 seconds.

The developer is exceedingly economical, and even when it turns yellowish-brown in colour it is by no means worked out. The colour merely implies that the time of development must be increased, perhaps up to twice the original time.

Blue-Black Paper Developer

Metol	18 *gr.*	2 *grm.*
Sodium sulphite (anhydrous)	220 *gr.*	25 *grm.*
Hydroquinone	53 *gr.*	6 *grm.*
Sodium carbonate (anhydrous)	306 *gr.*	35 *grm.*
Potassium bromide	7 *gr.*	0.8 *grm.*
Water: to	20 *fluid oz.*	1,000 *ccm.*

The normal development time for the papers noted above at 64°F. (18°C.) is between 45 and 60 seconds.

A cream paper base and blue-black tones do not go together: a white base is usually more suitable.

Warm-Black Paper Developer

Metol	9 *gr.*	1 *grm.*
Sodium sulphite (anhydrous)	220 *gr.*	25 *grm.*
Hydroquinone	53 *gr.*	6 *grm.*
Sodium carbonate (anhydrous)	175 *gr.*	20 *grm.*
Potassium bromide	44 *gr.*	5 *grm.*
Water: to	20 *fluid oz.*	1,000 *ccm.*

The development time at normal temperature is about 80 to 90 seconds. The developer can be used over and over again until exhausted. It is advisable to use the developer at a temperature some degrees higher than usual, *i.e.*, about 68°F. (20°C.). Not every paper is suitable for warm-black tones: the suitable papers belong to the *chlorobromide* class.

As a rule, warm tones are not pleasant on white paper. Cream, ivory and "chamois" papers are best.

Brown Developer

Hydroquinone	½ *oz.*	24 *grm.*
Sodium sulphite, cryst.	⅝ *oz.*	30 *grm.*
Potassium carbonate	1⅝ *oz.*	80 *grm.*
Water up to:	20 *oz.*	1,000 *ccm.*

For use, dilute with four parts of water, expose for three times the normal time, and develop for five to six minutes.

Farmer's Reducer see page 229.
Fixing Bath see page 229.

AND LASTLY THE NEGATIVE

Experience Already Gained

As has been explained already, we leave the development of negatives to the last—though it is usually put first—because the emulsion is very delicate and may be ruined once and for all by unskilful handling. Moreover, all the experience the beginner has gained in developing and fixing paper prints will stand him in good stead when he at last tackles films or plates.

The order of events is the same as it was for printing and enlarging: developing, rinsing, fixing and so on, until the dry, finished picture—in this case a negative—lies before you.

Individual Development Out-of-Date

Many years ago negatives were developed in the same way as prints and enlargements—one by one. The plate was watched in course of development, the action of the developer stopped at the critical moment, and the developer itself strengthened or diluted according to the nature of the negative—whether usefully or not is another story.

But nowadays 99 out of every 100 amateurs use panchromatic roll-films and individual treatment for every film on the spool is impossible. So we now develop our material "by time and temperature" whether we are dealing with roll-films, cut-films or plates. We can no longer watch the course of development, but rely on our thermometer and our watch to give us accurate results.

Any developer at 64°F. (18°C.) will produce in a given time a well-developed negative which, without examination, can be rinsed and fixed. For this it is essential that the film is reasonably accurately exposed. But that is an essential condition even if the exposures are to be handled individually.

"Timed" development makes a dark-room superfluous. After arranging your dishes by ordinary artificial light, you switch off the lights and put your plate or cut film into the developer in darkness. Rock gently, and at the end of the time indicated for development swill the negative and place it in the fixing bath. After a minute or so the light can be switched on again, provided the fixing dish is covered by a sheet of opaque cardboard.

Tank Development

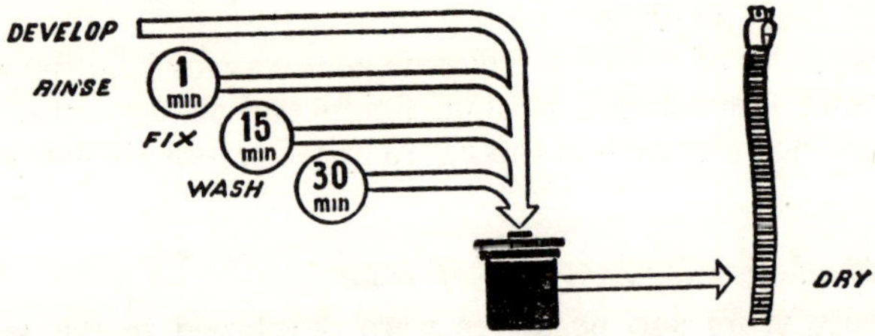

For developing roll films you will need a special tank. Some developing tanks can be loaded in daylight, so that the whole operation, including developing, rinsing and fixing can be done in the light. In other cases the film must be loaded in the dark, an operation that can be successfully performed by anyone at the second or third attempt. The cover is put on the tank and the remainder of the work can be done in daylight, with the film safely hidden away in the dark interior of the developing apparatus.

To make sure that the developer is kept well mixed and gets to every part of the emulsion the tank is shaken gently from time to time during the developing process.

After the allotted time for development, the developer is poured off and pure water is run in until the tank is full. After shaking and perhaps renewing the water once, you empty the tank and then fill it with the hypo solution which is allowed to remain for fifteen minutes, or ,with high speed fixer, 2 minutes. Finally clean water is run through the apparatus for half an hour to wash away all traces of the fixing bath.

The film is then removed with great care from the tank, and freed from superfluous water by wiping it carefully on both sides with chamois leather. Finally it is hung up to dry in a dust-free atmosphere. Wooden or plastic clips, such as those intended for hanging out the washing, can be used to weight the end of the roll.

The Suitable Developer

There is no lack of developers on the market. Of course you must use a *negative developer:* a paper developer would ruin your films.

There is now no point in experimenting with special developers unless you just like doing that kind of thing. Many years ago, emulsions were relatively slow and quite coarse-grained by today's standards. So special "brews" were developed for fine grain or for increased film speed. Now, fast films are available with grain at least as fine as that of the slow-to-medium films of the past.

In fact, considerations of grain size have given way to those of visual sharpness. The extremely fine-grained images produced by slow films and fine-grain developers can actually look less sharp than those of medium-speed films processed in the modern high-definition or acutance type developer. That is because modern films and developers concentrate on producing a sharp edge between adjacent areas of different tone which makes the image *look* much sharper.

This effect is produced by improvements in both emulsion and developer construction. The emulsion is thinner than it used to be and makes less use of larger grains for greater speed. The medium-speed emulsions, in particular, now have a very even, compact grain structure in an emulsion of microscopic thickness, so that clumping together of individual grains is reduced and sharp edges are more easily obtainable.

The developer is a vigorous type in dilute solution which exhausts rapidly where it does more work and does not easily carry over into areas where its vigorous action is not required. It is not a fine-grain developer and is not usually recommended for use with fast films. With these films, the straightforward metol-hydroquinone or Phenidone-hydroquinone developer is quite satisfactory.

Formulae are included on page 228 but making up your own developer is not generally worth while. The commercial brands are completely reliable and by no means expensive.

Once you have chosen a suitable developer stick to it for some time. Even if the first results are unsatisfactory, the remedy is unlikely to be found by adopting a second, or even a third make.

Probably the culprit for the early failures was not the developer. In photography as in all games of skill, you must first "get your eye in," and you cannot do this if you are constantly changing your apparatus.

For negatives use the same acid fixing bath as was used fixing prints and enlargements, but in a slightly more dilute solution.

A Thermometer Essential

A thermometer is an essential part of your equipment for developing. Most times prescribed presuppose a temperature of 68°F. (20°C.). Even a few degrees more or less make a difference. If the developer is too cold it slows up the developing process and if it is too warm it attacks the emulsion too quickly. The result in both cases is bad.

The Finished Negative

The negative cannot be judged accurately until it is quite dry. It should be examined by holding it up against the light. A moderately powerful magnifying glass (×3 to ×6) will enable you to judge sharpness and grain. The so-called "Linen counter" will serve the purpose best.

The dense parts on the negative, representing as they do the bright portions of the original, are referred to as *highlights* and the light parts are known as *shadows*, since they represent the dark spots of the real object.

The "Normal" Negative

In what are known as normal negatives these shadows should show detail, and should not be as clear as glass. The highlights, on the other hand, should be sufficiently dense without being solidly black. They should show every gradation from grey to black. A well-balanced negative of this kind does not usually appeal to the unpractised eye of the amateur. Yet, on normal paper, it will produce excellent prints without any trouble, and on hard paper, vigorous enlargements. Its detail shadows show that it has been fully exposed, and the well-graded highlights point to correct development.

Under-exposed

Hard negatives show violent contrast between the light parts and the shadows. There are two kinds of hard negatives. If the shadows are completely transparent and devoid of detail it is a case of under-exposure. Either the exposure was too short or the aperture too small. There is nothing to be done with a negative of this kind except to consign it to the dust-bin before it has a chance of spoiling a perfectly good sheet of printing paper with a very poor print.

Over-developed

If, on the other hand, there is detail present in the shadows, the trouble is due to over-development. In this case the hard negative can be saved. A soft paper in the printing frame or a normal paper in the enlarger will produce positives in which the violent contrasts are considerably toned down. Besides this, the excess of density can be reduced by treating the negative with *Farmer's Reducer*, formula, see page 229. And yet a third way out is to make a less contrasty duplicate negative.

Over-exposed

The weak negative shows lack of contrast between shadows and light. If the shadows are veiled and perhaps heavily covered at the same time, it is a case of over-exposure. Either the shutter remained open too long, or the aperture was too big. Negatives of this kind are by no means lost. If they are to be printed the time allowed must be considerably longer than for normal negatives, to allow the light to penetrate the dense covering. But for enlargements the time becomes so unbearably long that it is better to reduce the film in *Farmer's Reducer* first, formula on page 229. Or else, as before, a copy can be made on a direct duplicate film.

Development too Short

If the weak negative is too thinly covered, even in the light parts, then it has either been removed too soon from the developing bath, or else the developer was too cold and could not have its full effect in the given time. Such negatives must be printed or enlarged on hard paper. This may mean enlargements with coarse grain. Here again a copy can be made on direct duplicate film. There are also intensifiers which improve the density of the film, but which unfortunately emphasize the grain at the same time.

Chemicals

It is no doubt a most amusing pastime to mix your own developer according to a new formula in the hope of hitting upon some marvellous new product. Alas! you are wasting your time. So leave experiments of this kind to the experts in their laboratories, and stick to the well-tested formulae on page 228 *or, preferably, buy the well-known brand-developers.*

Special note regarding formulae: The "potassium" variety of chemicals may safely be substituted by the "sodium". A 10 *per cent increase in quantity is recommended. For example to make up the fixing bath (page* 229) *instead of* 25 *gm. of "potassium-metabisulphite"* 28 *gm. of "sodium meta-bisulphite" should be used to give the same results.*

Even though you do not go in for photography on a big scale, you will have a certain number of bottles on your shelf: developer for films, developer for prints, fixing solution of two kinds. So to avoid disaster: label each bottle clearly.

Developer stains on coloured material are almost impossible to remove. Even white material is very difficult to clean once it is stained with developer. The moral is, therefore, to wear old clothes or an efficient overall, so that the question of cleaning your good clothes never arises.

Fixing salts: this light, white substance, in powder or crystals, can be the plague of the dark-room unless you handle it very carefully. It will get into your developer and spoil your prints. So keep your hands free.

Instead of performing miracles of legerdemain by pouring developer, etc., from a dish back into a narrow-necked bottle, why not buy a plastic funnel? It really makes things much simpler.

To remove deposit from trays, bottles, etc., use a 2 *per cent solution of hydrochloric acid, or ready made "dish cleaner".*

Some brand-developers in powder form consist of two separate powders. These should be dissolved as directed by the manufacturer (usually the smaller packet is dissolved first) in rather less than the full amount of water and then made up to the correct volume by the addition of more water.

Developer kept in a half-filled bottle deteriorates on account of the air, or rather the oxygen, with which it comes into contact. One way of filling up this unwanted air space is to drop glass marbles into the bottle. This is an old wrinkle which usually has only one drawback: namely, the number of glass marbles required.

Another idea is as follows. When the developer has been poured back into the bottle, suspend half a lighted match in the air space above the surface of the fluid by means of a piece of thin wire passed through the neck of the bottle. As soon as the match goes out push in the cork. The idea, of course, is to use up the oxygen present inside the bottle. The match must not be allowed to fall into the developer.

Do not put the fixing salt into the tray and pour water on to it. If you do, it will form hard lumps. First pour your water in and shake the salt into it gradually, stirring to help the dissolution.

Do not try to revive a fixing bath by adding more salts. Throw away the used solution and make a fresh supply.

In 1 *litre* (20 *ounces*) *of fixing bath* 25 *miniature film strips of* 36 *exposures* (24 × 36 *mm.* = 1 × 1½ *inches*) *or* 30 3¼ × 2¼ *inches* (6 × 9 *cm.*) *films of* 8 *exposures may be safely fixed.*

Developing

Most developers can be used more than once, provided they are kept in well-corked bottles, filled, if possible, to the top. The time allowed for development must be lengthened for the second or third time of using in accordance with the instructions on the packet or bottle.

If you carefully warm your developer up to 68°*F.* (20°*C.*) *and then pour it into an ice-cold developing tank, it is hardly surprising that the temperature of the liquid will fall, with the result that the negative will not get fully developed in the time allowed. So bring the developer up to at least 70°F. (21°C.) first of all and after pouring it into the dish, wait until it has settled down to the right degree of warmth.*

Metal developing tanks lose heat very quickly in a cold room. It is advisable to warm the tank by standing it in water of the correct temperature for a few minutes before pouring in the developer. Make sure that the top is secure and that no water can seep into the tank. If your workroom is very cold, wrap something round the tank during development to prevent it cooling off.

Ten or even fifteen minutes is a long time to wait. So while your films are "cooking" inside the pot you might as well pass the time as pleasantly as possible. You merely have to put your alarm clock on the table and set it to go off at the right moment. You can then read your paper in peace and the time will pass like a dream. But agitate the tank periodically.

A few drops of acetic acid added to the rinsing bath between developing and fixing will stop further development and prevent the transference of traces of developer to the fixing bath, and all the ills which arise therefrom.

Your Negatives

A contrasty negative is by no means the same thing as a sharp one. Yet many people persist in confusing the two. A negative with strong highlights and empty shadows proves to be less promising than it looked at first sight.

In the print, or still more, the enlargement, its failings become apparent. If the printing time is short the highlights are chalky and flat. If the time is lengthened the missing details appear in the highlights, but the shadows are one unrelieved black mass. Much better a well-balanced negative in which neither light nor shade is over-emphasized.

Of all the once popular reducing and intensifying agents the only one which does not deserve to be consigned to oblivion is

Farmer's Reducer. A negative which is too densely covered is immersed in the reducing bath until it has been sufficiently reduced. After washing and drying, the negative will give a good enlargement in a few seconds instead of, as formerly, in as many minutes.

Farmer's Reducer can be used for improving hard negatives, provided the defect is due to over-development and not to under-exposure.

Chemical treatment of an unsatisfactory negative has many drawbacks, even if that most innocent of preparations, namely, Farmer's Reducer, is the one used. Nowadays it is quite simple to make a copy of your negative, but without the faults of the original. With the help of copy film or lantern plates, you can print a positive transparency just as you would a paper print, correcting faults when you make it. You can then use the positive transparency to print a duplicate negative.

If your original negative is too dense, you will need a longer printing time to give you your medium density positive transparency. With a negative that is too thin, on the other hand, a short printing time will give a better positive. A hard negative, after medium exposure and a short development, will give a softer positive; and a weak negative, with the same exposure and a longer development, will produce a more vigorous positive.

Once the correct positive transparency has been obtained in this way, you can then print it again on to copy film, but this time you use standard exposure and development. The positive then gives an exact duplicate of the original negative, but with the faults corrected so that it is easy to produce good prints without any further trouble.

One great advantage of this method is that should a mistake occur, the loss is confined to the copy, which can easily be replaced, leaving the original unaffected.

If a drop of water falls on the emulsion side of the dry film or plate, the negative must be soaked completely in water and dried all over again. Otherwise a mark remains which shows up on the enlargement.

Scratched negatives can be treated with "Repolisan", which makes small scratches completely invisible and does its best even with more serious ones. It also protects the emulsion from subsequent rough handling.

If the water used in the dark-room is very hard, it sometimes leaves a white, powdery deposit on negatives. This can be dissolved away by putting the film after washing in a 2 per cent solution of acetic acid.

Film negatives should not be left in the strip. The constant rolling and unrolling will wear them out. They should be cut into single exposures and the good ones stored in a proper negative holder, while the bad ones should be thrown into the dust-bin where they belong. Miniature films should be cut in strips of six and stored in special wallets.

A USEFUL TABLE

Safelights for the Dark-Room

It is not enough to have any piece of red glass in your dark-room lamp. The road-mender's lamp looks red, but it lets through all sorts of other light rays. So be quite sure that any glass you use really lets nothing through which can influence the emulsion of your film. The same thing applies to safelights of any colour.

DARK GREEN for pan material. Lighting must be indirect—reflected from the ceiling, for example. Time-development in the dark is preferable.

DARK RED for ortho films and enlargements. Experience needed to estimate development of paper prints correctly.

ORANGE for contact prints and enlargements.

LIGHT GREEN ditto. But only with indirect lighting. Gives a bright light and is, therefore, more useful than orange or red.

YELLOW for contact papers. Not essential, provided developer tray is shaded and fixing bath covered with cardboard.

Tank Developer (Normal)

Metol	18 *gr.*	2 *gm.*
Sodium sulphite (anhydrous)	2 *oz.*	100 *gm.*
Hydroquinone	44 *gr.*	5 *gm.*
Borax	18 *gr.*	2 *gm.*
Water: to	20 *oz.*	1,000 *cc.*

The metol is first dissolved in about 2 fluid ounces (100 ccm.) of water at 95–105°F. (35–40°C.) and the solution placed in a bottle or flask. The sulphite is then dissolved in small quantities of 10 fluid ounces (500 ccm.) of water at the same temperature. When it has dissolved, the borax is added and the solution added to that of the metol. The hydroquinone is then dissolved in about 4 fluid ounces (200 ccm.) of water and also added to the rest. After cooling to room temperature, the bottle or flask is filled up to full volume.

This is now the standard rollfilm and 35 mm. film developer. At 68°F (20°C) it will develop most films in 7–10 minutes, depending on the contrast required. Use undiluted.

Tank Developer (Acutance type)

Metol	2.2 *gr.*	0.25 *gm.*
Sodium sulphite (anhydrous)	30 *gr.*	3.5 *gm.*
Glycin	6.6 *gr.*	0.75 *gm.*
Potassium carbonate (crystals)	66 *gr.*	0.7 *gm.*
Pinacryptol Yellow 1 : 2000 *solution* ..	300 *minims*	3.5 *cc.*
Water to	20 *oz.*	1000 *cc.*

This formula (due to Geoffrey Crawley, British Journal of Photography) is suitable for slow medium speed films which it will process to average contrast in 12–18 minutes, depending on the make of film. Use undiluted.

For Softer Results

Metol	131 *gr.*	15 *gm.*
Sodium sulphite (anhydrous)	1 *oz.*	50 *gm.*
Sodium carbonate (anhydrous)	1 *oz.*	50 *gm.*
Potassium bromide	9 *gr.*	1 *gm.*
Water: to	20 *oz.*	1,000 *cc.*

For use, the developer should be diluted with twice its own volume of water for very fast films and plates, and with four volumes of water for all those emulsions which tend to give hard negatives, such as fine-grain films.

The development time should be about 6 minutes.

For Contrast

(*A*)

Sodium sulphite (anhydrous)	1 *oz.*	50 *grm.*
Hydroquinone	220 *gr.*	25 *grm.*
Potassium bromide	220 *gr.*	25 *grm.*
Water: to	20 *fluid oz.*	1,000 *ccm.*

(*B*)

Caustic soda (stick)	220 *gr.*	25 *grm.*
Water: to	20 *fluid oz.*	1,000 *ccm.*

The working developer is made by mixing equal parts of (*A*) and (*B*) just before use. The solution should not be allowed to touch the fingers. Plate or film clips, or rubber gloves, are required.

The time of development should not exceed 4 minutes, and since the mixed developer does not keep well, it must be thrown away after use.

Fixing Bath

Hypo (sodium thiosulphate)	4 *oz.*	200 *grm.*
Potassium metabisulphite	½ *oz.*	25 *grm.*
Water up to	20 *oz.*	1,000 *ccm.*

Farmer's Reducer

(*A*)

Potassium ferricyanide	2 *oz.*	5 *grm.*
Water	40 *fluid oz.*	100 *ccm.*

(*B*)

Hypo crystals	220 *gr.*	25 *grm.*
Water	10 *fluid oz.*	500 *ccm.*

Immediately before use, mix one part (by volume) of (*A*) with five parts of (*B*).

The negative can either be dry or wet, and if it has just been fixed it need not be particularly thoroughly washed before reducing. The degree of reduction can easily be observed, but since the process continues for a short time in the washing water, reduction should be stopped rather before the negative has reached the desired stage. As soon as this point has been reached, the negative is well swilled under the running tap and then washed really thoroughly.

Solution (*A*) must be kept in a brown glass bottle. Both stock solutions keep well, but the working solution decomposes very quickly. If the reducer becomes slow during the reduction of a negative, it should be thrown away and fresh reducer used.

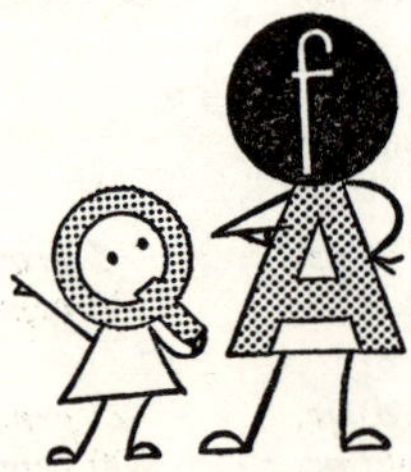

If you have any difficulty drop us a line at

FOCAL PRESS LTD.

31 *Fitzroy Square, London, W1P 6BH*

We shall be glad to help you—free of charge, of course. But matters will be simpler for us if you enclose a stamped addressed envelope for our answer.

INDEX

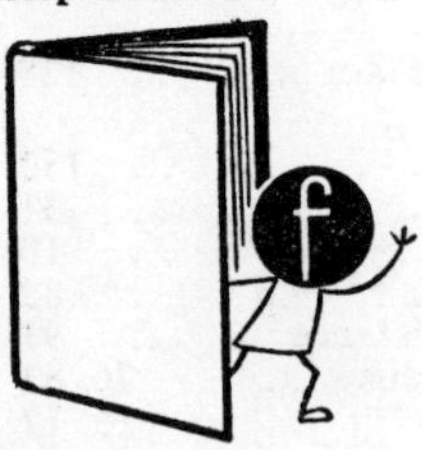

ASK FOR THE LATEST ILLUSTRATED CATALOGUE OF THE FOCAL PRESS, 31 *FITZROY SQUARE, LONDON, W1P 6BH*